If These
WALLS
Could **TALK:**
DALLAS COWBOYS

If These
WALLS
Could TALK:
DALLAS COWBOYS

Stories from the
Dallas Cowboys Sideline,
Locker Room, and Press Box

Nick Eatman

TRIUMPH
BOOKS

Library of Congress Cataloging-in-Publication Data

Eatman, Nick.
    If these walls could talk, Dallas Cowboys : stories from the Dallas Cowboys sideline, locker room, and press box / Nick Eatman ; foreword by Darren Woodson.
        pages cm
    ISBN 978-1-60078-937-3 (paperback)
    1. Dallas Cowboys (Football team)—History. 2. Dallas Cowboys (Football team)—Anecdotes. I. Title.
    GV956.D3E37 2014
    796.332'64097642812—dc23
                                                        2014014656

This book is available in quantity at special discounts for your group or organization. For further information, contact:

    Triumph Books LLC
    814 North Franklin Street
    Chicago, Illinois 60610
    (312) 337-0747
    www.triumphbooks.com

Printed in U.S.A.

ISBN: 978-1-60078-937-3

Design by Amy Carter

Photos courtesy of James D. Smith unless otherwise indicated

For Olivia, my superstar, my angel, and my world

CONTENTS

FOREWORD

On April 26, 1992, I figured my life was about to change. My dreams of making it to the NFL were about to happen. It was the day of the NFL draft, the biggest moment of my life. At the house we had the draft on, but I didn't watch it. I couldn't watch. Instead, I went out for a round of golf...and I didn't play golf.

Living out in Arizona, I had never gone golfing, but that's how much I wanted to get my mind off the draft. There was so much buildup and speculation that I just couldn't take it. I heard I'd be selected anywhere from the second round to the third or fourth.

At this point I just wanted the process to be over. I was on the golf course when somehow my mom got me on the phone and congratulated me. Then my best friend, Floyd, called and said, "You just got drafted by the team you hate."

I was so excited. All my dreams had finally come true. I was just happy to be in the NFL. But he was right—I hated the Cowboys growing up. I was a Steelers fan. Living in Arizona back then, we didn't have a team, so I rooted for anyone Dallas was playing. And it wasn't just dislike; it was hatred. I hated Drew Pearson and Roger Staubach. That's how intense it was. My heroes were "Mean Joe" Greene, Lynn Swann, and Rocky Bleier. Those were my guys.

But when I was drafted by the Cowboys, everything changed. When I got to Dallas and saw Jimmy Johnson and Jerry Jones, reality just hit me: *I am going to be a Dallas Cowboy!* That's all I kept saying to myself.

And I actually knew a little bit about the Cowboys. Everyone talked about Emmitt Smith, Troy Aikman, and Michael Irvin, but the guy I was excited about meeting was Ken Norton Jr. For some reason I just loved the way he played. Every time I caught a Cowboys game the year before, he was the guy I liked. He was just tough and nasty. He played the game the way I wanted to play—physical from start to finish.

But from that moment on, I was hooked. A team I grew up hating was now my team and my life. And I couldn't have been happier.

When I got there in 1992, we were ready to turn that corner. There's no way I could've gone anywhere better, especially after we won two championships in my first two years and then a third Super Bowl ring in my fourth year. I had four seasons in the league and three rings. A part of me thought I might get seven or eight before it was all said and done. But man, I never dreamed I wouldn't even come close to a fourth one.

In my next eight years, we never made it to the NFC Championship Game. We went through four more head coaches, and to this day, I'm the only Cowboys player to have played for five different head coaches. I still don't know if that's a good or bad thing.

The longevity is nice, even though I still wish I would've played longer. One of my biggest regrets is not having more time with Bill Parcells. He came in 2003, which turned out to be my last season, but I learned more from him in a few months than I had in about five or six years.

If I had played more with him, I guarantee I would have been a hundred times the player I was and I still think my career turned out pretty well. I never considered myself a cocky person and still don't, but I was always confident.

When I think about all of the players I played with, all of the players that came after me, and even all of the players that were before me, I still don't think there has been a more versatile player to ever suit up for the Cowboys than me. You could argue Deion Sanders, who played offense and defense and returned punts. He was an amazing talent.

But I remember one of his first games back in 1995, against the Giants, and he's got big Rodney Hampton in the open field. Deion is wrestling with him and trying to bring him down. And I'm over at my safety spot and I'm flying to the ball. Surely Deion is going to get him down, but he hasn't yet. I'm going full speed and when I get there I'm right behind Deion and just smash him in the back, right into Hampton, and we all three go down hard. Deion, with that high-pitched voice, looks up at me and yells, "Woody, are you crazy? What's wrong with you?"

I told him right then, "Listen, if I have to run my ass across this field because you're not making the tackle, I'm going to hit you, him, and anyone else I have to—to make the play."

That's just the way I played the game. I wanted to be all over the field and for the most part I was. I played safety, moved down to linebacker sometimes, and could play the nickel corner. In today's game, you see teams paying a lot of money for a nickel cornerback, but I played the slot my whole career. And I played all of the special teams, too.

One of the things I'm most proud of is knowing I played for a dynasty team and never really came off the field. I'm hoping one day to see my name up in the Ring of Honor, but that's out of my control. All I could control was what I did on the field, and hopefully my play spoke for itself. I certainly have no regrets. How could I? I got to line up and play for America's Team for 12 years.

I remember Nick Eatman when he was just a young kid out of college back in Wichita Falls. He's now covered this team for 15 years and will reveal some of the greatest untold stories over the last two decades. This book, *If These Walls Could Talk*, isn't about the history of the Cowboys. It's not about the Tom Landry era and really doesn't focus a lot on our championship runs of the 1990s. But Jerry Jones is the best owner in the NFL because he's managed to keep this the most popular franchise in the world even without another Super Bowl since 1995.

The stories in this book will focus on a team climbing to get back to those glory days. I was once a big part of that climb, a journey the Cowboys are still on today.

And as I've transitioned my career from player to ESPN analyst, I've grown to appreciate the Cowboys' brand even more. Even without the recent success on the field, there is no team more relevant than the Cowboys. In our production meetings at ESPN, we're always trying to talk about the Cowboys or Tony Romo because we know that's what sells.

The Cowboys have always been America's Team and always will be.

—*Darren Woodson*

CHAPTER 1
DYING DYNASTY

The first time I met Emmitt Smith was during his rookie season in 1990. I was just 14 years old and the Cowboys held an open practice at Texas Stadium, trying to make it a fan-friendly event that could hopefully boost ticket sales. Remember, the team was fresh off a 1–15 season, so they were pulling out all the stops.

I got him to sign a picture that I had ripped out of a Sports Illustrated. He didn't have a football card yet, and that's all I had. He said, "What's this?" poking fun at my piece of memorabilia. But Emmitt had yet to play a single snap for the Cowboys. Of course, how could I have ever known then that I would have a front-row seat for his last few years with the team?

So during my teens, I loved watching Emmitt play. He was the guy the Cowboys just couldn't win without, which was evident in the 1993 season when they lost the first two games when he sat out with a contract dispute but returned to win NFL MVP honors and lead the league in rushing.

Needless to say, I knew Emmitt the player and I more than liked the guy. Emmitt the person was a little different, at least when I got there in 1999. Success for the team was fading, and his play was deteriorating, though he was still producing at a relatively high level.

And after Troy Aikman and Michael Irvin were gone, Emmitt was really the only star left, something he made clear a few years after he left the team, saying he felt like a "diamond surrounded by trash" in his final seasons with the club. His premise was correct. The word choice was poor.

In 2000 I remember walking into the team hotel in New York before a Giants game, and Emmitt motioned me to come over by him. He then asked for my bag.

"You want my bag?"

"Yeah, let me have your bag real quick."

I handed over a less-than-impressive blue Nike gym bag, and Emmitt grabbed it with one hand and had his own personal luggage in the other. He then walked right through a massive group of fans who were in a frenzy trying to collect his autograph. Emmitt just smiled and kept going. Of course, he couldn't sign because…well…his hands were full.

Emmitt had passed the gathering and was approaching the elevators when he looked back, dropped my bag to the ground, and let out a thunderous laugh. I think he'd done that move before, but it didn't seem to get old. When I told that story to people who knew him better, the usual response was something like, "That's Emmitt."

But I've also seen other sides of him. In 1999 the Cowboys lost to a miserable Saints team in a Christmas Eve game that seemingly knocked them out of the playoffs. The Cowboys managed to sneak in anyway, but during the return flight from New Orleans, it appeared their postseason chances were over.

Yet with the plane in the air headed back to Dallas, Emmitt went to the front and personally shook hands with every single person on the flight, wishing them a Merry Christmas. Even with people he didn't know, such as sponsors and guests or even new faces in the media he didn't recognize, Smith still shook all of their hands and genuinely wished them well.

And I'll never forget one day in 2002. It was a Thursday because Emmitt never talked on Thursdays in the locker room. If you approached him on a Thursday, he'd laugh at you for not knowing "the rules." But on this day, the mood at Valley Ranch was somber. The team's director of TV, John Chang, one of the more likeable individuals in the organization, had suffered a brain aneurism and was in critical condition. He eventually passed away from a cerebral hemorrhage later that day, but as of Thursday mid-morning, everyone was praying for the best.

My job was to try to get quotes from some of the veteran players who knew John, so I could write a remembrance article. In 2002, it was such a young team that Emmitt was really the only guy, other than Darren Woodson, that I could talk to.

Knowing the day of the week, I cautiously approached Emmitt, who was sitting at his locker. Before I could say anything, he stood up and asked, "You need me to talk about John, don't you?"

"Yeah, I'm sorry, Emmitt, but I do."

"Definitely, I'll talk about John Chang all day."

3

And he went over to another area of the locker room and shared stories and memories about John, whose talented vision carried the Cowboys' in-house TV department to new heights.

His ability to know his role and have the presence of mind to interview about a staff member was also a case of "That's Emmitt."

—Nick Eatman

Deion Mans Up

In the 1990s no team had swagger like the Dallas Cowboys. They were bold, brash, flamboyant, loud, and talented.

And then they signed Deion Sanders.

Deion joined the Cowboys in 1995 after agreeing to a seven-year, $35 million contract that was completely unheard of at the time for a cornerback. And that's part of the deal—he wasn't just a cornerback in Jerry Jones' mind, as the owner envisioned him playing offense as well, something Sanders did during his time with the Atlanta Falcons.

When Deion came to the Cowboys, he fit right in on Sundays as he expected to. "Prime Time" had style, flash, and a confidence that was unmatched. But what Deion wasn't expecting was the level of intensity in the Cowboys' workouts, which was always triggered by the one-on-one drills. When the receivers took on the cornerbacks, it was the highlight of practice.

Sometimes coaches from other positions would conveniently take "breaks," so they could catch a glimpse of the action. And it made sense to watch because they were certainly going to hear the players chirping about it all day and probably all week.

Deion signed two games into the 1995 season, but an ankle injury he sustained playing baseball prevented him from taking the field for six weeks. Once ready, Deion immediately jumped into the starting lineup during his first practice at Valley Ranch, which meant he took the first rep on the right side of the field. Five other players, a mix of cornerbacks and safeties, joined him, including Pro Bowler Darren Woodson. On the left side, there were a handful of other defensive backs. The drill consists of one-on-one matchups to the right, then to the left and so forth.

On the very first play, Deion got right up on Michael Irvin, one of the few receivers in the league who had enjoyed moderate success against him. Irvin ran 10 yards downfield and then made a hard cut to the outside where he hauled in a perfectly thrown pass from Troy Aikman. The two hooked up on that play for more than 10 years, and when run and thrown properly, they couldn't be stopped.

Deion certainly didn't stop it on this play, and Irvin proceeded to woof, slamming the ball down with a spike and then giving his trademark first-down sign. The receivers were going crazy, yelling and screaming that their boy, "The Playmaker," had just worked over the guy who was supposed to be the savior on defense. "Deion was hot," Woodson recalled. "He walked over to the side, and when the next corner came up—I think it was Alundis Brice—he told him to get off the field. Deion came over and said, 'All of ya'll should go on the other side if you want any reps. I'm taking every one of these fucking reps.' And that's exactly what he did."

Maybe that was his way of knocking off the rust, considering he had played baseball all summer and this was his first practice. Or maybe that's just how bad he wanted to prove the first ball to Irvin was a fluke.

The arrogance to send the rest of the defensive backs to the other side of the drill wasn't too surprising. That was Deion's reputation long before he came to the Cowboys. But what transpired over the next 12 snaps was nothing short of incredible.

Deion did take every rep on the right side. And he didn't give up another ball. Not a slant, not a deep ball, not another out route, even when Irvin tested him again. Deion stayed on the field and covered every fresh receiver that rotated in. And he mixed up his coverages, playing off at times, pressing the receiver on others. He had the receivers and quarterbacks out of rhythm.

Toward the end of the drill, when the receivers were getting frustrated, they started running deep every time. "I think he had three or four 9-routes in a row, and Deion ran with his guy every time," Woodson said. "It was unbelievable. In all my years of playing and watching guys do things in practice, that's the most amazing thing I'd ever seen.

Not only did Woodson enjoy the show but the break, too. He didn't go to the other side to get reps, and when defensive coordinator Mike Zimmer came over to see what was happening, Woodson told him what Deion had said. Zimmer then started yelling at some of the younger cornerbacks to get in there, but deep down he was pretty impressed and excited about his newest cornerback.

Everybody knew Deion could play. But they all quickly found out how hard he competed as well.

Muzzling Haley

When it comes to pranks, playful harassment or any other joke, there aren't many players off-limits for razzing.

Troy Aikman was usually the exception. He was the quarterback, the franchise, and the team's stoic leader, which typically gave him a pass from the locker-room high jinks.

However, Charles Haley was the exception to just about every rule. His loud mouth, wild personality, and "just-don't-give-a-shit" mentality had no filter. At times, knowing his teammates didn't mess with Aikman, Haley would purposely try to antagonize the quarterback. "Charles never thought he was getting his respect," equipment manager Mike McCord said. "He used to mess with Troy all the time. Charles thought he was the Golden Boy and didn't care. He'd mess with Nate [Newton], Michael [Irvin], Deion, and Emmitt [Smith], but he really liked to mess with Troy."

One day, Haley was in one of his typically playful moods, and his love for wagering on full display. It didn't matter the circumstance. Haley would often try to put money on it and make it a bet. From one side of the locker room to the other, which is about 15–20 yards, Haley spots Aikman getting dressed after a workout. Like always, Aikman stuck to himself, especially when the locker room antics were getting rather boisterous like they were on this day. But, Haley made sure Aikman was involved this time. "Hey, Troy. Hey, I'll give you $500 cash right now if you can throw this football in between these trash cans," Haley challenged. "The ball can't hit them either."

Aikman laughed it off and continued to get dressed, but Haley kept pressing. He had five $100 bills and was ready to give them up if Aikman could fire a ball across the locker room into this tight spot. Haley pushed and pushed, and Aikman finally just acknowledged the challenge by looking up to see that Haley had maneuvered a pair of trash cans so close together that one football couldn't even be placed sideways between two without touching one of them. And Haley wanted Aikman, who was known for his pinpoint accuracy, to fire this ball across the room and not hit them? "Ball," Aikman demanded with force, which riled up the onlookers, including Haley, who was trying to figure out a fair number of throws to give the quarterback to try this feat.

"How many throws you need to get it through there?" Haley asked.

Aikman never said a word. The only sound made was the humming of the hardest, fastest, tightest spiral he had ever thrown. The ball zipped straight through the two trash cans, smacking one of the lockers behind them.

The room went nuts. Here was their quarterback, their leader, the guy that takes them into battle, and he had just rifled a football across their locker room into a space that seemed impossible. Most of the players couldn't have delivered a handoff into a space that small, much less a 20-yard pass.

Not only that, Aikman did something that seemed even more impossible. For a brief moment, he actually made Haley speechless, probably a more impressive feat than the pass itself.

He Punts, Too?

Troy Aikman had to be perfect. That was his goal every practice, every game, and every season. With every pass that rolled out of his right hand, Aikman strived for perfection and demanded the same from his teammates, his coaches, and anyone else that was around him.

So when things weren't going perfect, innocent bystanders sometimes felt the wrath of "8-Ball," the nickname given to Aikman, the last player to wear No. 8 for the Cowboys.

One day during a practice in the early 1990s, the Cowboys were on the field during a heavy downpour. The team had yet to build its indoor facility, which actually collapsed during a practice in 2009, and chose not to travel to a local high school that had an indoor field.

At that time, the equipment staff also had only two people helping during practice: Mike McCord and longtime manager Buck Buchanan, whose son, Bucky, eventually replaced him and is still one of the team's two full-time assistants. There weren't a host of interns like today to shag balls and dry them off.

Aikman, who like most quarterbacks had trouble throwing a wet football, wasn't having much luck on this day. Usually tight spirals were slipping out of his hand on every throw, wobbling through the air like a kickoff.

In one particular drill, McCord played the role of the center, kneeling down in front of Aikman and either simulating a snap into his hands or giving him a shotgun pitch. In fielding the balls back from the receivers, McCord was also doing his best to towel them off before giving them to Aikman.

Still the weather was winning the drill. It was raining hard enough that the coaches considered stopping practice and waiting for the storm to pass.

Aikman didn't say anything, but his frustration was starting to show. He cursed after each fluttering pass, and his disgust was becoming more and more physical. "Troy was one of those guys who had really big hands, but he squeezed the ball so tight," McCord said. "That's why he always struggled at first in the Super Bowls because he was throwing brand new footballs. On this day the ball was soaking wet, and he's squeezing it so hard. It's just not going the way he wants it to."

Finally, Aikman had seen enough. After about the sixth straight pass that he failed to grip properly, the quarterback completely snapped. "Hey, McCord, can you just fucking give me one dry football?"

With that, Aikman took the ball and punted it about 40 yards to the other field. "And that was Troy," McCord said. "He didn't usually call you out, but if he was having a bad day, he was going to take it out on someone."

Fashionably Late

When it came to practice, no one pushed himself harder or performed better than Michael Irvin. He was always on time and never really displayed the overzealous showmanship that made him one of the NFL's most flamboyant players.

When it came to the team charter, though, that was a different story.

Irvin, of course, sported some of the loudest, most colorful suits of any player on the team, but a more pressing question than what Irvin would wear on each charter flight was when the wide receiver might get there.

Earlier in his career during the 1992 season, Irvin was left behind. His former college coach, Jimmy Johnson, ordered the team to leave without its star receiver, who said he simply overslept. The Cowboys went to Detroit, and Irvin had to catch his own flight. He was also punished by being benched for the team's first possession of the game.

Irvin never missed another flight, but he certainly could've.

As he got older, he realized more and more that he had enough skins on the wall, so a few extra minutes here and there would be tolerated. In fact it was often celebrated as someone regularly profited from his delay. "He was late every single time," equipment manager Mike McCord said. "It wasn't a matter of if he'd be late, but how late. We knew it every week. That's just the way Michael was."

McCord was one of the football staff members who made a game of Irvin's tardiness. Sometimes as many as 10 guys in the back few rows would place their bets on the exact time Irvin would arrive. Usually they were $1 bets for fun, but sometimes the pot was $5 each.

If the plane was scheduled to leave at 1 PM, around 12:45 is when the bets would start coming in. Of course, Irvin wasn't there yet.

"I'll take 12:58."

"I've got 1:02."

"Hmm, how about 12:54?" A bold prediction of Irvin actually being rather early would receive some oohs and ahhs.

"Nah, let's go 1:07," which would be late enough to get the head coach, whether it was Johnson, Barry Switzer, or Chan Gailey, to at least consider the possibility of leaving without him.

Every week Irvin would make it a show. And more often than not, he'd come in through the back door yelling, "All right, who won? Who had 1:05 on the nose?"

The players made tons of money, but the football staff always could use some extra cash. For one guy, it was a nice jumpstart to the weekend—all because of a receiver's consistent lack of punctuality.

Did Dat Just Happen?

One of the more popular third-round picks in Cowboys history joined the team in 1999. To the avid college football fan in the state of Texas, Dat Nguyen was already a star. He had won the Bednarik and Lombardi Awards in 1998 as a senior at Texas A&M and was a unanimous All-American selection. Throw in his lack of size, as well as being one of the first Vietnamese players to reach the NFL, and he instantly became a favorite of the Cowboys' faithful.

And the organization loved him right away as well. The coaches thought he was a smart, instinctive player who would swarm to the football. They were confident he could eventually be the starting middle linebacker in their 4-3 defensive scheme.

But the best part about this situation was the lack of pressure on Nguyen to play right away. He needed to get bigger, stronger, and more acclimated to the game, so with veteran Randall Godfrey already in place, Dallas was the perfect fit. Godfrey had one year left on his deal and was expected to be a free agent in 2000. Until then Nguyen would have quite the leader from which to learn.

However, Godfrey sensed the plan and tried to get a new contract in place before the 1999 season. During the first full team minicamp of the summer, he held out, hoping his absence might force the club's hand to give him a new deal. What it did instead was force Nguyen into the starting lineup for his first practice with the entire squad. He had participated in the rookies-only camp after the draft and, as expected, stood out among the group of 20-something hopefuls.

But during the veteran minicamp, it was Nguyen who looked out of sorts. The knock on him from the start was that opposing linemen were simply too big for the 5'11", 235-pound linebacker. Initially, though, the entire moment seemed too big as well.

When the first team drills began, the Cowboys opened up with the starters on each side of the ball facing each other, first-team defense

11

against the first-team offense. Nguyen got the signal from the sideline, and with his back to the line of scrimmage, he blurted out the play-call for the defensive unit. "I turned back around, and that's when I saw Troy Aikman coming up to the huddle," Nguyen said. "I was like, 'Wow, that's *Troy Aikman*.' And then I saw Emmitt Smith behind him. And Daryl Johnston. And there's Larry Allen. And I look to my right, and there's Michael Irvin. I was thinking about making it to the NFL and playing against all the great players...and they snapped the ball. I didn't move. I just froze right there. I got completely starstruck."

Nguyen just stayed in the middle, and the entire play rolled to his left. Finally, the rookie linebacker gathered himself and shuffled to the ball, which by the time he got there was already being tossed back to the middle of the field for second down.

Nguyen couldn't believe what he had just done. Linebackers coach George Edwards yelled, "Dat, what the hell are you doing? You're with the big boys now!"

But it wasn't Edwards who Nguyen remembers the most. "I looked over to the sideline and saw Dave Campo," Nguyen said of the defensive coordinator at the time who would eventually become head coach of the Cowboys in 2000. "I just remember 'Camps' had his face buried in his hands, and he was shaking his head."

For a brief moment, it was as if all of the critics, who said Nguyen was simply a good college player but not big enough, fast enough, or talented enough to make a difference in the NFL, were on point.

But it was only one play. Nguyen actually turned things around and had a great first practice. It prompted Godfrey to return to the team, and he finished out his contract with a solid 1999 season.

Nguyen was a good role player on the nickel defense and special teams that year, but when Godfrey signed with the Titans in free agency, it made Barron Wortham, who was a free agent himself with Tennessee, expendable. The Cowboys then signed Wortham, and he started 11

As the Cowboys' third-round pick in 1999, Dat Nguyen became the first Vietnamese American to play in the NFL. He led the team in tackles three times between 2001–04. *(Dallas Cowboys)*

games in 2000 before giving way to Nguyen later in the season. Nguyen remained the team's starting middle linebacker for the next four years.

Three of those seasons occurred under Bill Parcells. The head coach was blunt about his desire to have bigger, bulkier linebackers who could consistently battle with offensive linemen. Guys like Nguyen and Dexter Coakley, both under 250 pounds, weren't considered "Parcells guys."

But over time, they became favorites of Parcells, especially Nguyen, who was so reliable that Parcells said he often overlooked him. "You have to be careful with a guy like Dat," Parcells said more than once during the 2003 season, his first as Cowboys head coach. "He's someone you can count on. He's where he needs to be. He's on time. He knows the calls. He doesn't make a lot of mistakes. He's one of the guys you just don't ever have to say anything to. He's not one of my St. Bernards. I've got a few St. Bernards here on my defense; you have to hit 'em with a stick to get them to do anything. Even guys like Dat, you have to make sure not to forget about them sometimes. But he's a real professional."

Nguyen played seven years before injuries eventually took their toll. He then joined the Cowboys' coaching staff in 2007 with Parcells' replacement, Wade Phillips. After three years on the sidelines, and still missing the game as a player, Nguyen decided to move on from the pro ranks and went back to his alma mater to coach linebackers at Texas A&M for two seasons. He is now a talk radio host in San Antonio, where Cowboys coverage is king. "I'm always going to be a Dallas Cowboy," Nguyen said. "Even now that I'm in the media, I'm still a Cowboy at heart."

Earning His (Pin)Stripes

By the end of the 1990s, the colorful personalities were almost too much for one locker room. Of course, there was the original in Michael Irvin, but Deion Sanders definitely rivaled him, if not surpassed him. When it came to fancy clothes, tailored suits, fur coats, and gaudy jewelry, you couldn't beat Deion and Michael.

However, some would always try.

Then again, the imposters were never really welcomed, mainly because they just weren't good enough on the field. Sure, other players had nice suits and looked the part, but Michael and Deion were the fashion police of the locker room, and they didn't let just anyone into their proverbial club. Imitators were greeted with harsh criticism and embarrassment.

One of those who attempted to match the superstars' flashy ways was linebacker Darren Hambrick, a fifth-round pick in 1998. Hambrick had unreal athleticism for his position. At 6'1", 227 pounds, he looked like a big safety, especially when he ran sideline to sideline.

With the potential to be good, especially in the Cowboys' 4-3 defense that coveted linebacker speed, Hambrick started 12 games during the 1999 season. But despite working his way up the depth chart, he was still a relatively young player on a team that featured all of the Triplets—Irvin, Emmitt Smith, and Troy Aikman—along with Sanders, Daryl Johnston, and Darren Woodson.

Of course, that didn't stop him from trying to look and act the part. Hambrick grew up in Dade City, Florida, and idolized both Sanders and Irvin, who also hailed from the Sunshine State. He relished their fame and celebrity and wanted so badly to be on their level. And Michael and Deion weren't opposed to taking youngsters under their wings. But they made sure to put them in their place when needed.

Michael once decided to poke fun at Hambrick's stylish attempts and stood up on his locker to get everyone's attention. "Hey fellas, we've got this guy, Darren Hambrick. Man, he's always hanging out with us," Irvin said with that trademark chuckle before and after each sentence. "This Hambrick, he wants to be one of us. But you know, he's just not ready. You know, when you go look at my suit, when you look inside the jacket, it says, 'Exclusively Made For The Playmaker.' You look at Deion's suit, it says, 'Exclusively Made For Prime Time.' You look at Emmitt's jacket, it says, 'Exclusively made for The Zone.' You look at Darren Hambrick's suit. You look on the inside, and what does it say? It says 'X...X...L!'"

The locker room erupted with players rolling on the floor in laughter. But Hambrick was one of them. He could take a joke, which was a good thing because they didn't always stop.

In 2000 Hambrick led the Cowboys with 154 tackles and was having another solid campaign in 2001, the final season of his original four-year contract. Once asked by reporters about a new deal, Hambrick expressed his desire to get a big payday. His actual quote referred to his hopes of purchasing a "25-square-inch house" like many of his high-rolling teammates.

So, never one to hold back from a joke, the athletic trainers had some fun, taking an empty trash can and building their own house with toy cars in the garage and a towel that symbolized a carpet. Of course, the house measured exactly 25 square inches.

Once again, Hambrick was playful and usually was with the players in the locker room and often the staff. He did have his moments, though. For the first offseason practice before the 2000 season, Hambrick opted to wear his cleats from the previous year instead of getting a new pair. That was fine with the equipment managers, Mike McCord and Bucky Buchanan, who were already giving out new pairs to certain players. To them, Hambrick re-using his old cleats was a good thing.

But when the feisty linebacker noticed a buildup of grass on the bottom of his shoes, he went straight to McCord, sat down, plopped his feet up in McCord's face and said, "Wipe me off, Mike." What makes the Cowboys' locker room so unique is that the trainers and equipment guys, really the entire football staff, refuse to back down from the players. They'll take the jabs and shots but will also fire some back. McCord laughed in Hambrick's face and told him, "I'll get you another pair before I do that."

Hambrick had some off-the-field troubles before and after his playing days, but he was always a free spirit on the field—sometimes a little too much so.

Near the end of a demoralizing 40–18 loss to the Eagles in a Sunday night matchup during the 2001 season, Hambrick made a late-game tackle right in front of the Philadelphia bench. Instead of scurrying back to the huddle, he ran 10 feet from the sideline and did a gravedigger dance, mimicking himself with a shovel as he gyrated his hips, seemingly forgetting that his team was down by 30 at that point in the game.

The Cowboys eventually released Hambrick, who signed with the Panthers, where he finished out the 2001 season. He then played one more season with the Browns in 2002 before his NFL career came to an end.

Odd Scoring Threat

After the Cowboys survived a wild 41–35 overtime win over the Redskins in the 1999 season opener, defensive end Greg Ellis found himself with the football in his hands the following Thursday in practice.

Ellis had intercepted a deflected pass, and with his eager defensive teammates rushing up to either congratulate him or help him score a touchdown, he instead made a dumb decision, turning and pitching the ball backward to an unassuming defender. The ball hit the ground, and tight end David LaFleur picked it up.

It didn't take much to get defensive coordinator Dave Campo riled up, but he completely lost it in practice, screaming so loud at Ellis that it sounded like his voice was already giving out. And this was only Week 2 of the regular season. "If you get the football, go score with it. Don't try and get cute," Campo screamed at Ellis. "You're an athlete, too. Just get your ass up the field and try to score."

Ellis simply nodded, seemingly thinking that scenario wouldn't come up any time soon. Sure enough, just four days later Dallas was taking on the defending NFC champion Atlanta Falcons at Texas Stadium on *Monday Night Football.* Late in the game, the Cowboys saw a 17–0 lead narrow to 17–7 with the Falcons driving once again. That's when Atlanta quarterback Danny Kanell tried to dump the ball short on a screen. But the charging Ellis read the play perfectly from the start, jumped in front of the pass, deflected it up, and then caught it in midair, one step behind Kanell.

Just a few days earlier, Ellis had been looking for someone else to run with the ball, but this time the only Cowboys uniform he saw ahead of him was being worn by Rowdy, the team's mascot, who was jumping up and down in the end zone. So Ellis took off running, showing off that athleticism Campo had been yelling about earlier in the week.

Ellis made it to the end zone for an 87-yard touchdown, which not only put the game out of reach, but also stirred the Texas Stadium crowd into a frenzy. Grabbing an oxygen mask on the sidelines, Ellis received numerous high-fives, shoulder pats, helmet slaps, and, of course, an "I told you so" from a giddy Campo.

But it didn't stop there. In the next game against the Cardinals, the Cowboys dominated Arizona for most of the game, but now in the fourth quarter, they were trying to keep their opponent out of the end zone. While playing goal-line defense, Ellis was knocked to the ground on a running play when he noticed something odd right at his feet—the ball. Cardinals quarterback Jake Plummer was going to attempt a sneak from the Cowboys' 2-yard line but was never able to get a handle on the snap from center. The ball trickled out toward the end of the line where Ellis alertly got to his feet, scooped it up without being touched, and then quickly started the long dash back the other way.

Once again, he focused only on the green turf ahead of him. While this was an afternoon game with temperatures in the 70s, the sun had been beating down on the players for four quarters. Ellis was gassed already, but the chance to score twice was too much to pass up. "My first instinct was to fall on the ball, but I had a lot of green ahead of me," Ellis said. "I was running with it and could hear some guys yelling, 'Pitch it back.' I guess they didn't think I would make it. But I wanted to get into that end zone."

Anything not to hear Campo in his ear again.

Big Brother Troy?

Troy Aikman was the No. 1 draft pick in 1989. He was the MVP of Super Bowl XXVII. He made six Pro Bowls, led his team to three championships in a four-year span, and was inducted into the Pro Football Hall of Fame in 2006. So finding something negative about the face of the franchise is not only petty, but also nearly impossible.

If there was a popular complaint from some of his teammates and employees on the football staff, it was Aikman's lack of camaraderie, especially with the younger players. Now, Aikman ran around with his buddies, Jay Novacek, Dale Hellestrae, and Mark Tuinei, but for the most part, he didn't associate with all of his teammates on a daily basis. "To me, he was a lunch-pail guy," safety Darren Woodson said. "He would show up in the morning and go right into meetings. You rarely saw him. He was a part of the team, but he took his job so seriously. He didn't hang with us. And we didn't expect him to."

For Woodson, through his first few seasons, which included trips to the Pro Bowl for both he and Aikman, there weren't many extensive conversations with the quarterback. Aikman wouldn't avoid him or his other teammates, but most of the dialogue between the two was on-field related, either in a game or practice. "Great play, Woody," was really the extent of their talks.

But that changed after a 1997 newspaper report revealed that Woodson was among several pro athletes who lost money when his financial advisor was caught stealing. Woodson, Junior Seau, Tony Boselli, Rob Johnson, and Stanley Richard were the most notable to be scammed by John Walter Gillette, who was eventually charged with 38 felony counts for swindling more than $9 million from his clients. "It was all in the papers one day," said Woodson, adding that the original report stating he had lost $2.5 million was extremely false, and that the amount was closer to about $100,000. "It was still embarrassing. You still couldn't believe that something like that would happen to you."

Woodson was asked about it a few times by his teammates before Aikman wandered over to his locker one day, the first time the safety remembered him ever doing so in six seasons. "He came over and sat next to my locker," Woodson recalled. "He just said, 'Hey, if you need anything from me, don't hesitate to call me. But don't even worry about it. Get your mind right.' I then met with his financial group, and we just talked about different things other than football."

Actually, aside from the embarrassment and instant money loss, the incident turned into a positive for Woodson, who ended up receiving more than $2 million in a lost-wages suit filed against Gillette. Recouping the cash was sweet, but it also ignited a relationship with the team's most visible superstar. "After that point is when I really got to know him better," Woodson said. "This is really when my relationship with Troy changed. And I still call him a good friend to this day."

While he usually kept to himself, Aikman wasn't above socializing with younger players. In 1999 Dat Nguyen was a rookie, and Dexter Coakley was just a third-year pro when the quarterback approached them on his way out of the complex one summer afternoon. Aikman asked both of the linebackers if they wanted to grab some food. "I remember Dexter leaned over to me and said, 'Hey, if he asked us, that means he's going to pay, right?'" Nguyen said. "We were young and didn't know if we could hang with some of the places Troy went to."

As it turned out, Aikman didn't take them to a fancy place, but instead a quiet sushi restaurant just a few blocks from the Valley Ranch complex. Neither Coakley nor Nguyen had ever tried it. "This is funny to me because I'm Asian," Nguyen said. "And Troy Aikman is the one who introduced me to sushi. You would think it'd be the other way around. But he took us there, and he ordered like four bowls of food. We loved it. And I love it now. I just think it's amazing that here I am, one of the few Asian players ever in the NFL, and Troy Aikman is the one who got me to eat sushi."

CHAPTER 2
QUARTERBACK
HEART-AIK

*I*n the offseason of 2000, I was still carving out my place within the organization. Sure, I was the team's website writer, but it hadn't fully been determined how much exclusive information I would be privy to. But I soon found myself getting a few heads-up calls when the team began signing veteran free agents.

I can remember sitting in a Dairy Queen in Decatur, Texas, on the phone with Cowboys' Executive Vice President and Director of Player Personnel Stephen Jones, writing out the base salaries, roster bonuses, and the overall terms of a contract for tight end Jackie Harris, who played in Dallas for just two seasons. I then had to type out the story in my car that the Cowboys had signed Harris.

But Stephen and I shared another exchange that spring. During one afternoon at work, I heard the Cowboys were close to signing Randall Cunningham and that the deal could be completed later in the evening. I was instructed to call Stephen, whose number I didn't have until that day, at about 10 PM.

I made sure I called right on the dot, but he didn't answer. I called back at about 10:20, and he answered only to say he'd call me right back. About 10 minutes later, he did and told me they were still talking to Randall and his agent, but it was close and to be ready. Of course, with my story written, I was just waiting for the green light to publish.

Since this deal hadn't been leaked to the press, we were waiting for it to be official before posting anything on the website. These days, stories like this typically get out, so we would've likely written a story reporting that the deal is almost done or that the two sides are talking.

So I called Stephen back around midnight, and one of his cousins answered and said he was on another phone and would get back with me. I recall Stephen ringing again around 1 AM to tell me they were still negotiating and to "hang in there." Meanwhile, I was keeping our webmaster, Alan Larkin, informed because he was responsible for posting the article to the site. Good thing Alan was the biggest night owl I've ever seen.

About 3:45 AM, Stephen woke me up from a dead sleep to tell me

Cunningham's deal was done and to run with the story. I called Alan, who was actually still awake, and we got it out first.

To this day Stephen will see me in the hallway and yell, "Nick at Night!"

—Nick Eatman

Releasing the Franchise

On March 7, 2001, the Cowboys officially went into rebuilding mode. One could argue that happened earlier—maybe when Dave Campo was hired in 2000 and the Cowboys played the season with one-third of their salary cap tied up in dead money. But as long as Jerry Jones has a franchise quarterback, as he still did then, he would give himself a puncher's chance.

On that day in early-March, though, Jones said good-bye to Troy Aikman, who was cut for financial reasons. To this day he calls the move one of the toughest he's had to make during his ownership of the team. The Cowboys issued a statement from Jones that afternoon, which read: "If you're in my shoes and have been able to get up for the last 12 years and have a franchise quarterback, that's a luxury in the NFL. I'm going to miss that personally, and we're going to miss that as an organization."

Even Jones himself had no way of knowing how true that last sentence would be. Although the NFL game has evolved over the years, the priority of having a top-flight franchise quarterback has not changed. Aikman was the first player Jones ever drafted when he took the can't-miss UCLA quarterback No. 1 in 1989, a year that also produced fellow Hall of Famers Barry Sanders, Deion Sanders, and Derrick Thomas among the top five draft picks.

When a guy like Aikman comes along, you don't pass on him. Even Jones, the Arkansas businessman who quickly became known as the guy who fired Tom Landry, already had enough football smarts to know that a player like Aikman is a rare commodity.

Two aging pillars of the franchise, Troy Aikman and Emmitt Smith, helped ignite a 21-point fourth-quarter comeback to stun the Redskins in the 1999 season opener. It was the lone road victory of an 8–8 season. *(Dallas Cowboys)*

Of course, the quarterback proved to be everything Jones, head coach Jimmy Johnson, and the rest of the organization could've dreamed, guiding the Cowboys to three Super Bowl titles and six NFC East crowns from 1992–98. But when Aikman's skills slowly started to decline, as well as the talent surrounding him, and the concussions began to pile up—including two in the 2000 season alone—the Cowboys knew it was time to move on.

On December 10, 2000, Aikman rolled out to the right, looking for an open receiver in the end zone when Redskins linebacker LaVar Arrington decked him to the ground, giving the quarterback his 10th NFL concussion, which proved to be the last of his career. In the press box at Texas Stadium, one veteran reporter for *The Dallas Morning News* turned around and said to a group of writers, "Folks, that might have been Troy Aikman's last play of his career."

No one really believed it, considering Aikman usually found a way to get off the mat and play the next week, if not return to the same game. But the reporter was correct. Aikman never played another snap. After he was released, he flirted with the idea of moving to another team, entertaining the thought of reuniting with former offensive coordinator Norv Turner in San Diego. But ultimately he announced his retirement on April 9 with a teary-eyed press conference at Texas Stadium. (In 2013 Aikman said the real reason he retired stemmed more from his back issues than concussions.)

Michael Irvin had hung up his pads a year earlier, and now it was Aikman's turn. While Emmitt Smith was still around to chase Walter Payton's NFL rushing record, the Cowboys were clearly turning the page.

And it wasn't because they didn't have talented players on the roster. The reason was because they didn't have a quarterback. Aikman's departure left a major void and left the Cowboys searching every football field—and even a few baseball diamonds—to find his replacement.

When Pigs Fly

When Jerry Jones purchased the Cowboys in 1989, the tag "Arkansas oil man" or "Arkansas businessman" usually prefaced every mentioning of the team's newest owner. Without a doubt he had his strong ties to The Natural State but seemingly not in the War Room. Not until Jones' 20th season with the Cowboys did he draft a player from the University of Arkansas, when Dallas took running back Felix Jones in the first round. But that doesn't mean America's Team completely shied away from Razorbacks.

In 2000 Clint Stoerner might not have made any NFL roster, but Jones decided to do his former Razorbacks head coach, Frank Broyles, a favor. Broyles, the Arkansas athletic director at the time, had once coached

Jones, who was an All-Southwest Conference guard on the Razorbacks' 1964 national championship team. Broyles knew Stoerner was on his way to a tryout in the Canadian Football League that summer and was making a stop in Dallas.

It just so happened to be the same weekend that the Cowboys were having a rookie minicamp for their newest draft picks, undrafted free agents, and first-year players. Stoerner, an above-average college quarterback with limited athletic ability and arm strength as well as below-average measurables at 6'2", 210 pounds, was a fan favorite in Arkansas, and Broyles wanted him to get a shot in the NFL. He phoned Jones and asked him to let Stoerner attend the minicamp on a tryout basis, which is a common practice in the NFL anyway. (Without any veterans on hand, teams don't usually have enough arms to get through a weekend of practices.)

Jones agreed to let Stoerner work out during the minicamp, though he didn't get a ton of snaps behind Anthony Wright. Because of that, on the last day of the camp, Stoerner was asked to go back out on the field for a few more throws, allowing the coaches and scouts to get a better read.

There was only one problem, and it was really just Stoerner's issue: Valley Ranch was being deluged by an extreme downpour. But nobody ever said opportunity knocks when it's sunny and 72 degrees. Stoerner went out in the rain and conducted a regular workout. He took snaps from center and shotgun and sprayed the ball over the field. He wasn't perfect, but the Cowboys knew that going in. The guys evaluating him were also getting drenched, so that had to be taken into consideration as well. One of the last throws of the session was a deep strike down the sideline to a rookie receiver that probably wasn't too thrilled with the extra work.

Whether or not Stoerner impressed the Cowboys through his ability to function in the rain, throw a wet ball with accuracy, or something else, he was signed to the roster soon after that camp and made the team in 2000, appearing in one game as a backup to Troy Aikman and Randall Cunningham.

Everyone remembers the Terrell Owens-George Teague showdown in the 2000 game at Texas Stadium when Owens celebrated at the 50-yard line and was eventually decked off the star by Teague. But there won't be many who recall Stoerner playing in mop-duty for the Cowboys after that T.O.-Teague incident and leading the offense to a touchdown.

Stoerner got the call to start two games in 2001, a season that saw four different quarterbacks start for the Cowboys. Stoerner led the team to a 17–3 win against the Cardinals at Texas Stadium and one week later had the Giants on the ropes.

For a quick moment midway through the third quarter, the doubters who thought Stoerner was too small, slow, or simply not good enough to play in the NFL were preparing for a three-piece meal of crow. When he found Rocket Ismail over the middle for an apparent touchdown, the Cowboys were poised to take a 31–7 lead against the Giants at the Meadowlands. Stoerner was playing a near-perfect game and was close to having a 2–0 record as a starter.

But Ismail was flagged for offensive pass interference, negating the score. And on the very next play from the Giants' 15-yard line, Stoerner was picked off in the end zone. It was just his first interception of the game, but he was about to throw three more…on three straight possessions.

The Giants rallied back, and even though the Cowboys benched Stoerner for newly signed veteran Ryan Leaf, the damage was done. New York would get the game into overtime and win 27–24. The next start for Stoerner was with the Dallas Desperados, an Arena Football League team owned and operated by the Jones family.

Stoerner ended up sticking around with the Cowboys for three years and four training camps but eventually lost his job not because he didn't outplay a rookie in 2003—but because Bill Parcells thought there was more upside in keeping some guy named Tony Romo.

Don't Bank on It

In between the release of Aikman and his retirement ceremony, the Cowboys tried to get a short-term answer in the form of quarterback Tony Banks, a five-year veteran who flashed a few moments of talent in his time with the Rams and Ravens. Overall, his signing didn't excite many, especially the spoiled Cowboys fan base who were used to Roger Staubach, Troy Aikman, and even Danny White sandwiched in between.

But Banks had started 61 games (25–36 record) before he got to Dallas and seemed a more viable option than youngsters Anthony Wright, who started the last two games of 2000, or even rookie Quincy Carter, who was drafted a month after Banks signed with the club in March.

The Cowboys never would've even drafted a quarterback in the second round, particularly a reach such as Carter, if they thought Banks was something more than a stopgap. The expectations weren't that high on the Cowboys' end, but imagine their disappointment when Banks even failed to meet those.

The veteran quarterback didn't exactly get off on the right foot with his new team. Banks opted to skip half of the Cowboys' practices at an April quarterback school, which back then was what they called OTAs (Organized Team Activities). His reason was logical to him: he was moving. Who can be bothered with learning a new offense as the starting quarterback of America's Team when there's a U-Haul to be unpacked, right? "He really didn't give a shit," said safety Darren Woodson, one of the vocal leaders and few holdovers from the Super Bowl era. "You could tell he really didn't care about being a part of the team or being a leader. That's just who he was."

Some Cowboys coaches were miffed in training camp when Banks missed a few days with a groin pull that wasn't exactly strained but sore. Playing with pain is something the Cowboys needed from their veterans, especially the starting quarterback in his first year with the team.

When owner Jerry Jones and head coach Dave Campo told reporters at a training camp press conference that the quarterback position was open for competition, Banks was visibly annoyed when the media relayed the information to him. "Well, that's news to me," Banks said. "I'm the starting quarterback until they tell me different."

And they told him, all right—by showing him the door. Just two games into the five-game preseason schedule, the Cowboys waived their starting quarterback. (And get used to that because it actually became rather trendy for the team when they trained in Oxnard.) But one morning in sunny California, the Cowboys were preparing for a morning practice when Banks was approached by a football operations assistant during his routine warm-up throws. Already in full uniform for practice, Banks was told to go back into the locker room, where he was then informed by the coaching staff and eventually Jones that his days with the Cowboys were over.

Banks was upset, but it wasn't his style to show it. He was reserved, almost in a too-cool-for-school fashion that gave off the impression to his teammates that he simply didn't care.

So the quarterback didn't bother waiting around. He said a few good-byes to the players in his path, packed his bag quickly, and, while the Cowboys were in the middle of practice, rolled his suitcase through the apartment-style hotel of the Residence Inn followed by a few reporters who had caught wind of the developing story. "I'm out," Banks said, never slowing his stride while getting asked questions from the media. "I guess I'm not Jerry's guy. You all saw practice and how I was playing. I didn't see this coming. I feel like my dad hit me with a baseball bat."

And Banks kept walking right in to a Cowboys-issued company car with a driver ready to take him to Los Angeles International Airport and a flight back to Dallas.

Just like that, the Quincy Carter era had begun. Carter played decent in the first two preseason games and did have a couple of moments in the exhibition opener at Oakland where his elusiveness bought some time in the pocket and led to touchdown passes. With Carter flashing promise, coupled with Banks' blasé attitude and less-than-stellar performance, the Cowboys pulled the trigger on a move that Jones later called "bold, but something you have to do with a young team."

Carter went on to start the season opener but saw action in only eight contests that year because of injuries. And the Cowboys actually played two games against Banks, who caught on with the Redskins and started 14 games for Washington but went 0–2 against the Cowboys.

Quincy's Rise and Fall

On August 14, 2001, the team's official website, DallasCowboys. com, set a new record for daily page views. The surprising release of Tony Banks, the projected starting quarterback, in the middle of training camp was enough to get the nation's attention. On August 4, 2004, the website undoubtedly set a new record. The Cowboys did it again, this time cutting Quincy Carter in the middle of training camp in Oxnard, California.

Something about Oxnard wasn't sitting well with starting quarterbacks. Two visits out west resulted in a pair of starters leaving the practice facility well before the rest of the team. The Cowboys' decision to cut both players came as a direct result of the same person. Banks was cut because of Quincy Carter. Quincy Carter got cut because of…Quincy Carter.

While Banks never played a down for the Cowboys, Carter actually led his team to the playoffs in 2003, the year he won the starting job in training camp by outlasting Chad Hutchinson, who had supplanted him in the starting post midway through the 2002 season.

As the story eventually unfolded, though, Carter had essentially benched himself that year when he reportedly failed his first drug test. That didn't get him in trouble with the league but simply with the

Cowboys, who turned the reigns over to Hutchinson. And that might have been the preferred direction anyway for the team, which courted the two-sport star from Stanford whose right arm was seemingly as golden as his California blonde hair.

The similarities to John Elway were seemingly too close to pass up. And when the former Stanford star decided to quit his time as a major league pitcher with the St. Louis Cardinals, the Cowboys were there in January 2002 to sign him, hoping Hutchinson might be the one to finally replace Troy Aikman.

But in those nine games of 2002, the quarterback looked more like a pitcher—and an erratic one at that. Hutchinson had plenty of rust to shake off and room to grow. Carter, meanwhile, took advantage of Bill Parcells' arrival in 2003, which wiped the slate clean. He won the job in training camp simply because he was better and continued to show that during the regular season, leading Dallas to a 10–6 record.

To this day, media members will argue that the 2003 season might have been Parcells' best coaching job despite the lack of playoff success as the Cowboys lost to the Panthers in the wild-card round. But the simple fact that he turned a 5–11 record into a 10–6 mark in one year—with Carter behind center and Troy Hambrick at running back—was enough to warrant the 2003 Cowboys as one of Parcells' best efforts.

Still, Carter was trying to become more than just the team's starting quarterback. He wanted the fame and success that comes with that title and was borderline desperate to get his name into the conversation with Don Meredith, Roger Staubach, and Aikman. The problem was Carter wasn't even close to Danny White's level either.

Carter wanted nothing more than to be associated with Cowboys quarterbacking lore. Every day in the locker room he was comparing his own record after 24 starts or 32 starts and seeing how it stacked with the franchise's greats. Perhaps the pressure of living up to that billing was too much for Carter to overcome.

That offseason didn't bring a ringing endorsement for the team's incumbent starting quarterback. The Cowboys not only signed a Parcells favorite in Vinny Testaverde to come in and help Carter's growth and development, but they also let Hutchinson go and signed another former baseball player who was seeking NFL fame. Drew Henson, who started over Tom Brady while at the University of Michigan, decided to forgo baseball after a failed attempt with the New York Yankees. Like they did with Hutchinson, the Cowboys simply took a flyer on Henson with the hope that he was destined for greatness.

Meanwhile, Carter was feeling the stress. He never believed that Parcells gave him overwhelming support, and the arrival of both Testaverde and Henson had him looking over his shoulder more than your average quarterback who had just taken his team to the playoffs.

However, it wasn't the two quarterbacks now on hand that was causing issues for Carter but rather the new wide receiver. In a trade that sent Joey Galloway to the Buccaneers, Parcells reunited with Keyshawn Johnson, a former No. 1 overall draft pick of the Jets in 1996, a year before Parcells arrived as that team's head coach.

Johnson came into the NFL talking and wrote a book entitled *Just Give Me The Damn Ball!* that covered his rookie season in the league. So by 2004 Johnson had no filter when it came to speaking his mind. One day during the summer of that first offseason, Johnson and Carter had a difference of opinion that led to some good-natured jawing, which then went from playful to tense when Johnson told Carter that he was a "broken-down Shaun King," referring to a former Buccaneers quarterback with whom Johnson had played in Tampa Bay. King's career was modest at best.

Here's Carter, who was hoping to someday be mentioned with Cowboys greats like Staubach and Aikman, and this new receiver, who was supposed to be on his side, just blurted out in the locker room his thoughts about his starting quarterback.

At least everyone thought he was the starter.

Cowboys executive vice president Stephen Jones, the team's director of player personnel, was sitting in the first row of first class as the Cowboys were flying to Oxnard, California, for the start of another training camp. Coming off a surprising playoff berth, and with the addition of key veterans such as Eddie George, Johnson, and Testaverde, expectation and optimism were sky high.

That was when Jones looked back and saw Carter in the aisle, needing to speak with him. Carter then informed him of another failed drug test, which was his second by NFL testing. Looking to build off last year's success, the Cowboys' starting quarterback was now likely facing a suspension. Of course, the Cowboys kept the news quiet. They privately did their homework on the matter, making several calls to the league to gauge just what was about to happen.

On August 4, training camp with the Cowboys seemed to be business as usual. It turned out to be anything but. Carter got a knock on his hotel room door around 6 AM. Football operations director Bruce Mays, who is known as the scythe-holding "Turk" for his standard role of informing players that they're about to be released, was outside Carter's door. Like he seemingly always did, he told the quarterback to come with him and bring his playbook.

Could this really be happening to the starting quarterback of the Dallas Cowboys just seven months after he led the team to the playoffs?

Around camp, word started to trickle out, and even then, it was hard to comprehend. Former pro scout Bryan Broaddus was finishing up a routine morning jog when he ran into his boss at breakfast. Veteran scout Larry Lacewell, the team's longtime director of scouting, was sipping a giant cup of coffee with a puzzled look on his face. "What's wrong, Lace?" Broaddus asked.

"We just fucking cut our starting quarterback," Lacewell snapped.

"What? We did what?"

"Yeah, we just cut our starting quarterback. Quincy is out."

Videographer Chris Behm, who joined the Cowboys in 1999 as an intern for the in-house TV department, had worked his way up to full-time status by 2004. He heard through the grapevine of Carter's release and immediately informed his supervisor, Scott Purcel, the team's director of TV. "Well, go get a camera," Purcel ordered. "Go find him."

So Behm raced to get a camera and then hurried through the hotel, which looked more like an apartment complex. He got back over to Carter's room where he saw Mays standing outside. "I wouldn't stand out here if I were you," Mays told Behm. "Quincy's in there and he's not happy."

But needing to get the shot, Behm found a row of bushes about 50 feet from the building. He wedged himself inside the bushes just enough to camouflage himself but yet have his on-shoulder camera out to film the quarterback's final days with the club. Carter soon exited the room with his duffel bag around his shoulder and a bowl of cereal in his hands.

Before he left in one of the Cowboys' company cars for the airport, Carter went to the training room to say his good-byes. "I can remember that morning. We're getting our ankles taped," linebacker Dat Nguyen recalled. "He walked in with a pair of Jordans that just came out —football Jordans. He had just bought them and was talking about them… But he came in and said bye to everyone. We're like, 'What the hell happened?' Nobody knew."

Carter definitely didn't know. His mother was in town to visit and was staying at a hotel down the street and hadn't heard from her son yet. That morning she was seen passing out T-shirts with her son's name and the No. 17 on the back. Those jerseys were the only No. 17s at camp that day or any other day through the duration of the team's stay in Oxnard.

Even Testaverde had no clue. He was walking into the training room when he overheard some equipment or training interns say, "We just cut Quincy." The veteran quarterback's eyes were like silver dollars. At the age of 40, Testaverde could definitely still throw the ball. He kept himself in impeccable shape for an NFL athlete, much less a man of his age. But to start for America's Team? Even Testaverde didn't expect that. Whether or not he was the least bit excited about the opportunity, he didn't let the media or even his teammates know, keeping a consistent, stoic face.

Fourth-string quarterback Tony Romo didn't share the same demeanor—maybe because he had suddenly become the third-string quarterback overnight. "Well, I know one thing," Romo said on the field as the players were stretching before practice. "I know I'm not getting cut today."

Up to that point, Romo's play in practice had been less than stellar. But what he lacked in physique, Romo made up for with his wits. Though he might have trouble reading an NFL defense, he could read a depth chart. He knew the addition of Testaverde and Henson probably doomed his chances of making the team a second straight year.

He went into camp knowing Carter was the starter, Testaverde was Parcells' guy, and Henson was the pet cat that was going to get plenty of time to develop. Romo knew something odd would have to happen for him to stick around.

Well, it happened.

When the Cowboys finally got around to a press conference following practice, both Parcells and Jerry Jones were extremely vague in their answers. The words "drug test" were never used, and it was a few days, if not weeks, before the facts started to come out as to why the Cowboys sent their starting quarterback home.

In actuality, Carter didn't go home—at least not right away. The quarterback told his driver, who was a Cowboys training camp intern, to take him to a nearby hotel instead of the airport. What happened after that remains a mystery. Maybe Carter stayed just one night, or maybe it was a few days. Regardless, it was clear his time with the Cowboys was over. And even though Jones and Parcells ultimately made the decision to cut him, it didn't come without disappointment. "Quincy brought his problems on himself," Parcells said recently. "He had his opportunity as the starting quarterback of the Dallas Cowboys...and he knows it. He brought his demise on himself. For some people they don't want the bar to be too high because they just can't handle it."

Carter eventually ended up with the New York Jets that season, backing up Chad Pennington. An injury to the starter forced Carter into the lineup for three games in November, and in helping the Jets make the playoffs, it seemed as if the troubled quarterback had turned things around.

And then, with his team set to face the Steelers in the divisional round, Carter told the Jets he needed to get back to Georgia to be with his ailing mother. Instead, it was later revealed that he had a relapse in his drug rehab and had failed another test. He was also rumored to have been diagnosed with bipolar disorder. The Jets cut him that offseason, and he never played in the NFL again.

For the next five years, Carter didn't give up on his football dreams. He had short stints in arena football and an even shorter stint with the CFL before his football career ended in 2009 after he played for the Indoor Football League in Abilene, Texas. Along the way, his off-the-field issues were just as prevalent and included multiple arrests, usually stemming from possession of marijuana or assault.

As the decade came to an end, it was a wild ride for the player the Cowboys once thought would be their eventual quarterback of the future. There weren't enough ups and were way too many downs in the Quincy Carter rollercoaster, which would have been quite the attraction at nearby Six Flags Over Texas.

What happened to Carter isn't really up for debate because those answers are rather obvious. But there's a better what if regarding Carter and his surprising release from the Cowboys on that early August morning: *if Quincy Carter makes it through training camp and the preseason without being released in 2004, what would've happened to Romo, who more than likely gets cut as the fourth quarterback?*

That's a question the Cowboys are glad they never had to answer.

CHAPTER 3
TUNA FOR BREAKFAST, LUNCH, & DINNER

One thing I've learned about head coaches, no matter their age, how big they are physically, or how in shape they appear to be, is that they always seem to show up in the hallways when you don't want to see them.

It can be something simple like working out in the weight room, which has always been allowed for employees, or talking to a player in the back by the locker room, or maybe even getting a plate of food about two hours after the players have eaten.

My first time meeting Bill Parcells was in the weight room on a Saturday morning, just a few days after he had been announced as head coach. Like everyone else in the building, we didn't know what to expect from him but had heard he was demanding on everyone, not just the players.

I was working out when he walked in. I wasn't sure what he was going to say. Parcells was old school to the point that he didn't like anyone who wasn't a player to be in his locker room, weight room, dining hall, or anywhere else that might interfere with what he called a sacred place for the team. But it was a Saturday, and when he got there, it made only the two of us.

He didn't say anything at first, and I nodded to acknowledge his presence. He smiled back, so I figured I was in the clear.

Moments later, my back is turned to him, and he says in a booming voice, "What do you do?" At first, my conscience probably thought I heard, "What are you doing?" so I asked him again, but he wanted to know my job title. I figured once I told him, he would then follow up with the "What are you doing?" question, but he didn't. He talked about writing his blog for NFL.com during his time off and said he admired good writers because it wasn't easy.

As I walked away, figuring our short conversation was up, he says, "So, are you good?"

I laughed and came up with something like, "Oh, I don't know. I think I'm okay. I'm still around."

Thankfully, we got off on the right foot, but over his four years, we did have a couple of small run-ins.

Once he was so upset about a photo on our website showing players working out in the offseason that he got his secretary to call me to his office. Fortunately, my supervisor, Derek Eagleton, was already in there, having it out with the coach. By the time I walked in, not only was the matter resolved, but I'm also sure Parcells had a newfound respect for Derek. You'll see later in this chapter how important it was to stand up to the coach.

Parcells stopped me once in the hallway before the draft and asked why we profile players the Cowboys might select. He was always worried about losing that competitive edge, and it bothered him that I wrote a story listing some of the potential picks.

"Don't be so descriptive, Nick," Parcells said. "You don't have to give away our board."

I didn't really have any more information than the next guy and I was a little miffed on how I was supposed to now cover the draft. Sarcastically, I responded with what I thought was a joke.

"Okay, so you want me to write, 'The Cowboys could take an offensive player or a defensive player.'"

"Yeah, do that. That's good."

He was serious and walked away. Obviously, we didn't do that, though we probably did tone down our draft coverage for the next few days.

And then there was the time I grabbed a plate of food at about 2:30 in the afternoon. The meal was catered in for the players, but staff members are usually allowed to have what's left over. Of course, as I'm loading up a piece of chicken, Parcells walks by, stops, stares at me, and asks, "So are we feeding everyone today?"

I just said, "Yeah, I think so" and kept serving myself. Looking back now, I must have been very hungry.

—Nick Eatman

The Introduction of Jerry and Bill

Wearing a three-piece suit with a tie will never be Bill Parcells' favorite look. Although he could dress with the best of them, he was more comfortable in a light windbreaker or long-sleeve athletic shirt with shorts.

But Parcells was always at home when he was talking football, which is what ESPN had the retired coach doing for parts of the 2002 season. And it was there during a break on the set when he made a statement to his friend and colleague at the time, Chris Mortensen. "I could work for that guy," said Parcells, who was wrapping up his third season away from the game. "I really could."

That guy was Jerry Jones, whose face had just popped up on their screens in the studio. Jones was conducting an interview, following another disappointing loss for the Cowboys in the midst of another disappointing season.

Parcells was aware of the issues between Jones and Jimmy Johnson back in the early 1990s that cut short a relationship that might have been even more successful. Together the two had won consecutive Super Bowls in 1992–93 and put a team in place to win another ring in 1995 before their split. Parcells didn't know exactly what had happened but also knew that he could make it work with anyone, especially an owner who had such a passion to win. "We had some mutual friends. I was very close with Al Davis and I know Jerry was, too," Parcells recalled. "I had a little background information from Al—not about working for the Cowboys, just about what they were trying to do. I knew Jerry had a lot of passion for his work and his job and his organization. I could name a few organizations I don't feel that about. The owner is just blasé about 'If we win, we win, good; if we don't, that's all right.' But I could tell Jerry wasn't like that. You want to be somewhere where it's important to the people, and certainly it's a high-profile franchise without question. I just felt like those are the kinds of things I look forward to. I was trying to do something at a place like that."

In January of 2003, Bill Parcells—standing to the left of Jerry Jones—became the sixth head coach in Cowboys history. In four years Parcells went 34–30 with two playoff appearances. (Dallas Cowboys)

Mortensen may be a TV personality, but he is a reporter at heart. And it wasn't long before he relayed Parcells' thoughts back down to Irving, Texas. Not long after that, Parcells and Jones met on Jones' private plane on the runway of a New Jersey airport late in the 2002 season. The Cowboys then had a nationally televised game with the Philadelphia Eagles when reports surfaced that Parcells had met with Jones to discuss a return to coaching. The only problem was Dallas still had a coach, as Dave Campo was putting the finishing touches on his third straight 5–11 campaign.

Days after the season concluded, Campo was fired as expected, and Parcells was introduced as the sixth head coach in Cowboys history.

It'll never last.

There's no way Bill can work with Jerry.

These two will fight about everything, and nothing will get accomplished.

Those were the strongest and loudest media opinions about this newly formed marriage in Dallas. Could a couple of headstrong personalities coexist? Parcells never had a doubt. "I knew I could work for him, and that's why I said that [to Mortensen]," Parcells said. "I understood how he was running the team, but I also had a very good understanding of what I would be allowed to do and change and I was fine with that. To me, it worked out pretty well—much better than anyone thought it would."

Change It All

Veteran safety Darren Woodson was ecstatic when he heard his team had hired Bill Parcells as its new head coach. The 11-year veteran had grown awfully tired of the changing culture within the only football franchise he'd ever known.

Long gone were the days when the Cowboys battled in practice as hard, if not harder, than the actual games. Gone were the days that players such as Troy Aikman, Michael Irvin, and Charles Haley forced every player on the team to be accountable for their actions, pushing each to reach their upmost potential. And more importantly, gone was the actual talent that led to the glory days.

Woodson loved Dave Campo, his first position coach when he arrived in Dallas and who he watched move up to defensive coordinator and then to head coach. But it was time for a change, and Woodson knew the no-nonsense Parcells was the right man for the job. "That was music to my ears when someone told me Parcells was coming in," Woodson said. "I didn't really know him. But I knew enough to know he was going to turn things around."

About two weeks after Parcells had taken the job, Woodson had yet to meet his new coach. With Parcells in and out of town, trying to relocate to Dallas, and Woodson enjoying some time off in his home state of Arizona, their paths hadn't crossed. Until one day Woodson's cell phone rang, displaying an unfamiliar number. "I answer the phone and hear, 'Hey, Darren, this is Bill Parcells.' He never called me anything but Darren," Woodson recalled. "He asked if I was in town and told me he wanted to visit. I said I'd be back in town on Monday and would come over."

Woodson returned to Dallas with the first order of business being to make his way to Valley Ranch and Parcells' office. After the head coach shook his hand and offered him a seat, Parcells got straight to the point: "Darren, have you ever heard of the scorched Earth process?"

"Umm, nope. What is that?"

"Well, the scorched Earth process is this: basically a new leader comes into a regime and sets up his own regime. He kills everything. He burns the grass, kills all the animals, kills all the diseases, whatever he wants. He just makes it his way."

"Umm, okay?" Woodson nodded, still unsure what this all meant.

"Let me tell you how this is going to be, Darren. It's going to be a scorched Earth process. And the people I don't want here are gone. People I want to keep—their ass is on notice."

Immediately, Woodson perked up. He was smiling ear to ear. He knew this was the guy for the job. "I remember thinking, 'Hmm, we've got a coach with some balls,'" Woodson said. "But right away, he had my attention."

Parcells revealed that he had called around about him, asking holdover coaches, trainers, equipment guys, operations assistants, and even a few players and had heard Woodson was a "stand-up guy" and the leader of the team.

"I'm sure you're going to be just fine with me because you're going to work," Parcells told him. "But we're going to butt heads. If you have a problem with confrontations, then we'll have an issue. All of these meetings you had to have with players and reaching out to them and closed-door, players-only meetings…that shit is over. I'm the guy that will meet with them. You just play football."

Woodson had three Super Bowl rings. He was already the Cowboys' all-time leading tackler and had made five Pro Bowls. Yet leaving Parcells' office that day was one of the highlights of his NFL career.

Barking Back

Birds chirp. Dogs bark. But when it came to his football staff, Bill Parcells did a little bit of both. He picked his spots, too.

Parcells didn't treat all of his players the same. He also didn't treat the coaches, trainers, equipment guys, or anyone else in his direct path the same. He liked to push buttons, but it was those who figured out how to push them back that Parcells ended up liking the most.

That was the game that some of them learned to play. The ones who never did probably weren't upset the day Parcells left the Cowboys in January 2007. The others still miss him to this day.

People like equipment managers Mike McCord and Bucky Buchanan have plenty of respect for Parcells, despite a few chew-out sessions.

Buchanan, whose dad, Buck, was the team's equipment manager for 21 years, started on the staff in 1994. So he was going on 10 official seasons with the Cowboys—in addition to all the times he just hung around the locker room, practice field, and sideline with his father—when Parcells arrived. Buchanan knew the job inside and out, but when Parcells showed up, it was like he had to interview all over again. "Man, he rode me every day for a while," Buchanan said. "He just had a particular way of doing things, and it took us a little bit to get it right. But once you screwed up one thing, he wouldn't forget it. And he wouldn't let you forget it either."

Buchanan's "one thing" occurred when the Cowboys were practicing short-yardage and goal-line situations. Parcells often liked to put defensive linemen and linebackers on offense for certain drills. Players such as Marcus Spears and Jay Ratliff would be goal-line tight ends, but since defensive players practiced in blue jerseys, they needed the white pullover pennys to simulate offensive players.

And amidst his many other responsibilities, including setting up the fields with the tackling dummies, sleds, and ropes, Buchanan simply forgot. "He jumped my ass all practice," he said. "I had to run back in real quick and get them, but it was a big deal to him. He just liked to do that and get on our ass because he knew if he acted like that to the players all the time, the message would wear off."

Buchanan took the ripping rather well for the most part, but the day he retaliated is probably the day Parcells grew fond of his veteran equipment manager. "I'm out there on the field setting up, and he's just sitting on the bench watching me, waiting for practice to start," Buchanan said. "I knew he was about to say something and, sure enough, he did."

"Buck, you know we got that shor…"

"I got it, Coach. Short yardage and goal line. I've got your damn jerseys right here."

Parcells smiled. He knew he had his football staff paying attention to the details as well.

During that first season, Buchanan felt Parcells' wrath early and often, but fellow equipment manager McCord had yet to get a tongue-lashing from Bill. It became a running joke how McCord continued to avoid so much as a surly comment from the volatile head coach.

That changed one day in Detroit.

The Cowboys were in the middle of wrapping up a rather easy win against the Lions when McCord took a call on the sideline telephone. It was public relations director Rich Dalrymple, who dialed down regularly to inform McCord of possible wardrobe violations by the players and other apparel issues. "Rich will call to tell us that a player needs to pull up his socks or maybe that we need to wear a sponsored cap on the sideline or something like that," McCord said. "So in this game, Rich called me, and I'm talking to him with my back to the field."

McCord hung up the phone and turned around to see the head coach with an awful look on his face. "What are you doing, McCord," Parcells barked, "ordering a fucking pizza?"

As Parcells quickly turned back toward the field, McCord simply shook his head, but with a smirk on his face, Buchanan walked by just in time to mutter his sentiments: "Welcome to my world."

One of the more well-liked members of the Valley Ranch staff is Todd Williams, whose current title is senior director of football administration. Over the years Williams has gradually worked his way up from being the operations intern who had to drive players to the airport in training camp to working directly under Stephen Jones, the team's chief operating officer and director of player personnel.

But his versatility can be seen on gamedays when Williams is on the sideline wearing an earpiece, so he can help relay information from the field to the owner's box. After the game he's not afraid to transform into an equipment staffer and pick up some bags and carry them out to the truck to help speed up the loading process. Williams does it all and usually with the same consistent smile.

But even he had a nose-to-nose encounter with Parcells during the Cowboys' 2005 training camp in Oxnard, California. "He was sitting out there on the tennis courts overlooking the fields," Williams said. "I was told to go to the training room and talk to [head trainer] Jim [Maurer], so I was hurrying to get in there before practice started, and Bill yelled at me, 'Hey Todd, get out of the training room.' I just told him I had to talk to Jim real quick."

"I don't give a shit. You don't go in my locker room."

"What? Are you kidding?" said Williams, whose orders came from someone with the last name of Jones.

"No, you stay out of there."

"The hell I will. I'll go wherever the hell I want to."

By this time, Williams and Parcells were just a few inches apart, not even hearing what the other was spitting out. Williams eventually walked into the training room anyway and never had another real issue with Parcells.

The coach just enjoyed ruffling feathers. Those who kept flying were the ones he grew to actually like.

Training Day

Other than the players themselves, no group on any football team had more verbal contact with Parcells than the Cowboys' athletic trainers. Before 2003 the staff of head trainer Jim Maurer and associates Britt Brown and Greg Gaither had never seen a head coach be more involved in the rehab process than Parcells, who had his own methods for treating injured players.

Fortunately, Maurer and Brown already had a major in with the new coach. Both had worked at SMU with longtime trainer Cash Birdwell, who was a trainer at Army for two years—1966–67—when Parcells coached there. During that same period when Parcells was with the Black Knights' football squad, Bob Knight was coaching the basketball team, which included a player named Mike Krzyzewski. "Cash used to talk about Bill all the time," Brown said, "So we knew what to expect. We needed a culture change, and I knew he'd come in and give us that. But sometimes you have to be careful what you wish for. I was nervously glad he was coming."

Before Parcells made his way to the training room, Maurer, Brown, and Gaither did their homework. Whether it was calling Birdwell again for a refresher course or talking to trainers from Parcells' previous stops with the Giants, Patriots, and Jets, the Cowboys' crew was already aware of the new head coach's stance on a few things.

They got rid of all of the TVs in the training room, a place Parcells wanted to be anything but cozy. He insisted the temperature be set in the high 50s and outlawed any food or drinks, making it so uncomfortable that players wouldn't want to go in there for treatment unless it was absolutely necessary. The area certainly wouldn't be a hangout.

When Parcells finished up his introductory press conference on January 2, 2003, he walked back with Jerry Jones to the training room to meet his new staff. Wearing a suit and tie, Parcells didn't even bother with the standard greeting. He asked: "Are you guys going to be hard on them or softballs?"

But once he learned of their connections with Birdwell, Parcells nodded, walked off, and said, "Ya'll will be all right. I'm sure you guys can figure it out."

However, that didn't stop the head coach from riding the trainers just as hard—and sometimes even harder—than he did his team. Parcells never wanted the players to be coddled in any way, so early on he disputed the trainers' approach to treating players.

Parcells saw everything on the practice field. When players went down or so much as limped off, he seemed to notice. But he didn't want his trainers rushing to their aid. One day Parcells handed all of the trainers fireman helmets and said, "All boroughs report…All boroughs report…9-1-1," suggesting his staff treated injuries a little too aggressively from the jump.

"I get that. I know what he's saying," Brown said. "He wanted them to get up. I see that. If you're hurt, get up. That was his basis. Give the player a chance to walk it off."

Along those lines, Parcells often gauged toughness in his players by their ability to play through pain. So the last thing he wanted was a coach or trainer removing them from practice until it was absolutely necessary.

Maurer once pulled a hobbling player out of a drill and off to the side—a move Parcells called "catching a player before he falls." After that practice Parcells went to the training room and congratulated Maurer, the team's head trainer since 1996. "Jim, you made the major league play of the week today," Parcells jabbed, causing a perplexed look on his target's face. "Oh yeah, you reached out there and caught him before he fell. That's the most unbelievable play I've ever seen."

Maurer had his ways of handling those moments with Parcells. Brown, arguably one of the more intense, if not confrontational individuals in the organization, chose a little different approach. As the director of rehabilitation, he is often in charge of getting a player back on the field, and it isn't always on the same timetable as the head coach.

In Parcells' first preseason, he hovered behind Brown as he was tending to cornerback Pete Hunter, who had an apparent broken forearm. Parcells asked, "What's wrong with Hunter?"

"Coach, we think he's got a broken forearm. We're going to take hi…"

"Oh, you don't know. You don't have X-ray vision."

"Coach, he's got a broken forearm. It's shifting."

Sure enough, X-rays revealed a broken forearm, but a week later, Parcells was asking why Hunter hadn't returned to practice yet. "Shit, I had open-heart surgery and I was out jogging from tree to tree in Jersey in two weeks," said Parcells, who used that line several times to the trainers, though they later learned his recollection of the recovery was quite embellished.

In fact, the trainers quickly discovered that Parcells would exaggerate just about everything. He once went to the trainer's room around 4:45 on a Friday afternoon and didn't see any of the staff, so he promptly left a sticky-note on one of their desks: "Guess you guys took the day off. If you decide to come in Monday, come see me."

Or heaven forbid they take a vacation. Brown walked in after some time off to find his office filled with bubble wrap, packing paper, and boxes, suggesting he must have moved if he'd been gone a whole week.

Those kinds of interactions always kept the trainers on their toes. One Saturday afternoon before a 2003 home game during Parcells' first season with the Cowboys, the training room was rather quiet, and

Brown was in a tucked-away office watching the only TV in the area while drinking a beer. Parcells, of course, walked around the corner and saw his veteran trainer, who had no clue how the head coach might react. "Britt... umm," he said, "you got another one of those?"

And the two sat down and watched a little college football that day.

The biggest incident between Brown and Parcells occurred in training camp of 2005 and involved guard Marco Rivera, who had a hamstring strain. Parcells had been pushing him to practice, even though the veteran guard could barely even run. But wanting to please his coach, Rivera told offensive line coach Tony Sparano one morning that he planned on practicing later in the afternoon.

Before too long, word got back to Parcells that Rivera could practice, though the coach was told by Brown that he wasn't even close. Parcells eventually launched an F-bomb-filled tirade that lasted several minutes, ending with Brown yelling, "Well, then fire me, Bill!"

Two hours later Brown is at practice with smoke still steaming out of his ears. Parcells then calls the trainer and Sparano out to the middle of the field to straighten out the matter. "I just remember going off on both of them," Brown said. "I told them both, 'I don't know where you guys got your medical degree from.' They tried to play me against both of them. I wasn't falling for it."

The next day Brown and Parcells still hadn't spoken to each other, but the coach called his fiery trainer out to the middle of the field again. He said, "You want to whip my ass don't you?"

"Yeah, I do. And if I got on you, it'd be over. But the problem is: I'd be the lead story on ESPN. And I just don't think that's a very good idea."

Parcells started laughing as did Brown. And with that their relationship grew even closer, though it took an F-bomb or 12 to get there.

50 Shades of Blond

After three NFL coaching stints in the northeast, Bill Parcells made his way down to Texas, where he saw plenty of blue-eyed blondes. During his first season with Dallas, one in particular showed up in his mirror every day.

The fiery coach, whose oddly shaped body resembled a tuna, never seemed to care much about physical appearances, especially in regards to changing hair colors. But in 2003 Parcells showed up to Dallas a little leaner in the midsection with the idea to add a "little" lighter look to his hair. Parcells wasn't gray anymore. He was as blond as the famously coiffed pro wrestler Ric Flair. For a few days, it was the blondest elephant in the room until one reporter simply had to ask. "It wasn't supposed to look like this," Parcells responded during a press conference. "I was getting my hair cut by a young girl, and at the time, she was pregnant. Well, she was supposed to just put a little color in there just for a second to keep it looking healthy, she said. So she puts it in there, but then she got a phone call and had to leave for a few minutes. So I'm sitting there and before you know it, it's too late. So, what are you gonna do?"

To the young girl's defense, she claimed Parcells actually told her she could leave and didn't need to wait around to wash out the color. He apparently told her he would do it himself in 20 minutes. But two hours later, he'd simply forgotten.

Either way, the blond locks didn't last long, and he eventually went back to the natural silver hair that we see today. But for a moment there in 2003, the NFL world enjoyed a rare look from Parcells…on the bright side.

Trick and Treats

The trainers felt the heat from Parcells on a daily basis simply because they were around more than anyone else, but Parcells didn't discriminate when it came to jabs. Even the team doctors, ranging from three to five orthopedists who accompanied the Cowboys at home games and on road trips, fell victim to the coach's playful, yet powerful, quips.

Parcells is known for seeing and hearing everything that happens—both on the field and off. In one classic case, he was standing in the middle of the field before a game with the Steelers at Texas Stadium on October 17, 2004, when he noticed his team doctors were on the visitor's sideline. In what had become a tradition long before Parcells came to Dallas, the doctors would exchange gifts—usually just caps or T-shirts—with their counterparts on the opposing team.

Parcells saw the swap, which was something he had actually witnessed a time or two before. But the following Monday he asked around, wondering what was going on over on the Steelers' sideline, and it was relayed to him that the doctors often trade "gift baskets" with their colleagues from other teams.

Gift baskets, huh? That's all Parcells seemed to hear.

Now, Parcells was famous for phrases like, "I'm up to my own ass in alligators," suggesting he had enough problems on his plate, but he made sure someone in the building could take care of this situation.

Sure enough, the next week the Cowboys were traveling to Green Bay, and as the doctors got to their seats on the team charter, some of which were in first class, they were shocked to see plastic pumpkins filled with gifts to hand out to the Packers' medical team.

The best visual was seeing these well-dressed doctors walking down the airplane stairs, holding their duffel bags, briefcases, and these bright orange pumpkins as they headed toward the team buses.

No one was above Parcells' ire.

Daughter Figure

Bill Parcells had three daughters who were all grown up by the time he arrived in Dallas, which ironically was the name of his youngest girl. She eventually married Scott Pioli, the former vice president of player personnel for the New England Patriots and general manager of the Kansas City Chiefs.

But the life of a head coach, especially bouncing around from job to job like Parcells did in the 1960s and 1970s, isn't always conducive to having a healthy relationship with one's children. Parcells had nine different jobs in the 16 years before he returned to New York in 1981, where he was eventually named head coach two years later.

Parcells always regretted not spending more time with his daughters, and while he made sure to better those relationships as they got older and had kids of their own, the guilt often weighed heavily on him.

About two years into his time with the Cowboys, Parcells met a young intern named Jancy Briles who was hired to work in the public relations department. While Parcells could be tough as nails and rough around the edges to any player, coach, staff member, and definitely the media at times, he had a soft spot for those who worked hard, kept to themselves, and didn't make waves.

Parcells noticed those qualities in Jancy long before he realized she was the oldest daughter of University of Houston head coach Art Briles, who eventually went to Baylor where he has since turned that program from a perennial doormat into one of the best teams in the country. Parcells immediately took to Jancy and eventually treated her like a daughter. Although Jancy has never once felt neglected by her own father, Parcells still felt compassion for her, knowing she's had to move around, change schools, and meet new friends all while her father chased his coaching dreams.

The head coach's adoration for Jancy became evident during a press conference one day at Valley Ranch. Standing off to the side with her back against a wall, Jancy's leg accidentally unplugged a power cord for local radio station KTCK "The Ticket," which was broadcasting Parcells' media briefing live on the radio. The engineer, wearing headphones and not realizing how loud his voice would carry, immediately freaked out and yelled at Jancy. "What are you doing? You just unplugged my cord. I'm off the air," the engineer shouted without any care that he had just interrupted Parcells mid-sentence.

With her red face already resembling a stop sign, Jancy fought off embarrassment and quickly plugged the cord back in, hoping Parcells would continue his thought and shift the focus off her. But he was having none of that. Instead, Parcells stared down the radio tech, who didn't even look up as he scrambled to get the conference back on the airwaves. Then Parcells got his attention and everyone else's, too. "You see that girl right there?" Parcells asked. "She can do…no wrong. You get that? No wrong."

From there, it was well known that Jancy was a Parcells favorite. He made it her job to bring him an oversized cup of iced tea every day as he walked toward the press conference. Parcells was notorious for chomping ice into the microphone as he pondered his thoughts.

If Parcells had a break in the action, he'd often spend some time chatting with Jancy about topics ranging from her career goals, her hobbies, Xs and Os (because she could do that with the best of them) to even her dating life. And that's when he realized that she not only had a boyfriend, but he worked for the Cowboys as well.

Rob Phillips was in his fourth season as a writer for Dallas Cowboys. com and had been dating Jancy for the previous seven months. The father figure in Parcells was intrigued. He asked her to point out "this fella" one day before he went to his press conference. So as the head coach made his way to the podium with a 44-ounce cup of tea in his hand, he was introduced to Phillips, an easygoing reporter whose face Parcells certainly recognized but didn't know by name. And he certainly didn't know that Parcells knew he was dating Jancy. As Rob reached out to offer a handshake, Parcells cut him off. "You watch your ass with her," Parcells said in a *Sopranos* tone of voice.

Phillips laughed, then downshifted to a smile, and then reverted to a straight face. Parcells wasn't laughing. He didn't smile. And he didn't even wait for a response as he walked off. But he turned to an embarrassed Jancy and said, "If he messes this up, I'm going to punch the shit out of him." And he said it loud enough for Phillips to hear.

With that, Parcells got to the podium like any other press conference. He announced injury news, the progress of quarterback Drew Bledsoe and the offense, and probably answered a question or two about the upcoming opponent.

Phillips didn't know if Parcells was serious, but he certainly seemed to be. Needless to say, Phillips didn't ask any questions in that press conference. He and Jancy dated for a few more months before eventually breaking it off, though they remained friends and colleagues until Phillips left the Cowboys in 2012.

Jancy and Parcells still keep in touch to this day. The former coach will sometimes call her up after a big win by Baylor, telling her to pass on his congratulations to her father. But he probably just uses it as an excuse to talk to one of his favorites.

Learning the AB Sees

This highly gifted, emotion-filled wide receiver was one of the most exciting players on the team during his rookie year. He wore No. 88 like other great Cowboys receivers Drew Pearson and Michael Irvin. Yet this was a new era, and this kid named Bryant was destined to be a star. And then eight years later, they drafted a player named Dez.

Long before Dez Bryant came into the picture, it was Antonio Bryant who figured to be the next superstar receiver in the making.

He had all the tools physically, but he often struggled to keep his emotions in check. Bryant wasn't afraid to speak his mind, and it often got him in trouble. He was arrested twice at the University of Pittsburgh, where in 2000 he was the Biletnikoff Award winner as the nation's best receiver and was named an All-American. But his character issues caused Bryant to fall to the Cowboys at No. 63 in the 2002 draft when just a few days earlier he had been projected as a late first-round pick.

Bryant had 733 yards and 44 catches as a rookie in 2002, a season capped off by a 170-yard receiving game in the finale against the Redskins. But his immaturity often flared up that year.

With the Cowboys getting beat 37–0 in a late-December game against the Giants in the Meadowlands, Bryant caught what appeared to be a meaningless score, though it did prevent a shutout. But even that didn't seem to warrant him sprinting to the goal post and dunking the ball over the crossbar with his team still trailing by 30 to their division rivals.

But that was Bryant, who did things his own way. And the next year, that style cost him quite a bit of money when Bill Parcells entered the picture. Bryant was getting fined left and right by Parcells, who clamped down on players for a variety of things, including tardiness to practices, a cell phone ringing in a meeting, or anything that the head coach deemed to be a team distraction.

You name it, and Bryant was handing over money for it in 2003. But the receiver didn't seem to mind too much especially since the fines were usually in the $1,000 range. Moving to the beat of his own drummer seemed more important to Bryant.

But Parcells still liked him as he did most of the players. Parcells was 63 years old then but still tried to relate to everyone in the locker room— even those some 40 years younger. One of the things on which Parcells prided himself was knowing one or two obscure facts about each player. That's how he connected with them and how he let them know he was on their side.

For a guy like Joey Galloway, Parcells learned his No. 1 wide receiver had an interest in purchasing an Arena Football League team. Parcells would then ask Galloway about the AFL and quiz him on some of its history. Galloway, a former Ohio State standout, eventually became a part-owner of the Columbus Destroyers.

But for other guys, it was something simple. Bryant walked past Parcells with a bright, neon-green shirt that couldn't help but catch the coach's attention. It might have even blinded him. However, Parcells liked it. "Antonio where did you get that shirt? I like that shirt," said Parcells, who was probably one of the only people in the building who called him by his first name and not by his nicknamed initials "AB."

"I don't know, Coach—at the store," said Bryant, who wasn't one for chatty small talk, unless it was with himself or his food. Bryant had a habit of talking out loud and even to his breakfast at times.

But the coach continued to press the issue. "No, I like that shirt," Parcells said. "I like that shirt a lot. Where can I get one for me?"

"For you? Coach, you can't have this shirt."

"Why not? It's a shirt. What it is? Nike? I need to get one of those. Help me out."

"No, Coach, you can't get this shirt."

"Why not?" Parcells said with a smile. And at this point, he was probably just playing up the conversation for the audience that was around.

But as Bryant kept walking, he answered his pestering coach: "Because they don't make this shirt in 6X."

That gathered group busted out laughing. Only two people didn't crack a smile: Parcells and Bryant, who really didn't think he was being funny.

Parcells mumbled something like, "All right, wiseass."

Throwback Jersey

If only the Parcells-Bryant battles were as friendly as the verbal jabs that would take place within the halls of Valley Ranch. By the 2004 season, Bryant's act was getting old for Parcells, who told the receiver that spring, "I've got one more good fight left in me. Don't let that be with you."

Whether or not the comment eventually provoked Bryant, the two would square off during a June workout at the team's indoor practice facility, a structure that collapsed in 2009 during a rookie minicamp practice that severely injured a handful of staff members.

But five years earlier, the indoor facility hosted quite a scene between Parcells and Bryant, who didn't take much to get agitated. During this practice, he was not only the third receiver on offense, but also was doing scout-team reps. Even worse, Bryant wasn't getting many balls thrown his way, so as he would run his routes, he began taking pot shots at the coaches. "Yeah, I'm just running these for my health," he said.

Bryant's frustrations likely stemmed from the fact that the Cowboys had acquired Keyshawn Johnson from the Buccaneers in exchange for Joey Galloway. And with Terry Glenn in the fold, Bryant was left as the third receiver, out of the starting rotation.

Finally, he was completely fed up. Bryant started yelling at the coaches and took off his jersey, tossing it to the ground. Parcells quickly stormed over, picked up the jersey, and threw it back at Bryant, ordering him to put it back on and continue practicing. What Bryant did instead was unprecedented, especially in Dallas.

Bryant grabbed the jersey, wadded it up in a ball, and then hurled it at the volatile coach. The sweaty practice clothing landed squarely in Parcells' face, prompting even more rage. Tight end James Whalen picked up Bryant and tried to remove him from the skirmish while Parcells was being held back by players and coaches, yelling for Bryant to leave the field. It took team security to get Bryant back to the locker rooms.

For many players around the league, a move like that is typically his last. But Parcells is no stranger to mixing it up with his team. When he coached the Giants, Parcells was known for having wrestling matches and even trading punches with players. Hall of Fame linebacker Lawrence Taylor was even involved in some of Parcells' dustups.

So a jersey in his face, in front of the entire team, was enough to infuriate Parcells, but not enough for him to cut Bryant. However, the tension between the two built up to a point where the Cowboys eventually did trade Bryant to Cleveland in exchange for veteran receiver Quincy Morgan.

Bryant had his moments in Cleveland but wasn't retained after the 2005 season because of his inconsistencies. He played most of 2006 with San Francisco but was suspended late in the campaign for substance abuse violations. He then returned to the league in 2008 with Tampa Bay and enjoyed his best year, posting 83 catches for 1,248 yards and seven touchdowns, which prompted the Bucs to place the franchise tag on him for 2009. Once again, though, Bryant failed to meet high expectations and had just 39 catches for 600 yards.

After hitting free agency, Bryant signed a four-year, $28 million deal with the Bengals, who then just five months later released him before the season began. Bryant hasn't played football since. Bryant's jersey toss at Parcells' face may not have had a major effect on his career overall, one filled with high hopes and disappointments, but it definitely did impact his time in Dallas.

He Said What?

Born in 1941, Bill Parcells was classified as old school during just about all of his NFL coaching career. Still that doesn't give him, or anyone else for that matter, the right to say offensive things, especially in public settings such as a press conference. Parcells knew this and understood it, but most head coaches have a slip of the tongue every now and then. His mouth, which often got him in trouble while growing up in New Jersey, caused a stir or two in Dallas as well.

The first misstep, which still stands as his biggest, occurred after a 2004 summer minicamp practice in his second offseason with the Cowboys. Reporters had asked Parcells about tempers flaring earlier in the day between a few assistant coaches. Defensive coordinator Mike Zimmer was heard yapping with quarterbacks coach Sean Payton during a team drill, and though the incident wasn't major, the media wanted Parcells' take on the matter. "You've got to keep an eye on those two because they're going to try to get the upper hand," Parcells said. "Mike wants the defense to do well, and Sean, he's going to have a few—no disrespect for the Orientals—but what we call Jap plays, okay? Surprise things." After a few seconds of silence, when reporters weren't sure how to react, Parcells continued with, "No disrespect to anyone."

Not only did Parcells fail to use the politically correct term "Asian," he referenced a sensitive subject concerning Japan's surprise attack of Pearl Harbor in 1941. Media members looked around with nervous laughter, but most knew the head coach had gone too far.

The most ironic aspect of the entire situation wasn't about the quote itself, though, but rather the fact that a reporter named Akira Kuboshima from *American Football Magazine* in Japan was actually in attendance that June afternoon. It was the only time Kuboshima visited Valley Ranch, and according to Cowboys' public relations officials, was the only time any Japanese reporter ever showed up at the facility to cover the team.

Kuboshima was interviewed by The Associated Press and said he was not offended by Parcells' statement but understood others from his country might be. "There is a chance for someone to feel offended," Kuboshima said. "To me, it was no big deal."

But some reporters in the audience that day made sure they found a few who didn't share Kuboshima's thoughts. John Tateishi of the Japanese American Citizens League, a national civil rights group, told *The Dallas Morning News* he was extremely insulted by the coach's comments. "Bill Parcells is a brilliant coach," Tateishi said. "Unfortunately, he is ignorant about racial slurs. I take great offense by what he said. Parcells ought to know better. He sorely needs more education on what is offensive and non-offensive to Japanese Americans. I am shocked that he would say this."

A Cowboys spokesman apologized on the team's behalf and Parcells later issued a statement: "Today during my news conference I made a very inappropriate reference, and although I prefaced it with the remark, 'no disrespect to anyone intended,' it was still uncalled for and inconsiderate. For that I apologize to anyone who may have been offended."

Parcells also met privately that day with Kuboshima. However, the coach obviously wasn't happy about the turn of events and could be heard muttering, "a bunch of (expletive) liberals" as he walked down the hallway.

While the coach managed to offend just a single race with that comment, he loaded up the offensive slurs during a 2005 press conference. And did so in just one sentence. When asked about safety Keith Davis becoming a valuable member of the Cowboys' special teams, Parcells attempted to explain the art of covering kickoffs, describing a balance between reckless and controlled. "You can't just go all Kamikaze," he said, "like some wild Indian yelling, 'Banzai!'"

Unlike the previous bomb, this quote received more chuckles from the group of reporters, who could only shake their heads, trying to figure out just how many different ethnicities the coach managed to offend this time around. But that statement certainly never caused a scene like the incident in 2004.

Parcells had other similar comments, but he usually provided more humor than anything else. The Cowboys had seven games decided by three points or less in 2005, including a loss in Seattle where a short field goal sailed wide in the fourth quarter. Their specialists included Canadian snapper Louis-Philipe Ladouceur, Australian punter Mat McBriar, and El Salvadorian kicker Jose Cortez, who was eventually cut and replaced by first Shaun Suisham and then later Billy Cundiff. The next season Parcells joked to a reporter, "I knew I was in trouble last year when my long snapper, my punter, and my field-goal kicker were all from out of the country."

So in 2006 the Cowboys signed veteran kicker Mike Vanderjagt, who had been released by the Indianapolis Colts but was still then the most accurate kicker in NFL history, making 88 percent of his attempts. But where is Vanderjagt from? Toronto, Canada. The Canadian kicker didn't last long, though, missing several key field goals during the 2006 campaign, which led to the Cowboys finally waiving him and signing Martin Gramatica, who hails from Argentina, of course.

Time to Fly Away

The head coach of the Cowboys is always issued seat 1A on the team's standard 757 American Airlines charter plane. It's the right-side window seat on the first row of first class. When Parcells was the head coach, especially on the return flights after games, seat 1A was rarely occupied.

No, Parcells wasn't typically a chatterbox on airplanes. He didn't watch the movie or fraternize with the other coaches and he certainly wasn't in the back talking with the players. This head coach was a little fearful of flying—even admitting it a few times to a small group of reporters. Parcells' anxiety was nowhere near the level of John Madden, the former Raiders coach and longtime broadcaster whose fear led to him riding all over the country on trains and later his own bus.

To Parcells, it was more of an uneasy feeling. His fellow coaches and others who worked with him think it was less about the fear of crashing and more about the lack of control. And since Parcells definitely couldn't fly the plane, he didn't stray too far from the guys who did. Parcells would often sit in the cockpit directly behind the pilots and talk about everything from the recently finished game to movies, family, and simply matters of life.

The pilots flying the Cowboys home after their wild-card loss to the Seahawks on January 6, 2007 were probably the first ones to know that Parcells was on his way out of Dallas. Like most coaches he seemed to struggle with the losses appreciably more than he relished the wins.

And in 2006 it appeared Parcells was about to lead the Cowboys to their first playoff win in 10 seasons. All they needed to do was convert a simple field goal, a 19-yard attempt, and then hold on for another minute. With that the Cowboys would've gotten out of Seattle with a first-round victory.

Instead, Parcells' nearly flawless quarterback, Tony Romo, wasn't so fortunate as the field-goal holder. Romo fumbled the snap, which prevented Martin Gramatica from attempting the kick, and then fell short of the goal line on his subsequent impromptu scramble. The Cowboys would also fall short of the win.

And for Parcells, whether he knew it at the time or not, he would never coach another game again. "That loss really, really hurt," Parcells recalled. "And it still hurts to this very day. I really thought we had something there. We had that game won, and to lose it like that really hurt. That 2006 team was on its way. I really think we would've gone up to Chicago [in the divisional round] and won the game. After that, who knows? But I know that team was good enough."

And that's why the loss was so painful to Parcells. He didn't want to be around his coaches, his players, or the team's personnel. He just wanted to go away and hide. The cockpit was usually the safest haven. "I just remember thinking right then, 'I can't take many more of these,'" Parcells said. "We're in a position to win the game and we need a field goal. It's an elementary play and we didn't execute it. It was a hard loss, and I told those guys, 'You know, this is probably going to be my last trip.'"

As an NFL head coach, it was. Parcells announced his retirement on January 22, 2007, ending a four-year run with the Cowboys. Many critics never thought he would last that long under Jerry Jones, but even to this day, Parcells says he's proud of two things from his time spent in Dallas: "I'm proud that we got the team better. We changed the course and got that team in position to do something. And I'm proud to call Jerry Jones a friend."

When Parcells was inducted into the Pro Football Hall of Fame in August 2013, he made sure the entire Jones family was present for his ceremonial party after the festivities in Canton, Ohio. Parcells also made sure all of the reporters who called for interviews prior to the event understood his relationship with the Cowboys' owner. "Jerry and I are pretty good friends. I don't know whether or not people know that. We talk a little bit. I wouldn't say frequently. We talk a little bit. It's good," said Parcells, who added he never had any serious issues working alongside Jones. "Jerry is a good businessman and a good listener. What you have to do is make sense to him. You've got to make sense to him. If he thinks you're making sense, he'll alter his opinion. I enjoyed him. I like him. I like him a lot. Overall, I liked my experience there. It didn't turn out perfect from a record standpoint. I understand all of that. But I learned a lot and I enjoyed working there."

CHAPTER 4
WOODY, WITTEN, & WARE

Darren Woodson played every game of his career in the shadows of someone else. He wasn't one of the Triplets. He wasn't the hired gun like Charles Haley or Deion Sanders. He wasn't even the best second-round pick of his decade because Larry Allen came in two years later.

So it was only fitting that Woodson's moment of glory occurred October 27, 2002 at Texas Stadium. Though it was lost in the moment, Woodson became the Cowboys' all-time leading tackler, surpassing Chuck Howley with 1,236 and eventually ended his career with 1,350, which ranks first. You know the game as when Emmitt Smith broke Walter Payton's rushing record. Chad Hutchinson made his first NFL start, replacing Quincy Carter. And when it comes to Woodson, some people remember his vicious hit on Seahawks receiver Darrell Jackson that resulted in a penalty, a $75,000 fine, and Jackson was taken to the hospital later that day after suffering a postgame seizure in the shower. "You know what I remember the most about that game," Woodson said 12 years later. "We lost. That's really all I remember. We had a chance to win that game and we didn't."

In 2011 the Cowboys had a showdown matchup with their division rivals on national TV. The Sunday Night Football game featured Dallas and Philly with first place in the NFC East on the line. But the Cowboys were punched in the mouth right off the bat and never had a chance. LeSean McCoy ripped through the defense for 185 yards, and the Eagles won 34–7.

DeMarcus Ware tied a Cowboys record and set his own career high with four sacks, which brought down Michael Vick. Obviously, the sacks made no difference in the outcome, but yet the record was at least noteworthy. "I don't even care about that," Ware said after the game. "I'd rather have no sacks and win the game. Sacks are nice if they help you win. But tonight we needed a lot more than that."

The next year the Cowboys were in Atlanta for a similar showdown with the world watching. Atlanta was a perfect 7–0, and Dallas was trying to keep pace in the playoff race. Jason Witten caught what appeared to be a routine 7-yard pass over the middle as the Cowboys were trying to claw back into the game.

But it wasn't just a normal catch. It was the 751ˢᵗ career reception for Witten, which broke Michael Irvin's franchise record. Witten just surpassed "The Playmaker," but the Cowboys couldn't surpass the Falcons on the scoreboard.

After the game Witten was no different than Woodson and Ware. "Records are nice, but this isn't the time for that type of stuff," Witten said. "Maybe someday I can look back and reflect on it. But right now we're trying to win games. That stuff doesn't matter if you don't get the W. I'm proud to play long enough and be able to be that successful, but it's hard to enjoy something like that after a loss."

Only one thing ever mattered to these three players. And while they didn't look alike or play the same spots, they were so much alike in their passion to win. Nicest guys you'll ever meet off the field. Just don't cross them on gameday. Check that, practice either.

One day in 2012 training camp in Oxnard, California, Witten made a catch over the middle, put a move on safety Brodney Pool, and ran past the entire defense for an apparent score. Witten jogged back to the huddle and yelled towards a group of us in the media standing on the sideline: "Get this fuckin' scrub outta here!"

Two weeks later, the Cowboys waived Pool, a veteran signed in the off-season to shore up the glaring needs at safety, a position that hadn't been fixed in Dallas since Woodson retired.

I was standing a few feet away from a livid Woodson late in a 1999 game against the Vikings when he got right in defensive line coach Jim Bates' face and started yelling in what appeared to be just a one-sided conversation. Woodson was irate because Bates was rotating some of his best lineman at key points in the game. "We don't have time for that shit. I'm tired, too," he said. "But get those guys on the field."

Woodson could say those things, considering he never left the field on defense or special teams. Woodson was pointing fingers at Bates and then some of the defensive starters such as veterans Greg Ellis and Chad Hennings. Players had to calm Woodson down, though he likely wasn't going to fight a coach or player. But you didn't know that judging from his eyes.

And speaking of eyes, I always wondered how a player with such an easy-going demeanor such as Ware could be that dominating on the field. But I saw it late in the 2013 game against the Lions where the Cowboys once again got creative in finding ways to lose. They had let a 10-point lead in the final minutes slip away, and Dez Bryant just couldn't stand it. Bryant and Witten went nose-to-nose when the tight end tried to calm him down and keep him focused for a possible Hail Mary attempt. But Bryant wouldn't stop yapping—that is until Ware stepped in. Ware, who was out of the game with a quad injury, grabbed the receiver by the jersey and got right in his face. I'll never forget the crazy eyes Ware had at that moment as he talked through gritting teeth. Whatever he said, Dez calmed down enough to get back on the field, though the last play came up short, as did the Cowboys.

We see the talent these great players possess, but rarely do we get to see the passion that drives them. Woodson, Witten, & Ware: three of the very best the Cowboys have ever had in just about any category. They're not exactly linked together by anyone—unless, of course, I get asked to name my all-time favorites.

—Nick Eatman

Uniform Ride

The 2000 season will go down as one of the more frustrating campaigns in Cowboys history for a lot of reasons. Expectations were high, but injuries doomed the offense right from the start, and the defense couldn't stop anyone, particularly on the ground, as three different running backs rushed for 200 yards in a game that year.

The Baltimore Ravens could've had a fourth player reach the mark, but Jamal Lewis was pulled in the third quarter with 187 rushing yards, and his backup, Priest Holmes, went for 64 in the final frame in what turned out to be a 27–0 victory for the Ravens, the eventual Super Bowl champions that season.

One of the explanations for the Cowboys struggling so mightily in the second half against Baltimore was the fact that their defensive leader wasn't on the field. And for part of the game, he wasn't even on the premises.

This mid-November matchup was the Cowboys' first trip to the newly built PSINet Stadium, which is now named M&T Bank Stadium. It was also the team's first visit to Baltimore since 1981, when the Colts were the city's main attraction.

While new stadiums typically have the newest equipment and technology, there are always exceptions, and the Cowboys' medical team found that out the hard way in the second quarter. Darren Woodson came off the field holding his right forearm, which he had broken earlier in his career, an injury that required a plate to be inserted. Now the Cowboys' training staff feared it was fractured again, just above the plate.

Veteran athletic trainer Britt Brown is perhaps the fiercest and most short-tempered member of the Cowboys' organization. He's the director of rehab so he's in charge of getting the players back on the field after injuries and he's never been one to back down from a confrontation of any sort. Needless to say, some of his battles with players and coaches have been epic. This time, a poor stadium attendant in the X-ray room felt the wrath of Brown, who nearly blew a gasket when he walked in with Woodson and learned the X-ray machine was broken. "Are you shitting me?" Brown snapped at the guy, who probably had no knowledge of the X-ray machine itself and was only there to tell trainers such as Brown that it wasn't functioning. "How the fuck can this be happening? We've got a game going on, this guy wants to play, and your X-ray machine is down in a brand new fucking stadium. What the hell are we going to do?"

The suggestion of taking Woodson to a hospital just two blocks away seemed to be the only solution. So as the second quarter is being played, Brown and Woodson, who is still in his full uniform, are piling into the back of an ambulance. "We walk into the ER, and Woody can't walk on the tile floors because it's slick and he's wearing his cleats," Brown said. "I'm holding him up as we walk through."

Darren Woodson won a Super Bowl ring in his first two seasons in 1992–93 and became the Cowboys' all-time leading tackler with 1,350 stops in his 12-year career. *(Dallas Cowboys)*

In the biggest hurry of his life, Brown immediately goes to the nurse and tells her what's about to happen. "I need an X-ray of his forearm. I need it now. I'm not doing any paperwork. You're going to do the X-ray, give me a copy of the X-ray, and we're going to leave. And you can send us the bill."

And that's basically what happened. The doctor did come out and tried to read it to Brown, who all but snatched the results out of his hand, shoved it in the protective sleeve, and hurried Woodson back to the ambulance and back to the stadium. "I think we were there five minutes," Brown said.

Unfortunately for Woodson and the entire Cowboys team, the X-ray results were what they initially thought—another fracture. Woodson wanted to play, but the nature of the injury, as well as the Cowboys 4–6 record at the time, were reasons enough to hold him out. He eventually went to injured reserve and missed the rest of the season.

Barking Back

When the 2003 training camp rolled around, the players were already realizing just how different things would be with Bill Parcells now in charge. In the past there might have been a dozen coaches on the field with a whistle. Now Parcells had the only one—and he had the only real voice as well.

It was Parcells' show, and everyone knew it.

Just a few days into camp, the head coach was annoyed by the morning practice, which included several defensive breakdowns, mostly stemming from a lack of communication. He went straight to the leader of the group. "You guys are stupid. You make stupid decisions out there. Just stupid," Parcells yelled, staring mostly at Woodson, who usually can handle the toughest of criticism and even welcomes it. That word, however, got under his skin.

"I know you're not calling me stupid," Woodson yelled back. "Are you calling me stupid?"

Without answering the question directly, Parcells used an analogy to make his point. "Well, Darren, if you throw a rock at a pack of dogs, the one who howls the loudest is usually the one who gets hit!" Parcells said. "Darren, if they're counting on you to make the calls and adjustments and you can't make the calls and adjustment, then they're following the stupid one."

"We went at it pretty good that day," Woodson recalled, "but it took me a little bit to realize what he was doing. Bill had an agenda. Everything he did was for a reason."

After that particular practice, Parcells called Woodson over and had a stern but important heart to heart. "Darren...shit rolls downhill. I told you that we were going to butt heads," Parcells said. "You have to understand that. When I jump your ass, these other motherfuckers see it. So you just have to get it. I like how you fight back with me. That's good. I can take it. But you have to take it, too, and know why I do it."

There was definitely a mutual respect between the two. Woodson had long desired to see a coach demand excellence in practice the way Jimmy Johnson did when Woodson first entered the league in 1992. Over the next 10 seasons, though, Woodson had seen a gradual decline in preparation. "The players we brought in just didn't know how to work. They didn't know how to prepare," Woodson said. "Under Chan [Gailey] and [Dave] Campo, the discipline just wasn't the same. When Bill got here, he focused on being a smarter team. I didn't like being called dumb that day, but he was right in that we weren't a smart team. We made a lot of dumb mistakes, and that's what he focused on right off the bat."

Woodson absolutely loved the Parcells hire. His only regret was that it didn't happen sooner, especially after his injury before the 2004 season cut his career short, which only gave him one year with Parcells as his head coach. But to this day, it sounds like Woodson spent a dozen seasons with the veteran leader. "Man, I learned so much under Bill Parcells…it's amazing," Woodson said. "If he was my coach when I first got to the league or if I just had about five or six more years with him, I would've been a hundred times better player than I was. There's no doubt about that. When he got here, I didn't think there was a lot about football I didn't know. I'd played 11 years already. He gets here, and it was amazing the stuff I learned from him…in four months."

One of the things Woodson admired about Parcells was his ability to coach everything on the field. You've got your defensive coaches. You've got your offensive coaches. You've got special teams coaches. "And then you've got your football coaches," Woodson said. "Bill was just a football coach. He coached the offense, the defense, the punters, the punt returners. But the thing I remember the most about Bill was his preparation. He got me that way. He got me to learn the umpires and referees. That's paying attention to detail like I've never seen."

Before a game early in the 2003 season, Parcells came up to Woodson and warned him about the tendencies of the assigned officiating crew. "Darren, this crew calls a lot of holding. Be careful with that today," Parcells said during the pregame warm-ups. "But they don't call a lot of pass interference, so be aggressive."

As amazed as Woodson was that a coach would take the time to know the officials and study them, he was even more floored about how on point Parcells was with his assessment. His coach didn't just know his team or his opponent, but the refs, too.

"I've Become *That* Guy"

When Woodson was a rookie, he found out right away that the team's quarterback was treated differently, and he acted differently, but Troy Aikman simply was, well, different. In every way Aikman carried himself like a star quarterback would and should. He was certainly a team guy, but he didn't associate himself with a lot of players, particularly on the defense. "He had to set the standard and he lived up to that," Woodson said of Aikman. "And he was an absolute perfectionist."

Woodson had a front-row seat for some of Aikman's practice tirades. He saw the quarterback punt the ball in disgust because he had trouble throwing passes in the rain. He saw him yell at receivers for running the wrong routes. "One time Troy was so pissed off at the offense that he walked to the middle of the drill and started cussing everyone out. He said, 'We're starting this whole fucking thing over. We're doing it again. All of it.' That's just the way Troy was. If you're not going to do it perfect, then we'll do it again until it's perfect."

Woodson admired that, but by 2003 he was the last of the star players from the 1990s still around. Aikman, Michael Irvin, Jay Novacek, and Charles Haley were all retired. Deion Sanders and Emmitt Smith had both moved on to other teams. Sometimes the last link to the glory years would have to say, "I've got three Super Bowl rings doing it this way."

One day during practice, second-year safety Roy Williams, who was seemingly the heir apparent to Woodson and expected to be the Cowboys' defensive leader for seasons to come, had two busts in coverage on consecutive plays. Williams was a young but very talented player and, as his running mate in the secondary, was someone on whom Woodson counted. After Williams missed another assignment, the veteran lost it.

Similar to what Aikman had done nearly a decade earlier, Woodson put his hands up, stopped the drill, and started cussing uncontrollably. He didn't just aim his anger at Williams but the entire defense. He told them practice "won't end today until we get this thing right."

As Woodson walked back to the huddle and put his helmet on, he realized what had just happened. "I thought, 'Oh wow, I've just become *that* guy,'" Woodson said. "Just like Aikman did, I was the exact same way. And that's really why we hit it off like we did. We both liked the same kind of structure. I was more like Troy than I was Emmitt or Michael or even Deion."

It just took Woodson about 10 years to realize it.

Third-Round Steal

Veteran coach Bill Parcells had a saying when it came to drafting tight ends. "Keep 'em coming," he would state as he made a come-here motion with his fingers. "They're so valuable to your offense. Every year...keep 'em coming."

But Parcells also had a theory about the center position, too. When coaching the Giants one year, he recalled the team "being held hostage at center" due to a combination of injuries and youthful backups. He saw the value there as well, so in the 2003 draft, his first with the Cowboys, Parcells was placed in a real dilemma. The first-round pick was rather easy, as Terence Newman fell to the Cowboys at No. 5. But in the second round, at No. 38 overall, the club had two players they coveted. And they were at two positions that Parcells always sought to shore up: tight end and center.

Do they get this crafty, yet undersized center named Al Johnson, who comes from a tough-as-nails University of Wisconsin program that loves to run the ball or take a chance on this 20-year-old, baby-faced tight end from the University of Tennessee? Parcells, to this day, says he probably loved Jason Witten as much as any other player in the draft. He saw a prospect who had a tremendous ceiling.

While the coaches, scouts and front-office folks were debating Johnson vs. Witten, Parcells told them to look deeper. He told them not to compare those two players but rather those two positions. "Which position has more depth?" Parcells asked the room. "This one is close between these two guys. Let's look at the third round. Can we get a good center or tight end in the third?"

And that's when the Cowboys decided the tight end position was a tad deeper. To get a center who could play right away, Johnson needed to be the pick, and that's what the Cowboys did. Parcells was sick to his stomach. He knew it was the smart move, but he saw Witten as a young Mark Bavaro, a complete tight end who starred for Parcells on his Giants teams of the 1980s.

As the second round started winding down, Parcells kept seeing Witten's nameplate among the available players up on the draft board. The picks were flying now, but that "Tennessee kid" was still there.

The Cowboys had him rated as a first-round pick. The team's protocol in such a situation like that where he's still there in the third round was to have a scout or coach quietly go to the other room and make a call to either the school or his agent just to make sure nothing has happened to cause the slide.

Late in the second round, two tight ends (L.J. Smith and Teyo Johnson) went off the board, causing somewhat of a scare. The Cowboys held the 69th selection, and once the third round began, Parcells was getting antsy, knowing they were just four picks away from getting an impact player. Talk of trading up was even discussed but never materialized as Chicago had the 68th pick, and tight end was an apparent need for the Bears as well. But when they opted for linebacker Lance Briggs—who was a steal in his own right, going on to make seven Pro Bowls—the Cowboys had their guy.

Or did they?

The phone rang right when they got on the clock. San Francisco was on the other end with a trade proposal. Trades always perk up the room, especially for owner Jerry Jones, who loves to wheel and deal. The 49ers wanted to move up and were willing to give their third- (89th), fourth-, and fifth-round picks.

From a point value, it more than made sense as the War Room constituents scanned over their charts. But Parcells wanted no part of it because he wanted Witten and wanted him badly. The tight end had already fallen 37 spots further than Parcells had ever dreamed, so waiting 20 more seemed far too risky.

But Jones has the final say. He called the 49ers back, and some in the room thought he was ready to make the deal. Then he asked the 49ers who they wanted to draft. "Uh-huh. Yeah? Is that right?" Jones said with the phone up to his ear. "Okay, well, I think we're going to pass."

He hung up the phone and told the room, "They wanted Witten. We're taking Witten."

The room erupted with cheers. Yes, they had seen Jones work his magic with trades and maneuvering before, but sometimes standing pat is the better play.

Eleven seasons, nine Pro Bowls, and a Cowboys' record 879 catches later, that decision is still one of the best the Cowboys have ever made.

Calling Out the Vet

Once Darren Woodson had established himself as one of the best in the NFL, the veteran safety rarely bothered covering tight ends in practice. "It was a waste of my time," Woodson said. "I covered Michael Irvin. I covered little guys like Kevin Williams. I even covered Rocket [Ismail] and Joey Galloway. So when it came to tight ends, I didn't really go over there."

By "there," Woodson meant the one-on-one drills in practice. Of course, he'll be the first to tell you how many times he was burned in the early part of his career by former Cowboys tight end Jay Novacek. "Man, Jay used to school me," Woodson said. "I couldn't believe it. I mean, I was covering the best receivers in the NFL—the fastest guys. But Jay Novacek? He was so crafty. He taught me a lot about the game. He taught me about angles and moving my hips. I got a lot better because of him."

And because of that, the post-Novacek tight ends like Eric Bjornson, David LaFleur, Jackie Harris, and Mike Lucky were no match for Woodson, though he admits that James Whalen "worked me pretty good a few times." For the most part, though, Woodson didn't worry about tight ends until the 11-on-11 team period of practice.

But in training camp of 2003, Jason Witten was ready to test his skills. At the end of the one-on-one portion of practice, the rookie tight end asked for one more rep. But he didn't want just anyone covering him. "Hey, Woody," he asked, "you ready?"

"You want some, Witten? Are *you* ready?"

"Let's go, baby!"

Woodson couldn't believe it. He was in his 12th year in the league, an owner of three Super Bowl rings, and he no longer really bothered covering tight ends anymore, especially since he was essentially the team's slot corner, handling inside receivers. But Witten was calling him out, and Woodson never backed down from a challenge.

Witten made sure Tony Romo, a fellow rookie, was the quarterback throwing to him. And instead of running something deep or to the outside, Witten ran a drag route, angling across the middle of the field. That's a solid play in any game situation, but in one-on-one drills, where there are no defenders to help, it's considered "bush league."

Witten made the catch and was jawing with the veteran, who barked back, "Run a real route, rookie. That's bullshit."

The two were both smiling, and there were no hard feelings. Woodson went back to the sideline telling his defensive buddies that he wasn't going to count that as a catch against him. But deep down, he was thinking about something more. "I remember thinking, 'This rookie just called me out. And he's a damn good player,'" Woodson recalled. "From there, I knew that I needed to face him. He wasn't just a normal tight end. Just like Jay got me better early in my career, I knew this kid would make me better later in my career."

Jaw-Dropping Streak

If there was one underlining theme to some of the changes Bill Parcells was implementing in his first season with the Cowboys, it was toughness. Parcells wanted the Cowboys to be a tougher team, and to do that, they couldn't be coddled, as he put it.

He often thought the Cowboys' training staff rushed to the aid of players too quickly. There were some battles between Parcells and his trainers where he blurred the line between proving a point and putting a player's health at risk. To Parcells it was always pretty simple: if you're hurt, get off the field. If you're not, keep playing.

Early in the 2003 season, he wasn't too happy when he learned his rookie tight end, Jason Witten, had suffered a broken jaw and would miss the rest of the team's game against the Cardinals. "I told him Bavaro played right through it," Parcells said, referring to former Giants tight end Mark Bavaro, to whom he often compared Witten, especially early in his career. "Mark had the same injury once, and I told him he could play through it."

Witten didn't return to the game that day and missed the next one against the Eagles as well because his jaw was wired shut. The rookie tight end had trouble eating solid foods, which meant he was losing weight. If he couldn't make his weight, Parcells said he couldn't return to action. "He came up to me and said, 'Do you want to get back on the field?'" Witten said. "I told him I did, and he said, 'Eat this right here.' He had a couple of jars of baby food. I don't remember what kind it was. I didn't know if he was serious, but he was. He said it would make me gain my weight back, and it was something I could eat."

Witten admits it was a good idea from his coach, who seemingly had a solution for everything, but Witten didn't eat the baby food, stating he "just couldn't do it." He may have spurned the baby food, but Witten wasn't really a complete grown-up either. He couldn't even buy a beer when the Cowboys drafted him in April 2003 and was just a 21-year-old when he was playing his rookie season.

While this 52-yard reception with no helmet in 2007 will go down as one of Jason Witten's most memorable plays, the NFL has since changed its rules, stopping the play when a ball carrier loses his lid.

Having already missed one game, Witten wanted to make sure he was back for the Cowboys' next matchup against the Lions in Detroit. But the rookie was worried about his weight, having dropped about 12 pounds since the injury. He needed to be close to 260 pounds, or Parcells was going to make him sit out again.

And that would mean another week of more Bavaro stories.

So Witten and associate trainer Britt Brown came up with a plan. When he went to weigh himself, Witten stepped up on the scale wearing his baggy sweatpants, and with Parcells watching, promptly came in at 258.

With eyebrows raised Parcells was impressed. He told his rookie tight end to keep eating but cleared him to play. Witten stepped off the scale, gingerly walked back to the training room and made sure Parcells wasn't following him. He didn't want the head coach to see the five-pound weights he had stuffed into his sweat pockets. "I had to get back out there," Witten joked. "Do whatever it takes, right?"

To this day the staff members who worked with Parcells say the head coach was the most knowledgeable and aware person they've ever been around, stating that nothing ever got past him. "I think this might have been one thing he didn't know," Brown said. "But who knows? Maybe he did and just overlooked it. He wanted Jason to play, too."

But Parcells had another agenda as well. "I was trying to see if he could push himself," Parcells said. "He was a tough kid, but sometimes they need to understand what they can do. He missed one game, but that was it."

Indeed, Witten returned the next week and hasn't missed a contest since, playing in 171 straight games through the 2013 season despite concussions, high-ankle sprains, lacerated spleens, and broken ribs.

Calling on Betsy

All Cowboys fans have seen the play. There have been T-shirts made up to commemorate it. Replays have been shown over and over.

Without a doubt, whenever Jason Witten is inducted into the Cowboys Ring of Honor or maybe even the Pro Football Hall of Fame, the shot of him in the 2007 game at Philadelphia will be shown over and over. There's something symbolic about Witten's over-the-middle catch, when he takes a hit from a defender and loses his helmet but continues to stay on his feet and run with no lid for a 53-yard gain. One of the toughest players the Cowboys have ever had showed it in one single play, one that will forever be associated with the greatest tight end in Cowboys history.

What few people know about that play is what was said on the sideline by the team's equipment staff when the helmet went flying off Witten's head. "There goes Betsy," said Bucky Buchanan, the team's longtime equipment assistant who actually named Witten's helmet for him as a joke that actually stuck. It's not only stuck for one helmet, but Witten is now onto Betsy 2.

The name actually started as a result of Witten being both superstitious about changing equipment but also extremely anal retentive in getting the look and feel to be exactly the way he wants it. Although other players were fine with changing out helmets every year or every other year, Witten kept the same helmet for the first five years of his career.

Even when the Cowboys tried to break in a new helmet during consecutive offseasons, the switch wouldn't last long. One day in a summer OTA practice, Witten was so frustrated with the helmet, that he ripped it off in disgust. He was fed up with the change.

But it's a good thing Buchanan was ready for it. "Hey, I've got Betsy for you if you want it," Buchanan said to Witten, who was trying to abide by all safety rules but just wasn't ready to make the switch.

"Yeah, let's do it. Let me have her back."

Buchanan went to a trunk behind a practice bench and pulled out Witten's old helmet, which actually had a blue sticker with the name "Betsy" printed on the backside of the headgear.

And that went on for years before Witten finally switched to a new helmet. Of course, the helmet is aptly named "Betsy 2." "In my era growing up, my dad use to nickname things," Buchanan said, whose dad Buck served as a Cowboys' equipment manager for 21 years, "like a boat or a car has a girl's name. He rode with it. We just put Betsy on the back tag. He's still the same way. It'll probably take a long time for him to get rid of Betsy 2."

However, during a game in 2013, Witten did play one snap without his trusted Betsy. Just as the offense is going onto the field for the first play in Detroit, Witten's chinstrap snapped in half as he's buckling his helmet for the first time. "Well, he just freaks out," equipment manager Mike McCord said. "He's throwing us his helmet. And, of course, he doesn't have a backup. So we just gave him James Hanna's helmet. It's not the same brand or style."

Witten goes out to the huddle fidgeting with the new and uncomfortable lid. He gets it snapped and goes to the line of scrimmage. Before he gets into his stance, he looks over once to see if Buchanan has fixed his helmet. Then he blocks a linebacker for a running play. Witten then looks over before the second-down play, and sure enough, his helmet is ready. Witten races toward the sideline and meets Buchanan at the numbers to exchange his helmet.

The crisis was averted. The Cowboys not only avoided a Witten blowup, but the helmet also got fixed before the Cowboys could use a three-tight end set involving Hanna.

What's My Name?

When it came to studying film, running a precise route, or making sure he used the proper blocking technique, no one paid more attention to detail than Jason Witten. What he learned from veterans like Dan Campbell, assistant coach Tony Sparano—who was Witten's first tight ends coach—and especially former head coach Bill Parcells was how important the little things were to being successful.

But that was on the field. Sometimes Witten could be a little spacey off it.

The Cowboys' locker room has been shuffled around quite a bit over the years, and Witten, like all of the longtime vets, has had different lockers. And with that he has certainly had many different locker neighbors.

For nearly two seasons, from 2009–10, Witten found himself next to Cory Procter, a jolly offensive lineman who was seemingly always in a good mood. Procter, who came over from the Lions during the 2005 season, even started 11 games in 2008. His versatility was valuable to the Cowboys, considering he could play both guard spots and center. Though maybe not the most talented player, that position flexibility allowed Procter to stick around—not only with the Cowboys, but also later with the Dolphins, where he played in 2010.

As is customary toward the end of the schedule in December, players will often get their teammates to sign memorabilia—for Christmas gifts or just to have. After the season is over, it's likely they won't see each other for a few weeks, if not months. So Procter wanted to make sure he got a jersey autographed by his locker neighbor. An autographed Witten No. 82 would be a treasured item for Procter's collection at his office or man cave. "Hey Witt," he asked, "you mind signing this jersey for me?"

"Yeah, no problem. Do you want me to make it out to anyone?"

"Yeah, it's for me. Just make it to me."

"Okay, no problem. I'll do it in a second."

A few minutes later, Procter came back to his locker and saw the jersey had been signed. But he was a little bummed. The note said, "To Corey." Witten had misspelled his first name.

"That work for you, Proc?

"Well, yeah, but you spelled my name wrong. There's no E in Cory. I guess it's okay."

"No, it's not okay. I'll do it again. Let me just flip it over, and we'll sign it on the other side. I'm sorry, man. I'll do it after practice."

Again, Procter was one of the more easygoing players on the team, so it wasn't a big deal to him at all. He forgot about the jersey until the next day when he noticed it was laid out on his locker with a sharpie on top of it.

He flipped it over to see how Witten had signed it. Once again it had another signature, another thoughtful message, and yes, another beginning with "To Corey."

All Procter could do was laugh. He said, "Witt, it's right up there," pointing to his nameplate above his locker.

Witten ended up getting him a jersey and signing it yet again—correctly this time. The third time was the charm in getting Procter's name right.

Flashing Before His Eyes

They say football is a game of inches. It's a game of minutes, too. One minute, a player's perspective can be centered on a game. The next minute, it can be about real life.

At 5:22 PM, DeMarcus Ware has only one thought racing through his head: get a stop, so we can get off the field. At 5:24 the Cowboys' best defensive player is wondering if he'll ever walk again, much less resume his already stellar NFL career.

That's how fast perspective can change in the game of football. Not long after chasing LaDainian Tomlinson around, Ware is having to wonder if he'll ever chase his two-year-old daughter in the backyard.

Without a doubt, December 13, 2009 will go down as one of the scariest moments in Ware's life. In the middle of a crucial home game against the Chargers, the Cowboys were tied with their AFC counterparts 10–10 early in the fourth quarter. That's when Ware awkwardly fell headfirst into the side of Chargers offensive lineman Brandyn Dombrowski. Ware's neck jammed straight into Dombrowski's side, dropping the Cowboys' pass-rushing specialist to the ground immediately.

Suddenly, everything Ware had ever worked for is flashing in front of him. "That's the scariest moment I've ever had in football," Ware recalled. "If you're immobile and can't move, but you think you're moving and all of a sudden you're getting strapped down and everything around you is quiet and all the guys around you are praying, and now you've got your face mask off…it's a scary feeling. I'm thinking, 'Am I going to come back?

Am I going to be able to walk again. Can I still play with my kids? Wow, I'm that guy. I'm that guy getting carted off that I've always seen before.'"

The one thought not going through Ware's head or anyone from the Cowboys' organization was the football game they had on the schedule in six days. That's when they were set to play the undefeated Saints with Drew Brees and Sean Payton, who had led that offensive juggernaut to a 13–0 record.

With Ware strapped to a stretcher and getting carted off and headed to the hospital, just playing again—ever—was the focus. Playing again this season would be miraculous, too. But next week? On a short week, too?

Cowboys associate trainer Britt Brown, who is the team's director of rehabilitation and was the member of the medical staff who rode with Ware in the ambulance, said he would've never dreamed Ware would play against the Saints in six days. "I would've said there's just no way," Brown recalled. "But he did have some movement of all of his limbs. That's a good thing. I knew if anyone on our team was going to do it, it'd be him or maybe a Jason Witten. Those guys just amaze you. What Ware did was amazing."

Ware didn't just play the next game in New Orleans. He played one of the best games of his entire career. What was supposed to be just a limited outing with only third-down snaps turned into a heroic performance that will go down as one of the best individual games in franchise history.

Ware sacked Brees twice, resulting in two forced fumbles for the defense, including one in the final 20 seconds of the game to preserve the Cowboys' stunning 24–17 win against the Saints to ruin their perfect season. "When I think of that game I think of No. 94," said current head coach Jason Garrett, who was the Cowboys' offensive coordinator at the time. "You didn't know if he was going to be able to play again, and he comes back the next game and plays like he did. It was just an incredible performance, and something I'll never forget."

Ware says the entire six-day journey is one he'll never forget either, starting, of course, with the frightening scene back at the place now called AT&T Stadium and ending in the Louisiana Superdome in New Orleans.

The journey to get there was courageous enough, but initially the outlook for Ware to play again, even walk again was in doubt. With 11:28 remaining in the game, the Cowboys are in a dogfight with the Chargers. The game is tied 10–10, and Dallas is 8–4, desperately need-ing to avoid a two-game losing streak after a tough loss to the Giants the previous week and the undefeated Saints looming ahead.

So that was the mind-set in the fourth quarter as tensions were riding high. But in a blink of an eye—or an awkward neck jam to the thigh—the outlook changed. The Cowboys' star player lay helpless—and motionless—on the turf.

The medical team rushed to the fallen star and immediately got his neck stabilized. Brown said one advantage the Cowboys, and many NFL teams have in these situations, is the luxury of having a specialized spinal surgeon on their sidelines. Dr. Drew Dossett attends nearly all Cowboys games and was at this one for Ware, who said part of that experience was a blur, but he does remember the sounds or lack thereof. "It was so quiet," he said. "I had a lot of people right there talking to me. But it didn't sound like a football game. It was so quiet. I could hear players talk-ing to me and praying for me. But that was scary just hearing how quiet things were around me in the stadium. That made me wonder, 'Wait, is this really bad?'"

Lying there on the field, confused, and somewhat out of sorts, Ware was asking why so much attention was around him. "People said you aren't moving. I was like, 'What? Are you kidding me. I am moving.' But I wasn't. I thought I was moving my arms, but they said I wasn't. That's what I remember the most. And I remember the whole feeling of them strapping me down and taking my face mask off. You can't forget a feel-ing like that."

After a few minutes of attending to Ware, Cowboys head athletic trainer Jim Maurer turned toward the corner of the stadium and crossed his arms in an X to signal for the medical cart. By then, longtime equipment assistant Bucky Buchanan had used his metal tool that unscrews the bolts on the face mask to remove it from Ware's face. That's a procedure teams use right away in all neck/spine injuries that gives more air for the players but also in case oxygen or ventilators are needed.

Still, something about the face mask being removed is emasculating for NFL players, who are already helpless as they lie flat on their back.

Fortunately for Ware by the time he was being rolled out, he had some feeling in his arms and hands—enough to flash a thumbs-up sign and then he made a "W" with his fingers to encourage his teammates and the fans to rally the Cowboys to a win. That didn't happen. The Cowboys lost 20–17, but none of that seemed to matter at that point. Ware's health had rightfully stolen the focus.

Brown remembers the ride to the hospital with Ware, who was undoubtedly worried but wasn't showing it. "Actually he was calm. He felt like we had everything under control. He was asking questions about what we're going to do when we get there," said Brown, who was there for similar incidents involving Emmitt Smith in 1996 in Chicago and, of course, Michael Irvin in Philadelphia in 1999. "[DeMarcus] had movement of all of his limbs. That's a good [sign]. With the history he had with all of his neck burners, we had to be careful with him. A similar thing happened with Emmitt. He was fine and he played. But you just have to be overly cautious. You don't have X-ray vision. You don't have an MRI yet. You're basing it on their symptoms and their pain level and where the pain is."

Avoiding all clichés, Ware simply had a massive pain in the neck, and it got worse once he made it to the hospital. That's when the All-Pro pass rusher said he eventually took matters into his own hands in terms of the rehab process. "I remember going to the hospital, riding in the ambulance with Britt," Ware said. "My neck was hurting worse. I was going through the tests and I passed the test. They put that neck brace on me, and it started to hurt even worse. So I told them, 'I'm not wearing it. It's hurting me more than it's helping.' The next day I came here and did some preliminary tests that I passed. So it was just a waiting game for me. We had to figure out if I was going to play again that year and then we had to figure out if I could play that week."

The latter seemed so unlikely. How could this guy have no feeling in his arms at one moment and be ready to play just a few days later? When Ware woke up Saturday morning—December 19—he says he still didn't know if he would play that night. Obviously he hadn't practiced all week. And even though they were less than 12 hours from kickoff, it was still 50-50.

On one hand, Ware had just sustained a scary sprained neck injury that had him questioning his quality of life at one moment. Then again, he had never missed a game in his NFL career, playing in 77 straight contests heading into New Orleans.

Ware had about 20 family members who had made the drive to that game, and they were all telling him to be smart about the decision. Ware said he felt no pressure to play the game for them or anyone else—except the guys he goes to war with each day. "When I walked into the locker room, I remember seeing their faces," Ware recalled about his teammates. "They had this look on their face. You knew this game was big. You knew how much it meant to them. And I knew how much it meant to me. I just decided I was going to give it everything I had to play."

About three hours before kickoff, Ware was on the field wearing shoulder pads and a helmet. The Cowboys' medical staff was putting him through a wide range of tests to check his range of motion and to see how the neck would hold up. Ware said it was a head-butt with Cowboys fullback Deon Anderson that proved to be the final test, proving to him he could hold up.

With that, he was cleared and he was playing. But he wasn't going to start. The Cowboys made the choice to play Ware on third-down situations while Victor Butler would start at outside linebacker in the base defense.

But that didn't last long. "Football is an angry game—a gladiator's game," Ware said. "I just remember one of the first plays of the game. I went out there, and it was third and 11. They ran the ball. I was like, 'They're insulting me. They're trying to hurt me.' It was the first third down when I went out there. I just thought I'd rush the passer, and they ran the ball to my side. I started saying, 'You know what, I'm getting a little angry.' They did it again a couple more times to test me. I just said, 'You know what, you're testing the wrong guy tonight.' I started getting my confidence back and then later I waved off Victor and said, 'No, I'm playing the whole game.' I was supposed to play third downs, but I started playing first and second downs. I thought, 'If you guys don't think I can stop the run, I'm staying out here for the running plays, too.'"

Ware said he was initially told to be on the field for about two-thirds of the plays. Instead he played almost all 62 defensive snaps and he did his damage rushing the passer—just like he's always done. He sacked Brees and forced a fumble before halftime that led to a field goal and a 17–3 half-time lead for the Cowboys, who were balanced on offense as well. Dallas led 24–3 before the Saints woke up and rallied in the fourth quarter.

The Saints had the ball back down seven before Ware struck again, sacking Brees with 12 seconds to play. Jay Ratliff recovered, and the Cowboys escaped New Orleans with the most improbable victory of all, thanks to an improbable week and a heroic performance.

Smith has a game. He played with a shoulder injury against the Giants and willed the Cowboys to an overtime victory that won the NFC East back in 1993. Garrett has a game when he beat the Packers on Thanksgiving in 1994. Clint Longley and Leon Lett are associated with games. So as great as Ware has been for his entire career, could this be his game—his moment?

Some of his teammates agree. "Nobody thought he was going to

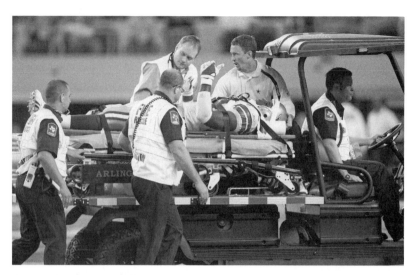

Despite being unsure of the severity of his neck injury, DeMarcus Ware gave a thumbs up sign to his teammates and fans during a Sunday game with the Chargers in 2009.

No one expected Ware to even play six days later in New Orleans. But he saved the game with two sacks, including this forced fumble in the final seconds, to beat the undefeated Saints.

play, and he willed himself into that game," Jason Witten said. "The place was rocking. To be able to beat them and really keep our playoff hopes alive, that was a special game, really just to watch him, watch DeMarcus will his way through it."

Long snapper L.P. Ladouceur recalls a late field-goal miss by Nick Folk that necessitated Ware's game-clinching play. "It was unbelievable. That to me is just the resiliency of that guy," he said. "We ended up missing a very short field goal that game, too and we got them close. We had to make a defensive stop at the end of the game."

But to Ware, he won't agree that night in New Orleans was his best game. "I haven't played my best game yet," said Ware, who signed with the Broncos during the 2014 offseason. "You're never going to have your best moment because there's always another level. There's always something else to strive for."

Ware to Go?

For about a two-week span during the Cowboys' 2013 training camp, anyone watching the daily matchup between defensive end DeMarcus Ware and left tackle Tyron Smith had to be somewhat concerned.

If you would've polled 100 people from the fans, media, or even coaches and said that one of these two would make the Pro Bowl after the 2013 season and the other would get released, the vast majority would not have picked Ware to be the player let go. He wasn't just dominating Smith. He was the best player on the entire team.

But after another injury-riddled year that saw a quadriceps strain force him to miss the first three games of his career, the Cowboys had a tough decision to make on a player counting more than $16 million against the salary cap with a base salary of $12.25 million. The team was already strapped for cap dollars and leery of paying more to Ware, who had actually spent the last two years battling a slew of injuries, including to his neck, back, shoulder, hamstring, and both elbows.

At the end of his 2013 season, Ware's pride perhaps got the best of him. Although he was clearly struggling to make a difference on the field, he refused to admit injuries were a factor. "I'm not hurt," Ware said after a game against Green Bay in which he recorded just two tackles, no sacks, and only two quarterback pressures. But not admitting injury, while it sounds brave, opens up the discussion for media pundits to criticize the performance of a self-proclaimed healthy player.

Down the stretch Ware struggled as part of a dismal Cowboys defense that ranked last in the NFL in yards allowed (415.3) per game, which is also the worst mark in franchise history. For the third straight year, the Cowboys again missed the playoffs thanks to a Week 17 divisional loss with the NFC East title on the line.

Personnel changes needed to be made, and it seemed to start with Ware, whose top priority—thinking solely about his family, which includes two kids—was to remain in Dallas.

After a quiet six weeks in January and half of February, Jerry Jones dropped his first hint of the Cowboys' possible life without Ware. He told reporters at the scouting combine that the team was considering cutting Ware because his production wasn't matching his cap hit, stating "you can't have it all."

The start of the NFL free-agent signing period loomed on March 11, 2014, which also seemed to be a soft deadline of sorts for the Cowboys and Ware to make a decision. Ware's agent, Pat Dye Jr., asked the Cowboys to come to a conclusion by then. That way, if Ware was to be released, he would have the same opportunity to sign with another team along with the league's other free agents.

On the Friday before the deadline, March 7, Ware met with Jones on the owner's private plane to figure out a middle ground. Ware understood a pay cut was needed and he left the meeting knowing the ballpark range he would have to drop his salary.

Through his agent, Ware then sent over a proposal to the Cowboys to reduce his salary by more than half of the $12.25 million base. That would've given Dallas a savings on the cap of about $6 to 7 million. And just cutting Ware outright only saved the team $7.5 million.

However, it appeared the Cowboys had decided to go in another direction. Jones and his son, Stephen, the team's executive vice president and director of player personnel, seemed ready to move on from Ware, wanting to get younger and healthier along the defensive line.

Jerry Jones and Ware met again on Tuesday morning, a few hours before the NFL's start of the new league year. That was when Jones informed Ware that his best interest was to test his market value and possibly sign with a new team. Of course to do that, the Cowboys would have to release Ware, one of the greatest defensive players in the team's storied history.

On March 11, 2014, the Cowboys cut Ware, sending out a press release in which Jones admitted the decision was difficult, though he left the door open for Ware to return if the market wasn't as kind to him as he hoped. By the end of Wednesday's business day, however, Ware was in Denver being introduced as the newest member of the Broncos. He signed a three-year, $30 million contract with $20 million guaranteed.

Denver wasn't the only suitor for Ware's services. In fact, it was rumored that the Eagles were offering even more money per season. But through his agents, friends, and other advisors, the defensive end still considered himself a Cowboy. He might not have been on the roster now, but he likely will be when he retires. Burning bridges and signing with a division rival didn't appeal to Ware, which is another reason he signed with the Broncos. Of course, getting the chance to play with Peyton Manning and joining a team that had advanced to the Super Bowl didn't hurt either.

Jones had to part ways with Troy Aikman, though he knew the veteran quarterback was likely going to retire. He had to cut Emmitt Smith, who played two more seasons with another team. And along the same lines, Jones had to release Ware, doing so just six months after he became the Cowboys' all-time sack leader. "DeMarcus has a unique spot in my experience with the Cowboys in 25 years," Jones said two weeks after the move. "He's a Hall of Fame player who likely has a lot of production ahead of him. But at his price tag—which was unavoidable—age and injury concern, and our situation, we can have three front-line players—front-line being a starter or significant backup—for what we were paying DeMarcus. That says a lot for DeMarcus, but it also says that we need three more than we needed one. Denver needed one more than they needed three."

The NFL has always been and always will be a business. Sometimes players feel that harsh reality sooner than they expect. Ware made a living sacking the quarterback, recording more than any player the Cowboys have ever had. But even he wasn't above being sacked himself.

CHAPTER 5

ROMO-MENTUM

I can't really say I remember much about Tony Romo's first season with the Cowboys in 2003. The focus was solely on the quarterback controversy between Quincy Carter and Chad Hutchinson. Truth be told, Clint Stoerner was better than Romo that preseason, but one long touchdown pass in an exhibition game was enough for head coach Bill Parcells and quarterbacks coach Sean Payton to hang onto him and see how he developed. Needless to say, that was a smart call.

But what I remember most about Romo's early years occurred in between his first and second seasons. In February 2004 I was playing on a flag football team with a bunch of guys from the Cowboys' staff. All of us were either in our late 20s or early 30s and playing in a rec league down the street. The team consisted of equipment managers, TV producers, security guards, and then some other friends of employees. But we were aptly named the "Cowboys" and wore old blue practice jerseys. (Side note: I wore No. 2 and after about the sixth game, I took off the jersey and tossed it down inside out. That's when I realized it was an actual jersey worn by Deion Sanders, who liked to wear No. 2 in practice. There was a small white patch inside the collar that said "Prime Time." But no, it didn't lead to any high-stepping touchdowns for me.)

Our team was pretty good and we had a good quarterback, too. His name was Andy, and he could run and throw. But we got greedy.

I remember warming up one day. (I'm not sure why because my athletic skills, or lack thereof, had me blocking on the line or rushing the quarterback.) But I could tell something was going down. The guys were acting weird, and the next thing I knew, Romo walked over to our huddle. He had cleats, he had basketball shorts, and he was ready to play.

"Hey guys, Tony is going to play with us today," said one guy on our team. "But don't call him Tony, okay? Just call him 'T.' He's not supposed to be playing with us."

But it didn't matter. The other team might have wondered who this guy with the rocket arm was, but they didn't recognize him. I guess they weren't *big fans of the preseason because up to that point, that's the only playing time Romo had seen.*

But he quarterbacked for us and he was, as expected, unreal. He threw the ball all over the field, which was only 80 yards, meaning he was pretty much in range to hit the end zone on just about every play—and he tried.

He threw five touchdowns that day, but I remember he was also the team's best defensive player. Even though this was his first game and probably our fourth or fifth, he was running the show. He called out defenses and put people in position.

I remember him telling me, a rush defensive end, not to go after the quarterback on this play and instead cover the running back on a screen pass to the flat. Sure enough, the ball came out there, and I was able to pull a flag for like a 2-yard loss. I was thinking, This guy is incredible. Romo also had a one-handed interception that showed just how athletic the guy is—especially when compared to a bunch of weekend warriors. This was a pure example of Pros vs. Joes.

Romo didn't play every game but most of them. And as far as I can remember, we won them all, and he was great. Our team made it to the playoffs where we faced a serious flag-football squad, one that had its own website, custom jerseys, and even a playbook. They were organized and they actually all spoke Spanish. During the play they would call out instructions to each other, and none of us knew what they were doing.

Our team didn't play well, and Romo was right there with us. He threw about four interceptions in that game, and we got blown out. And just like the big leagues, it wasn't all his fault, but he tried to force the ball into some tight spots. Over the years, we've seen Romo elevate the play of many receivers around him, but he couldn't do it with our group of stiffs that day.

None of us could have possibly known where Romo was headed. He certainly didn't appear to be the future face of the franchise and star quarterback of America's Team on the field that night.

—Nick Eatman

A Celebrity Quarterback? Not So Much

Few players in Cowboys history have a more engaging story than Tony Romo. Yet, he's probably the most polarizing player in the NFL.

He's had a fairy-tale ride from being an unknown, undrafted rookie out of Eastern Illinois University to the starting quarterback of America's Team. Along the way he's dated celebrities such as Jessica Simpson and Carrie Underwood, but when it was all said and done, Romo eventually married Candice Crawford, whom he met while she was interning with the Cowboys' in-house TV department.

Romo lived the celebrity life for a couple of years, which is ironic considering his first head coach, Bill Parcells, used to reiterate how he never wanted a "celebrity quarterback." He wanted the guy who loved to practice, loved to watch film, and competed every snap—whether it was Sunday in the fourth quarter or Wednesday's pat-and-go session to begin a practice. As it turns out, Romo is a lot more like the latter than the celebrity Parcells detested.

A sports junkie growing up, Romo played everything. When it was dark, which didn't always matter because Romo was usually still shooting hoops or throwing passes until he was ordered by his parents to come inside, he would shift his attention to the tube. Romo watched every game he could, and if nothing was on, he wore out VHS tapes of sports movies like *The Program*, which he quoted the first week he was named the starting quarterback, joking with reporters that he has his "place at the table," referring to a line in the movie that suggested he had arrived.

Romo loved flicks such as *Field of Dreams*, *Varsity Blues* and, of course, *The Natural*. He picked No. 9 because he idolized Roy Hobbs, the lead character of the movie, played by Robert Redford, who finds a way to stave off injury in his final at-bat and crush a game-winning home run that shattered the overhead stadium lights.

If it was an over-the-top movie played up by Hollywood, Romo was buying. He was such a fan of the *Rocky* series that after his first NFL start, a 35–14 win against the Panthers in 2006, Romo carried a personal boombox with him onto the plane. He then blared his *Rocky IV* soundtrack the entire flight home, which landed in Dallas around 2:30 AM. Anyone sleeping on that plane had to tune out songs such as James Brown's "Living in America" or "No Easy Way Out" by Robert Tepper.

Romo made everything a competition. Once on a 2008 bus ride from the airport to the team hotel in Denver, the quarterback had his laptop out, playing a variety of songs. He not only wanted the surrounding passengers, which were mainly coaches and other staff members, to guess the artist's name, but he was keeping score in his head to see who would win. Lovers of 1980s music were the only ones who really stood a chance since it was Romo's favorite genre by far. He tried so hard to stump the participants that he even played an instrumental theme for *Rocky*, and was impressed that someone still shouted out the correct answer—composer Bill Conti. Even in his own game where he plays the host, Romo liked to win.

Romo might have become the Cowboys' starting quarterback and a worldwide superstar, but it's hard to see that by just his appearance. "If you didn't know better, you wouldn't think he was the starting quarterback of the Cowboys," said equipment manager Mike McCord, who has been with the team since 1991. "I compare him to Troy [Aikman], and it's night and day. Troy usually carried his dress clothes with him on a hanger because he had somewhere to be after practice a lot of times. Tony, he isn't anything like that. He'll wear everything but his own clothes. He's got someone's sandals, pair of shorts…he'll grab someone's towel in their locker. He just doesn't care. Stuff like that doesn't matter to him. He comes in wearing old sweats and a T-shirt he's had for 10 years. In that regard he hasn't changed."

But there was a moment before his first press conference as the starting quarterback in 2006 when what he wore seemed to matter. Minutes before his first media briefing, which was rather informal since he

IF THESE WALLS COULD TALK: DALLAS COWBOYS

preferred—and still does—to sit at his locker rather than hold a podium-style press conference, Romo took a stack of baseball caps into the bathroom. One by one, he tried on different caps, some of which featured the Cowboys logo while others were from Major League Baseball teams. Romo settled on a Cowboys cap, which he wore backward.

For those who question his leadership, a common criticism of Romo over the years, they weren't on the field during a 2008 game in Arizona, when the Cowboys trailed by 10 with only a few minutes to play. A 70-yard touchdown pass to running back Marion Barber got the Cowboys back in position, and after the defense made a key stop to get the ball back, Romo went to the offensive linemen as they got up from the bench. Slapping all five starters on the shoulder pads one by one, Romo told each player the same message: "We're going to drive down the field and score," he yelled to Marc Colombo. "We're going to drive down the field and score," he screamed at Cory Procter. "We're going to drive down the field and score," he said, staring into Andre Gurode's face. "We're going to drive down the field and score," Romo roared, making fierce eye contact with Leonard Davis. "We're going to drive down the field and score," he shouted to Flozell Adams.

Sure enough, the Cowboys got the ball with just 50 seconds left and quickly moved into field-goal range for a game-tying kick. However, it proved to be a costly make as the Cowboys went to overtime, and Romo then broke a bone in his hand, forcing him out for three weeks. Punter Mat McBriar also ended his season with a broken foot on a blocked punt that was recovered for a game-winning touchdown by the Cardinals.

Romo doesn't just lead his own linemen on the offensive side of the ball. Against New Orleans in a December game late in the 2012 season, the Cowboys desperately needed to make a stop and get the ball back. Saints quarterback Drew Brees had a fourth and 1 near midfield and appeared to be going for the first down. During a timeout Romo put his helmet on, ran out to the defensive huddle, and told every defensive player, "He's not going to snap the ball. He's not going to snap it. Stay onside and don't jump."

As Romo predicted, Brees only hard-counted several times before pulling back from the center to call timeout. The Saints punted to the Cowboys, and Romo drove the offense down the field in a matter of seconds to tie the game and force overtime.

A scratch golfer, Romo hasn't met many shots he didn't like. You won't see a lot of laying up with Romo, who can crush the ball off the tee and will typically go for the green if it's anywhere close to within reach.

In 2007 Romo was competing in a U.S. Open qualifying tournament at a course in the Dallas area. Always cognizant of the score and what is likely needed to advance, Romo knew he needed to shoot a 68 or 69 this day to move into the regional round. As he approached 15, he kept telling his caddy and other onlookers that he needed two pars and two birdies to make it. When he bogeyed that hole, he kept the faith but changed his plan to "three birdies" on the final three holes. But when he bogeyed No. 16 as well, Romo kept smiling as he walked to No. 17, which was a short Par 4. "Anyone ever seen a hole in one?" He asked.

Romo didn't ace the hole but he certainly went for the green instead of positioning himself differently to get a birdie. He didn't advance to the next round that day, but it's that very mind-set that has both helped him excel on the field but also gotten him into trouble. Romo thinks he can make every golf shot—or quarterback throw.

One day in practice during the 2005 season when Romo was the No. 2 quarterback behind Drew Bledsoe, he was throwing routine passes to the running backs out of the backfield. In this seven-on-seven drill, the Cowboys used trash cans to simulate the offensive tackles, giving the backs a better idea on how deep to run their routes. After Romo connected on about four straight passes to backs who were running the same route, he decided to switch it up. Running back Tyson Thompson curled outside and as he turned up the field, Romo slammed the pass into the top of the upside-down trash can. The ball then ricocheted up perfectly into the hands of Thompson, who never broke stride.

Everyone looked at each other—not sure if Romo got lucky on that throw or made an unbelievable trick shot.

As he got ready for the next snap, equipment assistant Bucky Buchanan, who snaps him the ball for this drill, couldn't help but ask: "Are you shitting me with that last throw?"

"I've got more in the bag, Buck…more in the bag," he said with his trademark wink.

Eighth-Round Pick

Few players drafted in the NFL actually fit the position prototype completely. A few attributes usually stand out that sway teams in one direction or the other. Tony Romo didn't really have a lot of overwhelming qualities. There were a lot of good ones but nothing spectacular.

His arm was strong but not a cannon. He was athletic in the pocket, but his time in the 40-yard dash (5.0 flat) was slow by quarterback standards. He wasn't short, but he wasn't your 6'5" poster boy quarterback who made scouts drool.

Normally when you have good but not great qualities, players can get an edge if they at least played against stellar competition. Instead, Romo played for a Division I-AA school that didn't even have a long history of winning on that level.

Luckily for Romo, though, he didn't come from just *any* small school but one that happened to have a Super Bowl-winning head coach and a quarterbacks coach, who would later win a Super Bowl as a head coach himself, as prestigious alums.

To most of the NFL, he was just that quarterback from Eastern Illinois. But to Mike Shanahan and Sean Payton, he was Tony Romo, No. 17 for their beloved Panthers. And more importantly, Romo was a player they both wanted for their respective teams. Shanahan was entering his ninth season as the Broncos' head coach, having won back-to-back Super Bowls in 1997–98. Payton, meanwhile, had just joined Bill Parcells' staff in Dallas.

When the 2003 NFL Draft came to an end, the battle for Romo narrowed down to the Cowboys and Broncos, the two teams that knew Romo the best because of their EIU ties. But the quarterback actually helped his own cause at the scouting combine earlier that February when he was brought in as a "bullpen" passer.

Every year the combine invites around 15–20 quarterbacks as potential draft picks, but a few more prospects are added to help run other position drills. Romo was one of those guys in 2003, throwing the ball to defensive backs, linebackers, tight ends, running backs, and occasionally a receiver or two. Mainly, Romo was there to get the ball out and get it out quickly. His arm fatigue was of no concern for most teams, though Romo wasn't concerned either. "That was a great experience for me," Romo said. "I didn't care about being there all day. My arm was fine. I remember thinking every throw I make is being evaluated. I had to treat it that way. I knew if I went out there and threw the ball, someone would be watching."

Longtime Cowboys general manager and personnel man Gil Brandt, who helps coordinate and organize the combine even today, noticed Romo for more than just his arm. He helped Romo get the same treatment as the more high-profile prospects, taking him down to the media tables where he spent just as long if not longer talking to the press. Whether he was the center of attention or not, Romo made sure he took full advantage.

Shanahan and Payton already knew plenty about the youngster, especially Payton, who left EIU as the Panthers' leader in most passing categories. During the 2002 season, Romo broke Payton's school record for career touchdown passes.

Romo hoped to hear his name called late in the draft, and as the seventh and final round was wrapping up, the Cowboys pondered the thought of taking him. Payton knew there might be a battle with Denver in free agency, so he urged Parcells and Jerry Jones to get him with their last pick. But Parcells, who was in his first draft with the Cowboys, had sat through six rounds without getting an offensive lineman, and that's where his focus was. Sure enough, the Cowboys took Colorado guard Justin Bates, who never made the team.

Once the draft ends, that's when NFL coaches revert back to college-style recruiting. They get on the horn and call their targeted free agents, who typically sign deals based on two main factors: size of the signing bonus and chances of making the team. For Romo, it was about the latter, along with the opportunity to play for Parcells.

Payton called Romo and told him the Cowboys were offering him $10,000 for a signing bonus, which was considered average to slightly above average in 2003. Payton hung up the phone and then went back to Jerry Jones and relayed information that the quarterbacks coach had already known for a while—Denver was willing to pay more.

Romo informed the Cowboys that he was offered $20,000 by the Broncos, who take a different approach to rookie free agency. Denver typically will overpay four to five targeted free agents and then fill in the rest of the spots with very minimal deals that include little to no bonus. Romo was obviously one of those targets.

Jones asked Payton if he needed to sweeten the deal for Romo, offering to push it up to $15,000 and maybe even matching the Broncos' offer at $20,000. But Payton had a hunch. "Let me keep talking to him," Payton said. "I think we can get him for 10."

Payton wasn't offering more money but more opportunity. At the time he hadn't worked much with Quincy Carter or Chad Hutchinson or even Clint Stoerner for that matter. Romo was convinced he could not only come in and make the team, but also would eventually be in a situation to play. "He looked closely at his options and found a place that he felt comfortable," Payton recalled. "I think he knew if he came in and worked hard, he could make the team, and from there you never know what can happen."

Romo signed with the Cowboys for their original $10,000 signing bonus, exactly half what he could've made in Denver. He just wanted to make an NFL roster. He knew the money would eventually take care of itself.

Coached Up

Six days after agreeing to a rookie contract with the Cowboys, Tony Romo found himself all alone on a shuttle bus at the Dallas-Fort Worth International Airport. He knew more of his new teammates were coming, but the anxiety of getting to play professional football for America's Team was so overwhelming, he barely knew if the bus was empty or standing-room only.

He did manage to notice when a "goofy" guy eventually came aboard and sat down next to him. "I play quarterback. They signed me as a rookie free agent," Romo said to his new teammate, who introduced himself as Jason Witten, a third-round pick from Tennessee.

The Cowboys organization had different aspirations for the two, and neither of them knew much about the other. "I thought he was a kicker at first," Witten said. "I didn't know him. He didn't know me. We were just nervous kids not sure what was in store for us."

Clearly, they didn't realize then that they would both eventually be the faces of the franchise, outlast every player in that class, and still be standing together 11 seasons down the road as the two elder statesmen of the team.

Romo and Witten immediately established a friendship that hasn't wavered over the years. As grizzled veterans still grasping for the same goal, their journeys might have started on the same bus, but the routes to get to that point were completely different. Witten was just 20 years old at the time, and the Cowboys liked him so much that they had a first-round grade on him but managed to steal him in the third.

Even though Romo came to the Cowboys thinking he could knock off one of the three incumbent quarterbacks, the uphill climb was brutally steep. And his new head coach—the one person for whom he was excited about playing—wasn't exactly his best friend. Then again, Parcells was the very reason Romo came to Dallas. "I loved Bill because personality-wise he could be real tough on me," he said. "I can take tough coaching. I'm fine with either side of that. He could also be very funny at different times, but at the same time turn the switch and be extremely in your face."

Romo recalled an exchange during training camp of his rookie season when Parcells had been riding him for a few days. Every pass he threw either wasn't to the right guy, with enough zip, or out of his hand quick enough. And Romo recalled, if all that was correct, "He'd say my feet weren't right or something."

Following a rough morning practice that had Romo hearing plenty of Parcells' wrath, the quarterback was eager to turn things around in the afternoon. More importantly, he wanted to impress his head coach. As the rookie is warming up, though, he can feel Parcells' eyes burning a hole in him. "He was looking over and said, 'You're never going to get it. You know what you are, Romo? You're a ball in high grass.' And I'm just sitting there. He's just waiting for me. *Ball in high grass.* He's just waiting for me to ask. So I said, 'What, what does that mean?'... 'Lost!'"

But what Romo didn't know was Parcells had a reason for constantly riding him, and it wasn't solely because he was trying to push him to his limits. The head coach was trying to temper his assistants. David Lee, an offensive assistant who was assigned to work closely with the quarterbacks, was raving about Romo in one of the early minicamp practices in the summer of 2003. Parcells cut him off and shouted to the rest of the staff, "We've got Lee here who wants to put the kid in Canton. He's got a ways to go. Right now, the way he throws, he'll get every pass knocked down."

At a listed height of 6'2", though he's closer to 6 feet, Romo had somewhat of a side-armed delivery. He could get by with that in high school and Division I-AA college football. But in the NFL where defensive ends tower in the 6'5" range, Romo had to learn how to get the ball up higher.

Lee knew he could work with Romo and his mechanics but questioned if it was worth the time, considering he was an undrafted rookie from a small school and might not stick around anyway. Parcells, though, secretly saw the things Lee kept lauding and privately urged him to work with Romo's delivery, getting the ball higher over his head at the point of release.

At that point in Romo's life, throwing the ball was like breathing. As a teenager he could be on family vacations in a hotel but still find time—and light—to throw passes. Once when cooped up in the cold for hours, Romo spotted a vacant parking lot area right under a light post. He got the football out and asked (if not demanded) his father, Ramiro, to catch passes for him.

If he couldn't go outside, Romo figured out a way to throw the ball into the couch cushions at just the right speed with just the right touch to get the ball to bounce back toward him every time. While others simply watched the commercials during football games, Romo made up games of his own to throw and catch the ball.

And now he had to change his mechanics? But nothing like that ever fazed Romo, who quickly figured if Parcells wanted to tweak his delivery, he at least thought enough of him in the first place to do so.

He was right.

"He was eager, bright, and looking for an opportunity," Parcells recalls of Romo as a rookie. "I remember that he wasn't aspiring to just

Although he didn't make the switch until seven games into the 2006 season, Bill Parcells dropped hints nearly a year before that "this Romo kid" had potential to become the starting quarterback. *(Dallas Cowboys)*

make the team. Sometimes guys that aren't drafted, their goals are moderate and expectations aren't high. But he wasn't like that. And once I saw him do things, I knew if we could just channel it the right way, he could do well."

By the middle of that first preseason, Romo hadn't securely wrestled the third quarterback spot away from Stoerner. Carter eventually won the starting job in a close race over Hutchinson, but the third spot was up for grabs.

Potential usually wins out if the race is even. While Stoerner was slightly ahead, there was plenty of room and time to even the score. In the second exhibition game against the Texans, Romo launched a 60-yard touchdown pass to Randal Williams, a play that showed off his arm strength and mobility to get out of the pocket and throw on the run.

That was enough for Parcells to make his decision. Stoerner was a nice player but had probably maxed out his potential. Romo was just getting started—though no one could've predicted where this train was actually headed.

Veteran Approval

Starting defensive players in the NFL have enough to worry about. Facing some of the best quarterbacks in the league on a weekly basis is nerve-racking already. They aren't normally concerned about their own offense's backup—much less a rookie on the scout team. That's when their eyes typically light up.

In 2003, though, the veterans hated seeing Tony Romo. "We didn't like Fridays at all," linebacker Dat Nguyen said. "That's when we practiced two-minute defense, and that's when we saw a lot of Romo. We hated that. The kid was so good."

The Cowboys had Quincy Carter as their starting quarterback, and Chad Hutchinson was the backup. The year before, Carter started the first seven games but was replaced by Hutchinson. Neither was that effective for the 5–11 squad.

But the following season, Bill Parcells arrived and opened up the competition. Carter won the job outright, and Hutchinson went to No. 2. In an even closer race, Romo was able to convince Parcells during the preseason that he had more upside than Clint Stoerner. Romo loved his scout team role because the competitor in him wanted to play against the best. It didn't matter if it was a Friday afternoon in front of zero onlookers. He knew the coaches were watching and the film was running, and that was enough to get his juices going.

The reason the defensive starters had trouble with Romo wasn't so much his arm or even his feet. "He killed us with his eyes," Nguyen said. "As linebackers we're taught to read a quarterback's eyes. Usually, when he looks to our right, he throws it there. So you just drift to the side that he's looking. But Tony, oh man, he would look this way and then— boom—he's throwing it back the other way. It was sometimes like a no-look basketball pass."

Nguyen and Dexter Coakley were one of the best linebacking tandems in the NFL, and they were often made to look silly on Friday afternoons. Coakley left the practice field one day yelling at Nguyen, "Man, we're going to take this Romo and tie his ass up to the goal post."

Another veteran had some issues with the rookie quarterback, but they were more for competitive reasons. Darren Woodson didn't like losing at anything, even if it meant two-minute drills in walk-throughs. "I used to yell at Romo all the time because he held the ball so long," Woodson said. "There's no real pass rush, so you're supposed to just go back, make a read or two, and get rid of it. But he held it forever— sometime like 10 seconds—and then he throws it to [Jason] Witten or [Joey] Galloway. One day I just had enough and started cussing him out. 'Romo, you can't hold the fucking ball for 15 seconds…get the ball out of your hands.'"

But after practice, the easygoing Romo didn't want any enemies, especially the team's most vocal leader. So he approached Woodson in an attempt to get back on the safety's good side. What he got was an eye-opening statement that he never saw coming. "Woody, you mad at me?" Romo said in the hallway between the locker room and equipment room.

"Nah, Tony it's all good. You just keep playing."

Then Woodson stopped Romo and shot it to him straight. "Hey, Romo, let me tell you something," Woodson said. "I'm not bullshitting you here. You're the best quarterback on this team. You've got the most potential of anyone. And as far as I'm concerned, you're the best quarter-back right now. The best one this team has had since Troy. I promise you, you can be a great, great quarterback in this league."

Romo couldn't believe what he was hearing. The 12-year vet who owns three Super Bowl rings and has faced the likes of Brett Favre, Steve Young, Dan Marino, and John Elway is telling him that he's got what it takes. "Really?" Romo said in awe. "Are you serious?"

"I'm dead serious. You have the ability to be great. And don't you ever forget that."

Risky Sneak

Only 17 days after the Cowboys shocked the NFL world by cutting previous starting quarterback Quincy Carter, Romo hadn't done anything to seize the moment. In fact, he was going the other way.

In the preseason opener against Houston, Romo finished the game with a dismal 1.5 passer rating. He was 3-of-11 for 37 yards and two inter-ceptions, along with two sacks and another fumbled snap that resulted in a safety. Romo's game was so miserable that his own father, Ramiro, jokingly asked if the Cowboys were going to let him back on the bus afterward.

But it wasn't that funny to the Cowboys, as team scouts had lists of available quarterbacks who would be ready to join the team and perhaps replace or at least compete for a backup spot with Romo. Additionally, though rookie Drew Henson wasn't that much better, he was making the transition from baseball and had just signed a deal that guaranteed him $3.5 million. Henson wasn't going anywhere.

Romo could've been gone and might have been were it not for a defensive holding penalty on the Raiders the following weekend in Oakland. The Cowboys were trailing 20–14 with just 2:38 to play, and Romo again had yet to do anything impressive. He was facing a fourth and 11 near midfield when his pass over the middle sailed and was intercepted by a Raiders linebacker. That not only seemingly sealed the win but Romo's fate as well.

But a holding penalty on Oakland kept the drive alive. Romo converted a fourth-down pass to tight end Landon Trusty and then got the Cowboys to a fourth and 9 at the Raiders' 14-yard line with 23 seconds left and no timeouts. That's when Romo found tight end Sean Ryan over the middle for a 13-yard gain, though Ryan was stopped at the 1. He was actually knocked woozy and could barely get to his feet, and had Ryan been injured, the officials likely would've issued a 10-second runoff. Since the Cowboys were out of timeouts, that would've ended the game.

Fortunately, Ryan managed to get into his stance, and Romo hurried the team to the line to spike the ball. But that would've been too textbook for Romo, who grew up idolizing John Elway, Dan Marino, and Brett Favre. He had seen them make unorthodox plays to win games. So with time ticking off the clock, Romo improvised and got the snap and plunged forward for a quarterback sneak, surprising everyone, including his own linemen.

Romo managed to sneak the ball over the goal line just enough to get the touchdown with six seconds to play. The ensuing extra point gave the Cowboys an improbable 21–20 preseason victory. It also bought more time for Romo, who continued to develop and eventually became the No. 2 quarterback that season behind Vinny Testaverde. "If I wouldn't have scored," Romo said about that Raiders game, "I probably would've been on a bus back to Wisconsin."

Instead, he stayed and eventually became the face of the franchise.

Pregame Negotiator

When you're the backup quarterback, every practice is crucial. So you can imagine the approach Romo took to preseason games, especially in 2006, when he was the established backup behind Drew Bledsoe. In fact, rumors had started to spread a few weeks earlier that Parcells might be leaning toward playing the young quarterback over the veteran, if the situation called for it.

Romo handled every snap of the preseason opener that year, something that was rarely done, but that's how much head coach Bill Parcells wanted to see what he had in this player, who up to that point had yet to throw a pass in three regular seasons. He was about to enter the final year of his contract, and the Cowboys still didn't know what they had in Romo. But they were intrigued.

So as Romo entered Texas Stadium on August 31 to face the Minnesota Vikings, the quarterback was thinking about his final preseason opportunity when he saw owner Jerry Jones and Parcells approach him. They needed a word with him in private, so in a back room behind the locker room, the two tried to emphasize the importance of Romo adding another year to his contract.

Clearly, they were anticipating Romo playing with the Cowboys in 2006 but feared that if he was as good as they hoped, he would then become an unrestricted free agent after the season. All the grooming, all the adjustments to his mechanics, and all the coaching he received in four years would be utilized by someone else? The team couldn't allow that to happen, so Jones and Parcells tried to get Romo to sign a deal just a few hours before the start of the last preseason game. In fact, they even hinted Romo could be benched if he didn't agree. "We were stepping on his toes pretty good," Jones said of Romo, who joked to a reporter that the conversation had a "shakedown feel to it."

Not only did Romo not cave in, but he countered. Always considered quick on his feet on the field, Romo was quick in the dressing room as well. He told Jones and Parcells the money they were offering, in the $1.2 million range, wasn't incentive enough to play him if Bledsoe were to falter. The Cowboys wanted to buy an extra year for Romo, which was fine, but he wanted his price tag to be substantial enough that it would make sense for the Cowboys to pull the trigger and play him.

With the team fearing he could become a free agent after the year, Romo had the leverage, so the Cowboys bumped up the price, giving him a $1.9 million deal over two years with a $2 million signing bonus. Sure enough, Parcells named Romo the starter for the seventh game of the 2006 season, and as they say, the rest is history. Romo ignited a Cowboys' squad that went from 3–3 to 9–7 and into the playoffs, earning the young quarterback a Pro Bowl selection.

And, of course, in the middle of the 2007 season, Romo and the Cowboys agreed to a massive, $67.5 million contract extension that made him one of the highest paid quarterbacks in football. When Romo did get on the field, he quickly showed how well he could elude pass rushers and make plays on the run. It seems like he had some practice the day the owner and head coach tried to blitz him in the locker room.

Oh Snap!

In the Cowboys' storied history, which includes eight Super Bowl appearances and five titles, pretty much every feat has been accomplished. But as of 2006, no player in franchise history had ever returned a kickoff back for a touchdown in a playoff game.

But there he was: Miles Austin, wearing No. 14, an undrafted rookie from tiny Monmouth University, running down the left sideline with a huge smile on his face. The 93-yard touchdown against the Seahawks in the NFC wild-card matchup gave the Cowboys the lead and put them in prime position to win the franchise's first postseason game in 10 years.

Austin's score wasn't just the first playoff kick return for the Cowboys, but it was also his first career touchdown in the NFL. Obviously, he had to keep the football, right? So Austin went to the sideline and handed it to the equipment staff, who put the ball away in a storage trunk so he could have it forever. Little did anyone know how that moment would affect the course of the Cowboys' franchise and one player's national perception forever.

That game in Seattle is remembered for one play and one play only. Tony Romo, who had taken the league by storm in that 2006 season when he replaced Drew Bledsoe as the starter seven games into the schedule and led the Cowboys to a 9–7 record and a spot in the playoffs, had created a buzz for the Cowboys that hadn't existed since Bill Parcells' first season with the team in 2003.

Romo began the 2006 campaign as Bledsoe's backup and the holder for field goals and extra points. When he became the starter, the Cowboys didn't have a capable fill-in, so Romo continued to handle the holding duties as well. "I really didn't have a better option," Parcells said looking back. "Tony was the best guy we had, and I don't know if he still wanted to do it. If I had a better option, I probably would've changed."

The only reason the topic is still discussed today is what happened at the end of the game with the Cowboys trailing 21–20 in the final minute of play. Martin Gramatica lined up for a 19-yard attempt that would've given the Cowboys a commanding lead late in the game.

But Gramatica's foot never touched the ball, as the snap slipped right through Romo's hands just before the kick. The quarterback alertly scooped up the ball and darted toward the end zone only to be tackled from behind by Seahawks safety Jordan Babineaux at the 2—just one yard short of a first down. Had Romo picked up that first down, it probably would've been better than a touchdown or even the field goal going through. The Cowboys would've had more time to drain the final minute of play and then either attempt another field goal or go for the score.

But Romo was stopped short, and the team's playoff woes continued.

Just like that the player, who had helped the Cowboys get in position to win the game with his abilities at quarterback, lost the game with his inability to field the snap, one of the more routine plays in football.

The visual of Romo sitting on the turf with his hands clutching his face mask in disgust will forever be painfully etched into the memory banks of Cowboys fans from coast to coast. This was supposed to be the season things turned around, when they finally had a difference-making quarterback—but a quarterback that couldn't hold onto the ball.

Now, about that ball.

Before the game, the Seahawks' veteran equipment manager, Erik Kennedy, informed his ball boys working the game to try to use only one of the six kicking balls if possible. The footballs were brand new to start the game, so the assigned ball boys only worked up one ball to use. "They'll take the ball out of the bag, rub it down, work it in real good," said Cowboys equipment assistant Bucky Buchanan. "I didn't know EK [Kennedy] had told his guys to use just one. That's not really how we did it. But they just wanted to use only one ball for all kicks and punts, and that was for both teams."

In the third quarter, the kicking ball—numbered "K1" for kicking ball No. 1—was lost for good. It was now sitting in a trunk on the Cowboys' sideline for Austin's safekeeping after his exciting touchdown return. Luckily, the Seahawks ball boys had started to work up "K2" and they used that for the extra point, the ensuing kickoff, and then two punts.

But in the fourth quarter, Gramatica hit a 29-yard field goal, and the ball sailed over the back net and into the stands. That ball was now long gone, so the Seahawks quickly went to "K3," which was used for two kickoffs and two punts, including one that occurred after a Seattle safety.

By the time the Cowboys got in position to kick the game-winning field goal, the Seattle ball boys were already on to the third of the six balls. And had the field-goal attempt occurred immediately, it might not have mattered.

The third-down play was initially ruled a catch of seven yards by Jason Witten and would've given the Cowboys a first down at the Seattle 1. Instead, in a rather controversial decision, the replay officials challenged the spot and moved it back a half-yard, resulting in fourth down. Parcells then opted to kick the ball and take the lead.

In that additional period of a timeout and booth review, there must have been a discussion about which ball to use. Somehow, "K6" ended up coming out for that last kick, a ball that hadn't been used and likely hadn't even been touched before it was fired back to Romo. "The ball looked like a block of ice coming back there," said David Lee, the Cowboys' quarterbacks coach that season.

Buchanan said he's confident the ball was used for the first time. "I don't know exactly what happened there, but I promise you that ball had never been kicked," said Buchanan, who to this day still feels somewhat responsible for that play since he wasn't aware the Seahawks were using just one ball to start with.

Since then, NFL rules have changed as the league has implemented a sideline "ball official" that monitors the balls going in and out for special teams. Every NFL game now has an official wearing a maroon shirt and black pants, usually standing on the home team's sideline, who makes sure the balls are distributed evenly and are properly prepared before being used.

The Cowboys needed an official on that night in Seattle. The history of the franchise, the length of Parcells' coaching career, and the overall perception of Romo's ability to perform in the clutch could have all been very different.

CHAPTER 6

THIS MEANS WAR (ROOM)

I had one full offseason under my belt by April 2001, but the process was still somewhat new to me. Covering a football team is relatively easy when you have games and practices. The spring and summer is when finding a story gets challenging, and even after all these years, it can still be difficult to figure out what to write and who to cover.

That's why the NFL draft is great for filling up content. And it starts with the Senior Bowl in January and then February's scouting combine. That spring I attended both for the first time and will always remember the combine as one of the more eye-opening experiences of my life.

I got there not really knowing what my role would be. Covering the combine for a team's website is a bit tricky. The football staff doesn't really want you to reveal its wish list, and if you start profiling all of the players, you realize quickly that your team only has seven draft picks, so most of your work is all for nothing.

Somehow I got hooked up with our own scouting department and must have offered my services to help out. The next thing I knew, pro scout Bryan Broaddus put me to work. While the rules have since changed, back in 2001 the combine was vastly different.

In order to get players to come visit a hotel room filled with scouts, coaches, and front-office personnel, you had to go out and find the guys and bring them back. To say it's a chaotic scene is an understatement.

The players have no clue where they are going. The scouts have a list of guys they want, but just recognizing them is a difficult task. And the hotel lobby is so jam-packed with people it makes a shopping mall on Christmas Eve look rather tame.

But Bryan, who barely even knew me, offered a list of guys he was hunting down, and I went to work. I'm looking for some UTEP tight end that I first heard about when I looked down at the sheet. I remember trying to get Texas defensive tackle Shaun Rogers, but he had a foot injury and was in a wheelchair. Just walking through the crowd by yourself was hard enough, so getting Rogers to roll with me wasn't going to happen.

My claim to fame that year, however, was somehow getting Michael Vick to come with me to visit the Cowboys' room. Remember, at the time Dallas had the 37th pick overall, and Vick was slotted to go No. 1, which he eventually did.

But Vick was on the Cowboys' list, and somehow when I said, "Hey, Michael, I'm with the Cowboys, and we'd love to chat with you," his eyes lit up. He actually told the late John Butler, then the general manager of the Chargers, who had the No. 1 overall pick that year before trading it to Atlanta, that he'd be right back and he followed me. I remember being pretty proud of myself for corralling the best player at the combine and getting him there. The scouts and coaches seemed impressed and they hurried to gather their notes.

Just as Vick left his interview, which I was allowed to stay and watch, Leonard Davis came in. And that was a shock—not that he came into the room, but that he fit in the door. At a listed 6'7" and 330 pounds, Davis was probably the biggest human being I'd ever seen.

I remember thinking, Vick is going No. 1. Davis is probably going No. 2 (which he did). So why are the Cowboys wasting their time and the players' time by talking to them?

Six years later, I saw the point firsthand when the Cowboys signed Davis in free agency. Teams aren't just interviewing players for the current draft but for down the road as well.

—*Nick Eatman*

Moss-ed Opportunity

Ask Jerry Jones to name three of his biggest regrets since buying the Cowboys in 1989, and he'll always start with his mishandling of Tom Landry, whom he fired immediately after taking over. He's recently said he wishes he would've taken previous owner Bum Bright's offer to remove Landry as head coach himself and give Jones a clean slate. To this day, Cowboys fans still view Jones as "the man who fired Tom Landry."

Jones has also publicly regretted firing Chan Gailey as head coach after just two seasons with the team, 1998–99. Both years the Cowboys reached the playoffs but lost in the first round.

And then there's Randy Moss. In 1998 the Cowboys all but told the superstar receiver from Marshall University that they would take him with the No. 8 overall pick. He was tall, sure-handed, incredibly fast but also quick. And he simply loved to play the game. But Moss had a checkered past that resulted in Notre Dame pulling his scholarship and Florida State later kicking him off their team. Moss then landed at Marshall where he became a star, finishing fourth in the 1997 Heisman Trophy voting.

When he came to visit Dallas in the spring of 1998, Moss had played big-time college football but was still mesmerized by the simplest of things. When the Cowboys' scouts went to meet with him, they found Moss waiting in a top floor suite at a hotel near Dallas-Fort Worth International Airport. Moss was staring out the window, watching the comings and goings of hundreds of planes taking off and landing. "Man, I ain't ever seen anything like this," Moss said with a huge grin. "This is awwwesome."

Moss was certainly more interested in talking about the planes at the airport than his past, though he didn't mind discussing football, his true passion. Moss was a freak and he had everything Jones wanted. However, he didn't have a lot that Gailey wanted. The soft-spoken, strong Christian-valued head coach really wanted no part of Moss, especially considering the players already on the roster, including Michael Irvin, who had experienced their own share of troubles. Wide receivers coach Dwain Painter, another veteran coach, was on Gailey's side, and the two fought long and hard to distance themselves from Moss, whose name came up often during the team's pre-draft discussions. But it certainly wasn't Old School vs. New School in the Moss debate. The two most veteran scouts the Cowboys had, Walt Yowarsky and Jim Garrett, the father of current Cowboys head coach Jason Garrett, were strong supporters of taking Moss.

In one heated debate, Jim Garrett, who is now in his early 80s but was 67 at the time, raised his voice and got everyone's attention. "This is football for Christ's sake," Garrett screamed in the War Room. "It's not the Boy Scouts. This is the best football player in the draft. We have to take him."

Obviously, the Cowboys passed on Moss and picked defensive end Greg Ellis instead, a move the organization grew to regret—and not because Ellis wasn't worthy of the pick. He was a solid player who made one Pro Bowl, but Moss became one of the best receivers in NFL history.

After Moss fell to the Vikings at the No. 21 pick, he seemed to focus his anger solely on the Cowboys and not so much the other 18 teams that didn't draft him. (Cincinnati passed on him twice.) Moss loved the Cowboys and truly thought he would be playing in Dallas.

Instead, he made it his personal vendetta to annihilate the Cowboys every time he played them. And he did, starting with the Thanksgiving Day game during his rookie season. Moss caught just three passes, but scored on each, recording touchdowns of 51, 56, and 56 yards. And he continued that onslaught throughout his entire 14-year career, enjoying a perfect 7–0 record in games against the Cowboys.

There have been some controversies for Moss, both on and off the field, but nothing that should have prevented a team from drafting a player who now claims to be the best wide receiver in NFL history. Though that could be a stretch—and a debate with which Jerry Rice most certainly had issues—no one can deny what a remarkable talent Moss was during his time in the league.

Jones certainly can't and won't deny it. All the Cowboys' owner and general manager could do is make sure a mistake like that didn't happen again.

Millennium Miss

The new millennium wasn't that kind to the Cowboys' draft process. Of course, it only hurt matters that they didn't have a first-round pick in the first two drafts of the decade, thanks to the acquisition of Joey Galloway in a trade with Seattle on February 12, 2000. While the organization has found several good players in the later rounds through the years, history has shown that the Cowboys typically don't do so in seasons when they lack a first-round pick. Call it a coincidence or maybe just feeling the pressure to land quality talent.

In 2000 the Cowboys' first pick was in the second round, the 49th overall selection, after finishing 8–8 the previous season. This was Dave Campo's first draft as the head coach, and it was clear the former defensive backs coach, who was promoted to defensive coordinator and now to the top position, was looking for some secondary help. The club had decided to waive Deion Sanders in the offseason for salary-cap relief, and veteran Kevin Smith was aging, eventually deciding to retire a few days into training camp.

As the Cowboys waited their turn later in the second round, a pair of enticing cornerbacks were still sitting on the board. Dwayne Goodrich from the University of Tennessee and Mario Edwards of Florida State were two players the Cowboys coveted and conceivably wanted with the 49th pick. It was a close race between the two, who had actually squared off against each other in the first ever Bowl Championship Series (BCS) national title game after the 1998 season. Goodrich was the Defensive MVP of that game, helping the Volunteers to victory with a clutch interception return for a touchdown. After that performance he nearly came out of school early to enter the 1999 draft and likely would've been a late first-round pick. His decision to return to school proved costly, though, as he battled a back injury during his senior year. His stock dropped considerably, and some scouts actually had Goodrich as a middle-round prospect.

Cowboys scouting director Larry Lacewell, a former defensive coordinator at Tennessee, still enjoys close ties to the school and had a good relationship with John Chavis, a longtime assistant with the Vols who served as defensive coordinator for 14 years. The Cowboys listened to Chavis and others in the Tennessee program who spoke highly of Goodrich.

But Edwards was also a solid pick. The lanky cornerback was taller, listed at 6'2", and played with a swag the defense sorely needed with Sanders gone. So who better to replace the former Florida State standout than another one? And like Goodrich, Edwards was also coming off a BCS national championship, as his Seminoles defeated Virginia Tech in the title game a few months earlier.

So it was Edwards and Goodrich, both sitting there when the Cowboys went on the clock at No. 49. The debate was long and pretty even. According to witnesses in the War Room, it was getting close to a coin flip between the two. Jerry Jones and Stephen Jones were leaning in opposite directions. Ultimately, Lacewell seemingly proved to be the difference maker, and the team went with Goodrich. As the Cowboys' first pick of that draft, and with Sanders gone, Goodrich felt the pressure of being the savior in the secondary.

But he wouldn't be the only one. The Cowboys drafted two more cornerbacks, and shockingly enough, one of them was Edwards—in the sixth round. That's right, the guy the Cowboys nearly selected instead of Goodrich at No. 49 lasted 131 more picks, where the team finally took him at No. 180. In between, the Cowboys drafted twice, including another cornerback in Kareem Larrimore, a talented but troubled player from West Texas A&M, a Division II school near Amarillo. Larrimore had all the skills but he failed a drug test at the scouting combine, which was one of a few character concerns about him.

Former secondary coach Bill Bates, a fan favorite who played safety for 15 seasons with the Cowboys and was one of the best special teams players in franchise history, shared a story about Larrimore with the media after the draft. "We're watching a guy with him against Angelo State," said Bates, "and he's covering his guy every play, and the ball is going there. So I don't know what happened, but on the next play, the ball is snapped, and those two don't move. The receiver stands there. Kareem just stands there. And it went on like that for a few plays. So we don't know what went on there, but he's a talented player."

So talented that longtime scout Larry Dixon was giddy with the team's fourth-round pick after just one rookie minicamp practice. Heading out to the afternoon workout, Dixon turned to a group of reporters and said, "Larrimore has the quickest feet I've seen since Deion Sanders."

And in the same minicamp, Edwards also made quite an impression, but it wasn't with his feet as much as his voice. Bashful wasn't one of the descriptions listed on Edwards' scouting profile. He showed up at Valley Ranch with every bit of the swagger that came with the Florida State program during that time.

In his first morning practice, Edwards danced, hollered, strutted, and made a few plays, too. At one point in the practice, Edwards turned his attention toward the face of the franchise. "Hey, Troy! Hey, Troy Aikman," Edwards said to the quarterback in between plays. "I see you Troy. I see you No. 8. I'm here baby, I'm here."

This went on for a few plays and then finally, Aikman had enough.

"Hey Troyyyy! Whatup Tr…"

"Hey rookie, shut the fuck up!"

Edwards laughed it off, and so did everyone else from the players and the media in attendance. And actually, Edwards pretty much did shut up. He played rather well as a rookie and went on to start 47 games in four seasons. But he never really became the loudmouth showboat player that he was those first few days as a rookie.

While Larrimore started the first four games that season, Edwards proved to be a better pro in the long run. Larrimore only played 19 games in two years with the Cowboys and ultimately finished his pro career in the Arena Football League.

As for Goodrich, his season never got off the ground as he battled hamstring injuries in 2000, then missed all of 2001 with a torn Achilles before appearing in 11 games during the 2002 campaign. Unfortunately, he'll be remembered most for a fatal accident in 2003 when he struck and killed two pedestrians, who were helping pull another person from a burning car on the side of the highway, and left the scene before turning himself into police the next morning. He was convicted on two counts of criminally negligent homicide and sent to prison for seven and a half years, though five more years were later added. Goodrich ultimately spent six years in prison and was released in 2011.

The Goodrich incident was the final straw in a football career that never surfaced—and a draft class that didn't live up to expectations. Without a first-round pick, the Cowboys did nothing but reach in that 2000 draft. Even in the fifth round, the club took a chance on Ohio State running back Michael Wiley, though they didn't plan to use him at that position. Hall of Fame wide receiver Paul Warfield, himself a former Buckeye, served as a Cowboys consultant that year and convinced Jerry Jones and the staff to take a flyer on Wiley and convert him to a slot receiver.

And that's where Wiley started out. It's believed that he is the only player since Roger Staubach to wear the No. 12 for the Cowboys, even in a practice. Wiley wore it for a few days before switching to No. 32. That's about how long it took for the team to realize Wiley wasn't a receiver. Recalling that decision to try to convert Wiley, one former scout summed it up best: "When it comes to the draft, consultants are like pigeons. They fly in here, shit on everything, and then fly away."

It seemed like there were a lot of pigeons flying around that 2000 draft.

Right on Q?

In the spring of 2001, the Cowboys knew the time had finally come to get a replacement for Troy Aikman, who officially announced his retirement in a teary-eyed send-off at Texas Stadium that April. The Cowboys had moved on, having actually released Aikman and then signed veteran quarterback Tony Banks in March. But that wasn't enough to satisfy Jones, who couldn't help but notice a changing of the guard around the league. The Falcons' Michael Vick seemed a star in the making and Donovan McNabb's Eagles had just beaten the Cowboys twice the previous year. But those guys were first and second overall draft picks, respectively.

What Jones wanted was someone more like Aaron Brooks, a fourth-round pick of the Packers in 1999 who was sent to the Saints in 2000, where he played in eight games and went 3–2 as a starter. Brooks provided a jolt to the New Orleans offense, and that's what the Cowboys were needing.

The Cowboys' guy was Quincy Carter, the athletic playmaker from the University of Georgia, though many teams had concerns with his arm strength, accuracy, and some off-the-field issues from his collegiate days. There were wide differences of opinion on Carter. Some of his college coaches weren't too high on him, but his head coach, Jim Donnan, whom Jones knew and respected, thought the world of Carter.

Some of the Cowboys' scouts during that time remembered the team having a mid-round grade on Carter before a phone conversation between Jones and Donnan. In fact, all of the scouts were told to leave the War Room one day during their draft meetings, leaving just Jerry Jones, Stephen Jones, and Larry Lacewell. Once the scouts returned a few minutes later, Carter had been placed atop the second round on the draft board. Nothing was ever said, but everyone in the room knew it was pretty clear who the next quarterback would be.

The Cowboys didn't have a first-round pick that year, having sent it to Seattle in the Joey Galloway trade. And Jerry Jones was also dealing that draft day, moving back to eventually land two second-round selections, Nos. 53 and 56 overall.

As players continued to go off the Cowboys' draft board, there stood Carter, a guy that was probably more of a middle-round prospect for other teams. But the Cowboys weren't just another team. They were America's Team, looking for a quarterback to replace Aikman. It was desperate times, and sometimes that calls for a desperate move.

So as the draft got closer to No. 53, not only was Carter's name still up there, but another name, who was actually a legitimate high second-round prospect, was as well. He was a linebacker from Arkansas named Quinton Caver. The Cowboys were obviously very high on Caver. So much so that many in the War Room were upset when Jones traded back from the 37th pick. Linebackers coach George Edwards really wanted Caver, and he was still around with the Cowboys sitting on two picks.

Jones was getting giddy. Not only was he close to landing the quarterback he coveted in Carter, but he could also get Caver, who surprisingly enough would be the first Arkansas player drafted since Jones bought the team in 1989. Jones was a former captain on the Razorbacks' 1964 national championship team and raised his kids in Arkansas with his wife, Gene, a former homecoming queen at the University of Arkansas.

Even without a first-round pick, the Cowboys could make amends, in Jerry's eyes at least, by getting Quincy Carter and Quinton Caver. Yeah, that's not confusing. Actually, it was nothing but. So as the powers that be figured out what to do next, there was a difference in opinion, of course, in how to take these two guys. Jones had his eyes on the quarterback. He wanted to make sure the Cowboys got Carter. The scouts and coaches were worried Caver might get taken by another team. They had him pegged to be long gone by now, so they were pushing for Caver.

Even Stephen Jones, Jerry's oldest son who is the team's director of player personnel, was high on Caver. Jones was a backup linebacker for the Razorbacks in the mid-1980s, but that wasn't the only reason he was hoping Caver would join the Cowboys. Caver was 6'4", 245 pounds and he could run and definitely jump—a linebacker body with defensive back skills. So after a quick side meeting between Jerry and Stephen, all taking place during the 10 minutes allotted for second-round picks, the Cowboys were on the clock with the 53rd pick. The two men in charge then informed the rest of the staff in the War Room of their decision. "We're taking Quincy Caver," Jerry Jones said.

"Wait, you mean Quincy Carter?" One of the alert scouts shouted back.

"No, wait, Quinton Carter," Jerry said again.

"Who? Which one?" from the now restless scouts.

"Carter...Caver...Quincy Caver," said Jerry, who had one ear in the telephone as he was phoning the team's personnel up in New York that relay the picks to the commissioner.

Finally, someone spoke up—much louder than anyone else—to try and get a straight answer: "Are we taking Quincy Carter, the quarterback from Georgia? Or Quinton Caver, the linebacker from Arkansas?"

Stephen Jones stepped in and said, "It's the quarterback. Quincy Carter."

And that's what the Cowboys did. They drafted Carter, thinking it was a better PR move to get the quarterback first, considering he would be the focus point of this draft anyway. Plus, there was some minimal fear that the Cardinals might want to take Carter with the 54th pick.

Jerry got on the phone and talked to Quincy and passed it over to offensive coordinator Jack Reilly. High-fives were going around the room, though not everyone was excited, especially the scouts who feared Carter might have been taken a few rounds too soon. But those guys were about to feel better once Caver came aboard.

And that's when it happened. That's when the Eagles, sitting at No. 55, swooped in and drafted Caver one pick ahead of the Cowboys. Stephen Jones took his pen and tossed it across the War Room in disgust.

There might have been 10 people in the room dying to say, "I told you so," but no one did. Instead, they scrambled to try and make another trade, but time was running out.

The Cowboys went with Alabama safety Tony Dixon, a physical force for the Crimson Tide defense who was one of the smartest players in that draft. But Dixon didn't pan out, and the Cowboys eventually drafted safety Roy Williams with their first pick, eighth overall, the following season. Dixon played four years but only started 14 games.

As it turned out, none of the three mentioned players made it big. And Caver, who played in only 53 NFL games during his career, starting four, even landed back in Dallas in 2005 after a less-than-stellar four seasons with the Eagles and Chiefs. He was a non-factor in his time with the Cowboys.

Who knows if things would've been any different had the Cowboys taken Caver, not Carter, first.

2002—Using Every Second

The NFL has since reduced allotted draft times down to 10 minutes for first-round picks, but for many years, the league still gave its clubs a full 15 minutes to make the pick or a trade. In 2002 the Dallas Cowboys needed all 15 minutes—every one of the 900 seconds to be exact. Remember, this was Jones' first time back in the first round since 1999, as the Cowboys had traded away their last two first rounders for Joey Galloway. So in 2002 after a second straight 5–11 campaign, the Cowboys had the sixth overall pick.

Secondary was an issue despite drafting three cornerbacks in 2000 and a second-round safety in 2001. The Cowboys had two players on their wish list that year: Texas cornerback Quentin Jammer and Oklahoma safety Roy Williams. Both were exciting players and would seemingly be difference makers for a defense that had trouble against the pass.

At No. 6 it was clear the Cowboys would've been happy with Jammer, a big, physical guy who played a position that was clearly worthy of a high draft pick. But safety was a different story. There hadn't been many top 10 safeties in the past, and it was always a position that seemed to be addressed later in the first round, if even then. Williams, though, was a special player, a linebacker-type of guy who could run like a safety. But when Jammer went off the board right in front of the Cowboys to San Diego at No. 5, Jones got on the horn. Yes, he still wanted Williams, but he got greedy…almost too greedy.

Jones did not enjoy draft-day trades; he relished them. That was the one time when he felt like he was wheeling and dealing again like he used to do as an Arkansas oilman. When that clock was winding down and Jones was on the phone making deals, that's when he felt right at home. In 2002 Jones was working the phones like never before. The goal was to slide down a few spots and still get Williams, but he had to be positive that he wouldn't dip down too far.

Members in the Cowboys' War Room speculated that the Vikings, who had the seventh pick, and the Chiefs, holders of the eighth, both wanted North Carolina defensive end Ryan Sims, a player in whom the Cowboys seemingly had little interest. (They had already taken a pair of North Carolina defensive ends in back-to-back years, 1998–99, but neither Greg Ellis nor Ebenezer Ekuban had yet to produce consistently.)

With Sims not high on their board, Jones wanted to take advantage of a few teams that did covet the defensive lineman. So he called Chiefs general manager Carl Peterson to see about Kansas City moving up to the sixth pick and jumping the Vikings. However, he also had to make sure Minnesota wouldn't take Williams.

With one hand Jones had a phone up to his right ear with Peterson on the line. With his other hand he had another phone up to his left ear with Vikings personnel man Frank Gilliam on the line. "In my years of scouting, I've never seen anyone do what Jerry Jones did that day," said

Although Bill Parcells (left) still had a strong voice in the War Room, he didn't always get the players he wanted on draft day. *(Dallas Cowboys)*

former Cowboys pro scout Bryan Broaddus. "He got two teams to tell him who they were drafting. That's unheard of. Sometimes you get a team to tell you, 'We're going offense here. We're taking a defensive guy.' Maybe you get them to tell you a position. But that day Jerry got Carl Peterson to tell him they were taking Sims. And he got Minnesota to tell him they were taking [offensive tackle] Bryant McKinnie. It was the craziest thing I'd ever seen."

So the Cowboys had pulled off the trade, moving from six to eight while also picking up a third-round selection, 75th overall, in 2002 and a sixth-round choice in 2003—and they still got the player they wanted. But something was still missing.

In the midst of War Room high-fives and pats on the back, the TV still had the Cowboys' logo on the screen with just a few seconds remaining on the clock. Longtime scouting assistant Chris Hall calmly asked whoever was listening, "Did we turn in the trade?"

Nope. No one thought to call the NFL office and inform them of the swap.

That's when Stephen Jones did a Pete Rose impression and dove headfirst over a chair and desk to grab the phone. He smashed the speed dial button to the league office to tell them of the deal they had just made with the Chiefs.

The problem was the clock had hit zero. As far as the Vikings knew, it looked like the Cowboys had passed. Had their draft day personnel run up to the podium and turned in the card, they could've landed Ryan Sims. Then the trade would've been off the table.

It was complete chaos, not only in the War Room, but also on the ESPN set as well. Host Chris Berman, who has been covering the NFL Draft since the 1980s, was at a loss for words. Finally, it was announced the Cowboys' trade had gone through, and a huge sigh of relief was let out in the War Room.

Sims went to the Chiefs, McKinnie to the Vikings, and the Cowboys got their man, picking Williams at No. 8. They also used that extra third rounder to select cornerback Derek Ross, a player on whom they had a high second-round grade.

Minutes after taking Williams, the phone rang again. This time it wasn't another team but the league office. Joel Bussert, the NFL's senior vice president of player personnel and operations, had a message for the team. "Joel called us and said, 'If you ever do that again, we're not going to turn in the trade,'" Broaddus recalled. "Everyone was apologetic, but we knew we just pulled off a great deal. It was all Jerry."

Hall, who probably saved the day by alerting the room the NFL had yet to be notified, still gives the credit to his boss. "I really think that was one of Jerry's finest moments in the draft room," Hall said. "It was such a crazy scene. He was juggling two guys on the phone and playing them off each other. He pulled it off."

He'll Be Good for Someone

The night before the 2003 draft, Bill Parcells' first with the Cowboys, the new head coach went to dinner with both Jerry and Stephen Jones to discuss some last-minute strategies and to go over again how the process would work. However, the point of the dinner was more about informing Parcells that he wasn't going to get his way.

For the last few weeks, Parcells had pushed hard for University of Kentucky defensive tackle Dewayne Robertson, a massive 300-pounder the coach thought could plug up the middle in a 3-4 scheme. But Parcells was alone in his assessment and could hardly find anyone in the War Room to side with him.

The Cowboys needed cornerbacks, and Terence Newman was the logical choice if he was around when the team picked at No. 5 overall. But the Joneses knew Parcells was going to make a late push for Robertson, so at dinner the three of them discussed the plan for the next day. "Bill, we're not going to take your guy," Jerry Jones told Parcells. "It's just not the right move for us."

This was the type of confrontation that many people thought might cause a rift between the two headstrong personalities. Moments like this ultimately got the best of Jones' relationship with Jimmy Johnson. But Parcells was in a different mind-set that first year. He had opinions, but he chose not to push too hard. He would sit back and let the Cowboys pick the guy they wanted, though truth be told, he was pretty excited about Newman's potential as well.

But as it turned out, that conflict of interest never materialized. Robertson wasn't even around for the Cowboys to pick as he went off the board one spot earlier to the Jets, who grabbed him at No. 4. Everyone in the War Room was stunned. Everyone but Parcells, that is. "Good pick," Parcells said, chomping his ice from an already finished glass of tea. "He's going to be a good player."

But the scouts in the room weren't buying it. Pro scout Bryan

Broaddus went to grab Robertson's tag and place it up on the team's running draft board when he turned to the gratified head coach. "How many teams are you working for, Coach?" Broaddus playfully asked Parcells, who had been New York's head man for three seasons, 1997–99. "You sold the Jets on that kid, didn't you?"

"Nah, no way. They liked him. He's going to be a good player," Parcells said with a huge grin.

To this day the Cowboys scouts believe Parcells, knowing he couldn't convince his new team to take Robertson, eventually called his former team and got them on board. Unfortunately for the Jets, Robertson never became a star, playing just six seasons in the NFL. Meanwhile, the 2014 season will be Newman's 12th campaign, having played nine years with the Cowboys before joining the Bengals in 2012.

Ware vs. Merriman

In the week leading up to the 2005 draft, the debate around the War Room centered on only two players. With the Cowboys having two picks in the first round, 11th and 20th overall, it should've meant just about every player on the table was available. According to Jones that was the luxury of having two first rounders. The team had the ability to go up and basically get whomever it wanted.

But the guys the Cowboys wanted the most in this draft were probably going to be there for them to choose at No. 11. Both were game-changing pass rushers who seemingly would fit in rather nicely as the team continued its shift to a 3-4 defense—linebackers DeMarcus Ware and Shawne Merriman. If both players were available at No. 11, which is how the Cowboys scouts and coaches saw the draft shaking out, then it would literally be a win-win for the team.

Unless you were Bill Parcells. He liked both players, but neither was atop his wish list. The guy Parcells wanted—and wanted badly—was

Marcus Spears, the athletic defensive end with a 300-pound body who could move. The LSU standout was the guy Parcells had in mind, and he didn't want to risk waiting until the 20th pick.

So as the room debated for weeks on Ware and Merriman, Parcells held out for Spears. It wouldn't have upset him one bit had both players gone off the board before the Cowboys' selection at No. 11, so they could draft his guy Spears.

Before the draft you could've driven a line right through the War Room and found enough supporters for Ware and an equal amount for Merriman, who was the more polished of the two players at the time. The former University of Maryland standout was a beast off the edge and figured to enter the NFL ready to dominate.

Ware, who played for Troy State (now officially Troy University) in the Sun Belt Conference, was still growing into his own. A wide receiver as a freshman, Ware was trying to learn how to play the linebacker position. But many projected that once he figured it out, he could be one of the best ever. Even Parcells couldn't help but draw comparisons to Hall of Famer Lawrence Taylor, a player he coached while with the Giants.

This was about as close a call as the Cowboys would ever have to make. In their routine mock drafts, the scouts went through every scenario possible with the 10 picks ahead of them. And just about every time, it kept coming back to Ware and Merriman.

Without a doubt, they were going to have to make a tough decision.

But the night before the draft, Jones got a call from a friend in the media, someone he respected more than anyone and someone who did his homework when it came to the NFL Draft. This reporter was privy to some information about Merriman and some character concerns that had been kept under wraps. It wasn't enough to put Merriman in the proverbial "box," a separate destination on the Cowboys' draft board that meant they were deemed undraftable, but the issues were enough to break the tie.

So sure enough, draft day came, and the Cowboys were sitting at No. 11. Ware was there. Merriman was there. And yes, Marcus Spears was also still there with Parcells champing at the bit (and ice) to get him. But he was by himself on this one and virtually without a voice.

The Cowboys went with their instinct and chose Ware, who has gone on to become one of the best players in franchise history. Merriman went 12th to the Chargers, at the time coached by Marty Schottenheimer with Wade Phillips as the defensive coordinator. Two years later when Phillips became the head coach in Dallas, he told reporters that Ware and Merriman were ranked 1-2 on the Chargers' board in terms of defensive players. But he never revealed which player was rated higher.

For the first couple of seasons, Ware and Merriman were compared to each other just about every game. And for a while, Merriman got the upper hand. He earned Defensive Rookie of the Year honors and was named to the Pro Bowl in 2005, but any debate ended the next year when Merriman was suspended four games for violating the NFL's substance abuse policy. Reports surfaced that Merriman took steroids to enhance his performance.

And what about Spears? "When we took Ware, Parcells sat there and pouted for about two hours," said scouting assistant Chris Hall. "We had to convince him that we could probably still get Spears at No. 20. He didn't believe that at all. He wanted us to trade back up there and get him."

But the Cowboys had the draft pegged rather well. Parcells asked the room which teams ahead of the Cowboys might need a defensive end. Pro scout Bryan Broaddus spoke up. "The teams you have to watch out for are Cincinnati at No. 17 and Minnesota at 18. They both need ends," Broaddus said, trying to offer up the requested info.

"Why would you say that?" Parcells barked back to Broaddus.

"I was just answering your question."

But that was how intense this moment was for Parcells, who was just so enamored with Spears that he didn't want to hear any scenarios that would prevent him from being a Cowboy.

And like Broaddus had projected, Big Bill had to sweat out two defensive ends. The Bengals took Georgia's David Pollack while the Vikings picked Erasmus James of Wisconsin. The Rams grabbed Florida State offensive tackle Alex Barron at No. 19, paving the way for Parcells to finally get his guy.

At No. 20, about nine spots later than he wanted, Parcells was able to draft Spears. "After that he was the happiest guy in the room," Hall said of Parcells. "He was great for the rest of that draft. He got the guy he wanted."

Oddly enough, the Cowboys eventually landed four of the top 20 players taken in that draft. Not only did Ware and Spears play together for eight years, but Adam "Pacman" Jones, the sixth pick to Tennessee, and Barron both later wound up in Dallas for one season.

Breast Available Player?

The fact that Pacman Jones landed with the Cowboys in 2008 seemed rather implausible only three years earlier. And it's not only because he was the No. 6 player taken in the 2005 draft. Typically, top 10 picks don't change teams, especially before their original contracts expire after five years.

But other than his surname, nothing about Adam Jones was typical.

Even his nickname was original, and when the Cowboys visited with the talented cornerback from the University of West Virginia at the scouting combine in Indianapolis that year, the topic of that moniker was broached.

This is the time when it benefits the players to be honest. When stories about previous incidents or family matters are discussed, teams often know the answers already. They're just checking to see how the player responds.

In this case, the question was a simple icebreaker.

So Adam, how did you get the nickname Pacman?

And what followed will go down as one of the craziest scenes many in the Cowboys scouting department will ever recall. They've heard some strange answers over the years, but this might never be topped. "When I was little, my momma used to breastfeed me all the time," Jones said, "and they said that's all I ever wanted. When my momma popped out her titty, I just chomped on it like a Pac-Man!"

The nervous laughter then shifted to a more serious discussion regarding Jones' recent barroom fight while at West Virginia, where he reportedly hit a patron with a pool stick. "Well, that ain't no fight," Jones said, trying to give his honest recollection. "That was just two hits: me hitting him and him hitting the ground."

While head coach Bill Parcells was not in the room for this interview, many of the scouts still looked at each other in puzzlement, their facial expressions saying, *"We're not taking this guy."*

And the Cowboys never had to worry about it—at least not then. Jones went sixth to Tennessee, where his questionable decision-making expanded beyond more than just TMI to a bunch of coaches and scouts. Jones had a number of brushes with the law, but even though Pacman was arrested several times and eventually was suspended for a year by NFL commissioner Roger Goodell, he was never criminally convicted of any charges, which ranged from disorderly conduct to being involved in public fights and arguments.

The most infamous of these involved a nightclub incident during the NBA's 2007 All-Star Game weekend in Las Vegas, when Jones and his entourage, which included rap artist Nelly, were reportedly "making it rain" by tossing $100 bills in the air toward on-stage strippers. When the dancers tried to collect the money, figuring they were tips, that's when Jones and his camp got upset, and before too long, a massive brawl broke out. Shots were fired in the club with one bystander being paralyzed from the waist down. Jones, however, repeatedly told police he had no connection to the shooter.

After taking a plea deal for the charges, Jones served 200 hours of community service. But he was issued a one-year suspension from the league, which forced him to sit out the entire 2007 season. Tennessee eventually traded him to the Cowboys in 2008 for a fourth-round pick and some other late-round compensation. Although he spent most of the year accompanied by an off-duty police officer, Jones did have one incident in his time with the Cowboys. He and his bodyguard got into a fight in a bathroom at The Joule, an upscale hotel in Dallas, and though that did not result in any charges being filed, he was nonetheless suspended by the NFL for six games.

Although he played just one season in Dallas, Jones was again given another chance—simply because he could play. And he's still playing today, having finished his fourth consecutive season with the Bengals in 2013.

Hall Pass

Thanks to ESPN and the Dallas Cowboys Broadcasting Network, fans have had the opportunity to watch some behind-the-scenes footage of the War Room over the last few years. They've seen Jerry Jones and various head coaches and scouting directors discuss the process of making picks.

If you've looked closely, you've also seen an office in the background, and on draft days, it's usually unattended to. But on an everyday basis, it belongs to Chris Hall, a 24-year veteran of the Cowboys' scouting department who has worked his way from the bottom to now being one of the more respected members of the staff. Hall is currently the team's college scouting coordinator, but he joined the department not long after graduating from Southern Methodist University in 1990.

Benched earlier in the week as both a punt returner and starting wide receiver, Patrick Crayton, for whom scout Chris Hall lobbied during the draft, found a way to score touchdowns in both areas against the Falcons, including this game-clinching punt return.

Many of the scouts played football in either high school or college with some doing so in the pro ranks. Hall came to the Cowboys with an advertising degree; therefore, he started out as a scouting assistant responsible more for organizing player reports and sorting through the abundance of tapes and film sent to the staff.

But year after year, Hall continued to gain more responsibilities as well as respect. In the early 2000s he wasn't just sorting through the tapes. He was also breaking them down. And by the time Bill Parcells arrived in 2003, Hall was on his way to becoming a full-time scout.

Hall didn't hit the road like some of the area scouts as he continued his role as a scouting coordinator who helped organize the draft board.

But occasionally he would make it out to an All-Star game or two. In 2004 Hall found himself heavily in favor of an unknown receiver named Patrick Crayton, who did it all at little Northwestern Oklahoma State. "I had gone out to watch him in an All-Star Game in Las Vegas," Hall recalled, "and he caught everything. He was an option quarterback but making the transition to receiver. You could just tell he was going to make an easy transition. And that was before I was really writing reports on players. I was just back here organizing things, but I just for some reason had fallen in love with Crayton."

And it's not uncommon for certain scouts to do that with players. Before too long they get pegged as this scout's "guy" or that scout's "pet cat." And even without the skins on the wall, Hall made it clear Crayton was his guy. Several times during the draft he mentioned Crayton, who had a sixth-round grade and was drafted in the seventh round.

Soon after the pick, Parcells walked around and located Hall, who was grinning from ear to ear. "Well, do you have your skirt and pom-poms on?" Parcells asked with a smile. "You've been this guy's biggest cheerleader."

Needless to say, Crayton didn't disappoint Hall or the rest of the staff as he not only made the squad, but played six years with the Cowboys as a return specialist and valuable receiver, who even started during the team's 13–3 season in 2007. "Confidence-wise, it helped me," Hall said. "It let me know that I could identify a player and I could do this. I think it certainly helped me professionally. I think over the years I've been the guy who has been the voice of reason. Sometimes we get off track some, but I try to balance it out a little. But there are times when I voice my opinion, and that was one of them. I think it probably gave me a little credibility like, 'Maybe this misfit in the back might know a thing or two.'"

That might have been Hall's first big moment in the War Room, but his favorite occurred in 2011. By then his opinion was more than just heard occasionally; it was starting to be valued. That year the Cowboys had their sights set on taking a running back in the middle rounds, and two players in particular that figured to be options were LSU's Steven Ridley and Oklahoma's DeMarco Murray. Hall was admittedly a big fan of Murray's and let it be known early and often his feelings about the versatile Sooners tailback.

The room was seemingly split on the two guys, but Murray ended up with a late second-round grade while the Cowboys had Ridley valued at the top of the third. A few picks before the Cowboys went on the clock at No. 71, they wanted more assurance on Murray. So Jerry Jones picks up the phone and calls former head coach Barry Switzer, who was also a legendary coach at OU and was still an avid follower and supporter of the Sooners. "He got on the phone and said some good things but not a lot of great things about DeMarco," Hall said. "Barry liked the kid, but what he said just didn't have everyone convinced. So the guys were still a little unsure."

And sure enough, when the Cowboys got on the clock, the room started to waver again, wanting to revisit the Murray vs. Ridley argument. "Well, I'm getting pissed off because that's why we sit there and have all these meetings. We rank these guys up on the board, and then when the time comes we start playing hopscotch," Hall said. "So I'm saying, 'We've got Murray up there for a reason. Why are we going back now?'"

So time is running out, and it's clear the Cowboys will take a back but haven't yet decided which one. This is Jason Garrett's first draft as the head coach, and already he and the Cowboys had made a splash by taking USC offensive tackle Tyron Smith, the first offensive lineman selected by the Cowboys in the first round since 1981. Smith, who was picked on Thursday night, came into Dallas on Friday and visited the War Room before the second and third rounds began that evening.

As the minutes ticked off the clock, it appeared Jones was letting Garrett make the final decision on the two backs. That's when Garrett turned around and posed a scenario question to Hall. "It's January 1 in the Meadowlands. We're playing the Giants with a chance to win the game," Garrett said. "It's fourth and goal from the 1...Does he score?"

Knowing time was running out to make the pick, Hall fired back. "Jason, give him the fucking ball and run his ass behind the guy (Smith) we just drafted, and he'll score every time."

Apparently, that was all Garrett needed to hear as he nodded with approval. The rest of the room seemed convinced. The Cowboys had their guy and drafted Murray, who went on to start seven games as a rookie. His most impressive performance occurred against the Rams on October 23, 2011, in his first game with significant playing time. Murray's first carry was a 91-yard touchdown run, which set the stage for a record-breaking day. He rushed for 253 yards, eclipsing Emmitt Smith's 18-year-old single-game record of 237 set against the Eagles back in 1993. Garrett was a rookie quarterback that season and now as a first-year full-time head coach he had a front-row seat for Murray's unbelievable day.

The following day, Garrett sees Hall at Valley Ranch and is congratulated by the scout for the victory. "Hey, Chris Hall," said Garrett, who uses the first-and-last name combo with regularity. "When DeMarco was breaking that record yesterday, I kept thinking about you and your speech back on draft day."

Hall laughed it off to Garrett, but inside he knew that was a big deal. Scouts keep score, too. And that was another big victory for "the kid in the back office."

From the Same Tree?

Starting during the 2005 season, all through the early offseason in 2006, and most certainly as the NFL draft got closer that April, Bill Parcells had his own "pet cat" and he made sure everyone knew about him. Parcells didn't always like to show his hand on anything. He didn't want his picture to be painted by anyone. That was his way of having power in the room. Parcells was the guy who wanted to keep everyone guessing.

But he made an exception regarding Ohio State linebacker Bobby Carpenter. Parcells liked the kid. He liked him a lot. Sure, he was impressed with what he saw on film and always had a fondness for linebackers, but more than anything, Parcells liked Bobby Carpenter because of his dad.

Rob Carpenter was a bruising running back for the New York Giants in the early 1980s. He was definitely a throwback player, being one of the last white tailbacks in the NFL. But he had a linebacker's mentality and played with a ferocious style that always made him one of Parcells' favorites. Naturally, when his son came along, Parcells gravitated toward him as well. And it's not like he was completely reaching on Carpenter, who was graded a first-round player by nearly every team in the draft. "Bill talked about him all the time," one former scout said. "He was talking about Bobby Carpenter for months. He thought he was going to be a tough, hard-nosed player like his old man. And subconsciously, I think he convinced the scouts that he was better than he was."

So the Cowboys took Carpenter at No. 18 in 2006…and it simply never panned out. One of the problems was just finding a position for him. The Cowboys were transitioning into a 3-4 defense, but Carpenter played outside linebacker in a 4-3 at Ohio State, where he was overshadowed by A.J. Hawk, the No. 5 player taken in that same draft. Perhaps Hawk's presence made Carpenter even better.

The Cowboys tried Carpenter at inside 'backer in the 3-4, outside linebacker, and then strictly in the nickel scheme. He made plays sparingly but never could crack the starting lineup. His toughness was also in question, an issue Parcells never had with his father. During an interview with a reporter that was filmed behind the scenes by HBO's *Hard Knocks* in 2008, owner Jerry Jones called Carpenter a "finesse linebacker." And that same year, some of his teammates who blocked him regularly on the offensive line called him "Barbie" Carpenter—in part because of his long hair but also for a lack of toughness.

One day during a team meeting that involved some scouts, Parcells was clearly disappointed by the lack of progress from his rookie linebacker. When the scouts reminded him that he was the one driving that train from the start, the head coach cut them off before pondering his point. "You know fellas, I thought I was drafting his dad," Parcells said. "Turns out I was really just drafting his mom."

Carpenter spent only four seasons in Dallas before being traded to the Rams in 2010, though he did get the last laugh in a game against the Cowboys in 2011 when he was playing for Detroit. Carpenter's interception return for a touchdown sparked a remarkable comeback for the Lions, who trailed 27–3 in the third quarter before winning 34–30.

Still, Carpenter's name is always one of the first mentioned in the discussion of biggest first-round busts for the Cowboys.

Redemption for Randy

O*ne of the best receivers in the draft…An extremely talented player who could develop into the NFL's best…Has a passion for the game that is truly unmatched…But he's got character and maturity issues that might just be too much to deal with.*

No, that wasn't the Cowboys' evaluation of Randy Moss, but it sure could've been. Instead, it was an eerily similar situation 12 years later with Dez Bryant, the Oklahoma State superstar who didn't play during the 2009 season after he was ruled ineligible by the NCAA for lying about a lunch he had with former Cowboys cornerback Deion Sanders, which in itself did not violate any NCAA rules. Bryant missed what was projected to be a Heisman Trophy-caliber year.

When the Cowboys evaluated Bryant, obviously they looked closely at his game film from 2007 and 2008, but something from that 2009 season stuck out just as much. "The one quality I always come back to about Dez, which makes him who he is, is his absolute love for the game," said Cowboys longtime scout Chris Hall. "When he was at Oklahoma State, we heard things about him being suspended and couldn't practice, and he cried because he couldn't practice. The guy just wants to play football. When you're dealing with questionable character, the determining factor usually is: does this guy love football? Can he keep himself out of whatever trouble he's in because football is more important? That was our debate with Dez."

For Jerry Jones, he was dealing with the demons of passing up on Moss. In the team's pre-draft meetings, Jones sat and listened to the scouts talk about the good and the bad of Bryant. He kept listening and he kept bringing up Moss' name. It was almost like a déjà vu experience for Jones.

The Cowboys held the 27th overall pick and knew Bryant would likely drop in the draft but probably wouldn't get past the Ravens at 25. After their final meeting in the War Room, the night before the 2010 draft, Jones left the building, but a few scouts and personnel members stuck around. Executive vice president and director of player personnel Stephen Jones, director of scouting Tom Ciskowski, senior director of football operations Todd Williams, Hall, and a few others were chatting about the possibility of Bryant falling. "We knew how much Jerry wanted to take Dez," Hall said. "Our concern was taking the guy with the first-round pick, knowing you have to manage him and issues could pop up at any time. That's what we had to come to grips with. Jerry wanted to take that risk. We had to lay everything out there for him and make sure he understood everything that came along."

Jones wasn't going to let another Moss get away. Sure enough, Bryant fell like they expected, so the Cowboys traded with the Patriots and jumped Baltimore to get to No. 24, where they took the electrifying wide receiver.

In his four years with the Cowboys, Bryant has been everything he was first thought to be. He's had a few run-ins with the law, including an incident where he was arrested after his mother phoned the police saying her son pushed her, though the charges were later dropped. And his passion for the game sometimes gets the better of him, as seen on the multitude of NFL cameras that seem to follow every move he makes. But he's also shown incredible talent, posting two 1,000-yard receiving seasons with one Pro Bowl invite.

Like Moss was a decade earlier, Dez Bryant is one of the more polarizing players in the NFL. But unlike Moss (and most definitely because of him), Bryant didn't get past Jones and the Cowboys.

Daughter Knows Best

Before the 2013 draft, several of the scouts and coaches were spotted in the office of media relations coordinator Jancy Briles, whose duties usually involved writing press releases for the reporters and handling statistical projects for the coaches.

While she was an asset to several departments in the building, the focus this particular spring was less about her specific PR duties and more about her dad. The daughter of Baylor head coach Art Briles, Jancy was a coach's kid through and through. She was easily a favorite of many people at Valley Ranch because of her infectious smile, her willingness to help others with any tasks or needs, and her ability to work quickly and be a team player, even if it often meant going outside of her job description. More importantly, her knowledge of the game was impeccable.

Longtime reporter for the *Fort Worth Star-Telegram* Clarence E. Hill would often refer to her as the little girl from the movie *Remember the Titans* and would drop the line from the film—"Not gonna lie, I wanted the Hall of Fame real bad, coach"—when talking to Jancy, who certainly fit the bill of a football-loving daughter who was passionate about her dad's profession.

When she started working for the Cowboys in 2005, her father was the coach at the University of Houston, but when he went to Baylor in 2008, it made the 90-mile trek to Waco much easier for Briles' oldest daughter to attend the games. And since Baylor had turned things around dramatically on the field, it seemed as if Jancy was getting more and more requests from the coaches to give scouting reports about certain players.

Jancy was one of the first to warn Garrett about a receiver named Josh Gordon, who might become available in the 2012 supplemental draft. Her dad had called Gordon the most talented receiver he had ever coached, and that included guys like Wes Welker, Donnie Avery, and recently drafted first rounder Kendall Wright.

However, the rest of the league soon caught on that Gordon, despite off-the-field issues that eventually led to him getting kicked out of Baylor, was a freakish athlete with rare size and speed. He was a second-round pick of the Browns in the supplemental draft and eventually became a first team All-Pro in 2013, even though he missed the first game of the season because of a substance abuse suspension.

But while getting Gordon didn't work out, the Cowboys turned their attention the following year to another Baylor receiver. This time it was Terrance Williams, who the team thought could be an option in the first round but probably the second. Surprisingly, they were shocked to see Williams still on the board in the third round. Picking 74th overall, the Cowboys didn't pass this time. Following the advice of both head coach Briles and daughter Briles, they drafted Williams, a finalist for the Biletnikoff Award the previous season.

Jancy, admittedly frustrated the Cowboys didn't take Williams in the second round, was excited that it worked out. Her dad was pretty pumped, too. Minutes later, Jancy had to hurry to get off the phone with him because she received a phone call from the War Room, where she was asked to come over quickly. Without knowing why she had been summoned, Jancy hesitantly walked in. The elated War Room led by Garrett then asked the rather shy Jancy to give the entire room a scouting report on their newest receiver.

Completely caught off guard and with a face that was already three shades of embarrassed red, Jancy regrouped and reverted back to the girl who would often turn her back to her fellow high school cheerleaders at Stephenville High School so she could watch a key fourth-down play or who broke down film with her dad at the kitchen table. "Well, he's a great kid," Jancy stated. "He's got good speed, good hands, and can stretch the field."

The War Room erupted with cheers. The coaches, the scouts, and the front-office personnel had all done their homework on Williams. But for some reason, those short sentences offered up by the daughter of his head coach seemed to validate the pick even more.

CHAPTER 7
LONGSHOTS

When I went to college in the fall of 1994, I had two passions when it came to sports: the Dallas Cowboys and the Arkansas Razorbacks. Ironically enough, in a span of two months earlier that year, both were crowned champions. I didn't know much about the athletic teams of Midwestern State University (then an NAIA school that later moved to Division II). But over time my passion for the Indians, who are now the Mustangs, has grown to the level of my other teams.

My loyalty to MSU will last forever simply because it led me to a dream job I never knew existed. When the Cowboys decided to make my school, located in Wichita Falls, Texas, their training camp home, there's no way I could've known then that it would change my life. When I graduated in 1999 with a mass communication degree, I was fortunate enough to land a job with the Cowboys as the team's first full-time Internet writer. It was supposed to be a job that would look good on a résumé and help me land something else in the future. That day simply hasn't come yet.

As a proud alum of MSU, I've waited for the day when the Cowboys will have a Midwestern State player on the 53-man roster. It's been close a few times with a trio of players coming to training camp, but none has made the actual team. There are a couple of MSU guys, though, who didn't even end up at training camp that I can't seem to let go.

When the Cowboys got to Wichita Falls in 1998, they sought out MSU students to work various jobs for the team as interns. That's how I was first introduced to the organization, and it was the same for other students in other departments.

In 2000 the Cowboys needed a few operations interns whose jobs would often vary depending on the needs of certain players. One day an intern could be out in the triple-digit heat changing a tire on Peppi Zellner's car, and the next he's retrieving Erik Williams' wallet (stuffed with $100s) from his locker and bringing it back to his room. One intern had the task of running to Carl's Jr. every evening around 9 PM to purchase three Double Western Bacon Cheeseburgers for Larry Allen, who would give him a $50 bill before each trip and always say "Keep the change," which turned out to be around $41 each night.

One of those interns in 2000 was a football player named Dominic Rhodes. At MSU, which was just starting to compete with Division II schools, Rhodes was a campus stud. A one-time recruit at Texas forced to go the junior college route, Rhodes had a stellar 1999 campaign for MSU and was preparing for a decorated senior season that he hoped would draw interest from NFL teams.

As it turned out, Rhodes was right under the Cowboys' nose all summer long. Being a football player himself, he was never really asked to do a lot of odd jobs like the other interns. He would drive players to and from practice in golf carts, but he was hardly anyone's gopher.

The next year Rhodes went undrafted, and the Cowboys chose not to sign their former operations intern, who instead joined the Colts. Thanks to an injury to Edgerrin James six games into the 2001 schedule, Rhodes then became a starter and went on to become the first and only undrafted rookie to rush for 1,000 yards in a season. He spent nine years in the NFL, eight with the Colts, and is currently the 11th leading rusher (2,984 yards) in that team's storied history.

There was another former MSU player who enjoyed a marvelous football career in Dallas starring for a Jerry Jones team. It just wasn't the Cowboys. Will Pettis spent his final collegiate season at MSU after three years with the University of Houston and was a teammate of Rhodes' in 1999.

One Cowboys scout told me Pettis, not Rhodes, was the best player in the entire Lone Star Conference, much less MSU's team. But Pettis also went undrafted and eventually landed on the Dallas Desperados, a Cowboys-owned Arena Football League squad. He played cornerback in college but excelled as a two-way star. He was the epitome of an ironman, shining at receiver and defensive back.

In 2003 Pettis finally got an NFL shot, and with head coach Bill Parcells standing outside in the blistering Texas heat, Pettis lit up the workout, catching every pass thrown his way and running much faster than anyone on the staff *anticipated. Always hesitant to sign AFL players, Parcells was even impressed and gave the okay to add him to the roster.*

However, NFL rules stated that teams such as the Cowboys that owned franchises in both the AFL and NFL had to let the transaction sit on the waiver wire for 10 days, which gave other clubs the chance to claim him. On the ninth day, New Orleans decided to sign Pettis. They also ran the New Orleans VooDoo, a new AFL franchise that apparently wasn't up to date with the rules.

The Saints didn't contact Pettis until a week before camp, and he showed up with no knowledge of the offense. Consequently, he was released soon afterward, but New Orleans' plan all along was to keep Pettis around and have him play for the VooDoo. Of course, that didn't happen as his AFL rights remained with Dallas.

The Cowboys never gave Pettis another shot, and he continued to play with the Desperados until the team folded in 2009 when the original AFL league dissolved. Without a doubt, I'd call Pettis one of the best football players I've ever covered, and it still bothers me that he never got a legitimate chance to show the rest of the world.

Since the days of Pettis and Rhodes, the Cowboys have signed three players from MSU, but Daniel Polk, Zack Eskridge, and David Little never lasted past training camp.

To this day, I consider myself a long shot from Midwestern State University, so fortunate to be with the Cowboys. But I certainly wouldn't mind seeing a fellow MSU alum on the field.

—Nick Eatman

Living His Dream

Reggie Swinton was talking to a customer, trying to sell him a car when he was notified he had a phone call waiting for him. At this point in August of 2001, Swinton was pretty much a former football player, having recently been cut by the Arkansas Twisters of the af2, an Arena Football League. The Arkansas native was ready for life after the game when he found out the Dallas Cowboys were on the other line, trying to see if he could come to training camp in Wichita Falls, Texas, where their wide receiving corps was dropping like flies.

Good kickoff and punt returners must have a quick first step, so as you can imagine, Swinton didn't hesitate at the chance to make his NFL dreams come true—dreams with which he had toyed over the last three years as he bounced around from training camp to training camp with short stints in the Canadian Football League and both arena leagues.

By the next day, Swinton was in Wichita Falls, located about two hours northwest of Dallas. To everyone he was either "No. 15" or maybe just the "Arkansas kid," considering the ties the Cowboys' brass has with The Natural State. Jerry Jones and his family are all Arkansas natives and the director of scouting at the time, Larry Lacewell, was a former Arkansas State coach who still had plenty of connections. So it's likely someone up there tipped off the Cowboys that a savvy return specialist was available and ready to seize the opportunity.

At the start of Swinton's first practice, Jones hadn't yet made it up to the 30-foot scouting tower that overlooked the two fields. With a cold drink in his hand, something he would desperately need considering the afternoon temperatures in Wichita Falls in mid-August were typically well above 100 degrees, Jones walked near the end zone en route to his lofty perch.

Jones stopped to watch the action on the field, and it just so happened the play occurring was a bomb to the Cowboys' newest receiver. Swinton was streaking down the middle of the field with two defenders on his heels, and though the ball appeared to be thrown too far, the hungry prospect laid out to snag the pass deep in the end zone, which forced Swinton to slide a yard or two beyond the back of the end zone.

Swinton's momentum carried him right to the feet of an impressed

Jones, who said some encouraging words to Swinton before yelling to nearby fans and witnesses within earshot, "How 'bout that Arkansas boy?"

His first day on the job was impressive, and Swinton continued to make just enough plays to stick around, eventually earning a spot on the Cowboys roster. In his NFL debut September 9, 2001, against the Buccaneers at Texas Stadium, Swinton returned a kickoff 77 yards to set up a field goal. After the game he told reporters that he didn't expect opponents to kick in his direction anymore, a statement for which special teams coach Joe Avezzano, never one to hold back his emotions or feelings, gave Swinton quite a tongue-lashing.

But Swinton did have a nice career returning kickoffs and punts. He returned a punt for a touchdown against Denver on Thanksgiving Day of that same season to keep the Cowboys in the game and later had a kickoff return for a score at Philadelphia on September 22, 2002.

During Bill Parcells' first training camp in 2003, Swinton was on the outside looking in as the preseason was coming to an end. With just one game to play, the 53-man roster was nearly set, and it was clear that Swinton was on the bubble. He needed to do something against the Raiders to make it happen.

With the Cowboys leading 38–13 in the third quarter, Swinton fielded a kickoff near the left corner and proceeded to take it back to the middle. But again, knowing he needed to do something, Swinton cut it back down the left sideline, found daylight, hurdled a defender, and went 96 yards to the house for a touchdown.

Even the fiery Parcells couldn't cut him loose after that. Swinton stayed around just one week into the regular season, though, before being let go. He wound up with the Lions and then later spent 2005 with the Cardinals, playing a total of five seasons and 69 games.

Not bad for a guy who couldn't cut it in the af2.

Worth a Shot

In four seasons at the University of Arkansas, linebacker J.J. Jones was a productive player for the Razorbacks. He was a team leader, a great tackler, and could run well sideline to sideline. Like all players known by their initials, they usually are short for something else. Most people aren't born and immediately called J.J.

And Jones was no different. But not until he became a rookie free agent trying to make the Cowboys' roster in 2001 did he feel it was important to not only reveal but then also change back to his given name: Jerry Jones.

So just like that, rookie free agent J.J. Jones became rookie free agent Jerry Jones, a marketing ploy that obviously brought him some much-needed attention.

At the end of the day, Jerry Jones the linebacker didn't play much better than J.J. Jones likely would have. He appeared in all four of the Cowboys' preseason games before being released before the start of the season.

But he did catch on with the Saints and, after playing 13 games in 2002, is still today officially listed as J.J. Jones in the New Orleans' record books.

Double-Demotion Payback

A player losing his spot to another player is part of the game, a part of sports. Sometimes it's because of performance only. Sometimes it's injury-related. And sometimes teams just need to shake things up for the sake of change. Players lose their spots every week in the NFL. It just rarely happens to a player twice in the same week.

Patrick Crayton was the unfortunate exception to that rule during the 2009 season. The overachieving receiver, who wasn't all that fast, big, or quick, had stuck around with the Cowboys for six seasons, which is about six more than most people thought he would last when the team originally selected him in the seventh round of the 2004 draft.

The do-it-all star from tiny Northwestern Oklahoma State played quarterback, receiver, punt returner, and kick returner for the then-NAIA school in Alva, Oklahoma. (Actually, along with safety Lynn Scott, the Cowboys had two players from NWOSU on the roster in 2004–05, the only two players from the school to play for the Cowboys in the organization's entire history.)

Crayton wasn't on every team's radar, but having grown up in nearby DeSoto, Texas, a southern suburb of Dallas, he was able to attend a Dallas Day workout, which allows local high school products and any player from a nearby college to work out for the NFL team's coaches and scouts. The Cowboys had a couple of scouts who were extremely high on Crayton and finally convinced the guys in the draft room, including Jerry Jones and Bill Parcells, to take a chance on this long shot.

Six years later, they'd been proven undeniably right. Crayton even started 13 games during the 2007 season opposite Terrell Owens as the Cowboys went 13–3 despite a training camp injury to Terry Glenn that sidelined him for the first 15 games. Always a versatile player, Crayton filled in nicely. For his effort the Cowboys gave him a modest four-year, $14 million extension in 2007. It didn't break the proverbial NFL bank, but it was a nice payday for a local kid who dreamed of playing for the Cowboys and whose family worshiped the team.

The first year after Owens was released two seasons later, Crayton had earned one of the starting receiver spots opposite Roy Williams. At Tampa Bay on September 13 for the first game of the season, Crayton had 135 receiving yards, including a game-sealing 80-yard touchdown, which provided another jab to those critics who doubted Crayton's game-breaking speed.

But in Week Five, something amazing happened. Not to Crayton, though he did have a front-row seat for Miles Austin's coming out party in Kansas City. With Williams sidelined due to a rib injury, Austin stepped in and had the greatest game ever by a Cowboys receiver. With 250 yards and two touchdowns, including the 60-yard game-winner in overtime, Austin immediately became a star. And you can't spell starter without star, so inevitably he was going to take someone's spot.

Of course, it wasn't the guy he replaced in Kansas City. No, Williams was the team's No. 1 receiver, so that meant Crayton would be the odd man out. Never one to bite his tongue, Crayton was not happy about it.

What made it worse was how he found out. There wasn't a meeting beforehand from head coach Wade Phillips or offensive coordinator Jason Garrett. On the field during the next practice after the Chiefs game, Crayton was told just before a passing drill that Austin would take the first spot in line.

That's when Crayton realized he was no longer a starting receiver. When he was questioned by the media after the workout, his pride came to the forefront as well as some moisture around his eyes. Crayton didn't cry about the demotion, but he was clearly upset and hurt that the Cowboys would take his job, especially in that way.

To make matters worse, the Cowboys also wanted some help on special teams. The chance to sign journeyman Allen Rossum was too good to pass up, so they added the veteran, immediately putting him on both kickoff and punt returns.

So just like that, Crayton lost not one, but two starting gigs...in between games.

The Cowboys actually had a bye week following their victory over the Chiefs with a home matchup next against the upstart Falcons, who were much improved behind young quarterback Matt Ryan. Entering the game, Crayton was still activated as the third receiver and would play some on special teams, but his role was certainly diminished.

Things, however, have a funny way of shaking out sometimes.

On the Cowboys' first kick return, Rossum went 16 yards around the left side before his hamstring gave out. He limped off the field and never played another down for the Cowboys. His day was done, and he was released soon afterward. So Crayton took over as the punt returner, running the first Atlanta punt back 12 yards. He also muffed another punt later in the first half.

At receiver, Crayton was always going to be involved as the third wideout, a spot that often requires a crafty player who can get open when the play breaks down. Just before halftime with the Cowboys out of timeouts but knocking on the door at the Falcons' 5-yard line, Tony Romo kept a play alive with his feet, scrambling away from two would-be sacks before finding Crayton in the back of the end zone for a touchdown catch that gave the Cowboys a 10-point lead going into halftime. Then in the fourth quarter, the Falcons punted it away to Crayton, who sliced through the biggest hole imaginable and coasted to the end zone for a 73-yard touchdown that put the game away with Dallas cruising to a 37–21 win.

Benched during the week as a receiver, Crayton catches a touchdown pass. Benched as the punt returner, Crayton returns one for a score. He even came back the next week and took another punt to the end zone against Seattle. He finished the year fourth in the NFL with a 12.1-yard average on punt returns. Demoted twice, Crayton rose to the challenge…twice.

Snap Decision

The Cowboys have always had a tremendous following in the state of California. They spent 27 years in Thousand Oaks for training camp and have made eight trips to Oxnard since 2001. The combination of the weather and a loyal fan base makes it an attractive place for the Cowboys to train.

During the 2005 regular season, though, the club decided to spend a full week in California in between a pair of road matchups against the 49ers and Raiders. The idea was to cut down on the travel of back-to-back games and keep the entire team and football staff out on the West Coast, avoiding two long trips.

But they never dreamed that decision would help land them one of the most consistent players in franchise history. The Cowboys had just finished beating the 49ers in the first of the two Bay Area games, but head coach Bill Parcells was overly concerned about rookie long snapper Jon Condo. Three games into his career, the undrafted Maryland product had been less than stellar. His bad snap on an extra point against the 49ers resulted in a miss by Jose Cortez, who made the mistake of complaining too loudly. The kicker then caught the wrath of future Hall of Fame guard Larry Allen, who gave him a facemask tug for the ages. Cortez kept his job, but Condo did not.

Parcells decided he needed to make a change and asked his scouting department to get him some help. Since the team was in California, the staff started its search in the San Francisco area, hoping they could find someone close enough to join the Cowboys in time for that Wednesday's practice on the campus of San Jose State University.

As it turned out, the University of California, Berkley had recently graduated a snapper who actually went to training camp with the Saints a few weeks earlier. No one could pronounce the name Louis-Philippe Ladouceur, but fortunately he went by L.P., and that was good enough. The Cowboys were more concerned about just getting him in for a quick tryout. Being less than 30 minutes away from the practice facility, Ladouceur was able to arrive on time for a morning workout. Former scouting director Tom Ciskowski recalled, "As long as he didn't put any on the ground, he was going to get the job."

Sure enough, Ladouceur had a solid workout, and the Cowboys signed him on the spot. Asked about the switch that day in practice, Parcells chalked up the Condo release as a business decision. "We had too many balls on the ground," Parcells said. "We'll look at this guy for a couple of days, see what happens."

A couple of days turned into the rest of the season. It turned into two more contracts, and now Ladouceur is arguably the best snapper in franchise history, along with Dale Hellestrae, who played 11 years with the team. But Ladouceur finished his ninth season with the Cowboys in 2013 and has yet to have an errant snap in his entire career.

In the last 20 years, the Cowboys have only stayed on the road between consecutive games away from home just that one time in 2005. Without a doubt, Ladouceur used some good fortune to land his gig. But he's done the rest over the last decade to keep it.

250 Miles

The reason that millions of people love sports is because it's the ultimate reality show. It's not scripted. It's not rehearsed. And when things happen on the field that completely blow your mind, those events are talked about and remembered for years to come. One of those types of events happened in 2009 in Kansas City. The Cowboys were 2–2 and heading into a bye week against the winless Chiefs, coached by first-year head coach Todd Haley, a former Cowboys assistant.

Although it was early October, it didn't feel that way for two reasons. First, the wind was rather brisk on this day, creating temperatures in the low 40s. Secondly, the Cowboys already had their backs against the wall. They couldn't fall below .500 and head into the bye week with a damaging loss.

But to win they would need to do so without their No. 1 receiver. Roy Williams suffered a rib injury the previous week at Denver, propelling Miles Austin into the starting lineup. Austin was a four-year veteran who had just 23 catches in his career prior to the Chiefs game. He was big and fast and loaded with potential, but to that point had sporadic hands and was prone to minor injuries. However, this was going to be his chance to shine. And on a day where the sun never surfaced, Austin shined brighter than any receiver has ever shined in a Cowboys uniform.

The ironic part of Austin making his first start in this game was the coach on the other sideline. Haley was the Cowboys receivers coach in 2006 when Austin was an undrafted rookie from tiny Monmouth University in New Jersey. To this day many people around the team believe Parcells had a soft spot for Austin because they were both New Jersey natives. Haley, a rough-around-the-edges assistant, fit in nicely with Parcells. Both were bold, brash, and not afraid to tell it like it is.

In 2006 the darling of training camp was another undrafted receiver, Sam Hurd. The Northern Illinois product made a highlight grab seemingly every day. And it didn't hurt that Hurd became Terrell Owens' pet cat that year. The two stayed late after practice, catching balls, and before too long, it was clear Hurd would have a spot on the team's roster. With T.O., Terry Glenn, and Patrick Crayton already on board, it was unthinkable to assume the Cowboys would keep *two* undrafted receivers.

During one afternoon practice in particular, Haley was upset with Austin during a blocking drill and screamed at the wide-eyed rookie: "Come on Miles…Sam does *everything* better than you!"

But they both made the team that year and over the next five seasons of playing together, each had his share of moments. In 2006 Austin became the first player in Cowboys history to return a kickoff for a touchdown in a playoff game, a game against Seattle that would end painfully with Tony Romo's botched field-goal snap.

Hurd started a handful of outings and was a solid special teams player. The week before this Kansas City game, he was Romo's intended receiver twice in the end zone against the Broncos. Hurd battled with Denver cornerback Champ Bailey, who got the best of the matchup, and the Broncos prevailed for a 17–10 win.

But against the Chiefs, the Cowboys went with Austin—a move they would never regret.

It started out rather unceremoniously as Austin made four catches for 71 yards in the first half. The yardage was nice, but he was targeted seven times and had a key drop in the end zone that would've been a touchdown. Instead the Cowboys settled for a field goal in a game they trailed 10–3.

While the temperature only got colder, Austin heated up in the second half. He had an Alvin Harper-like catch early in the fourth quarter, bringing back memories of the former Dallas receiver when he outjumped Chiefs cornerback and future Cowboys teammate Brandon Carr for a 34-yard gain that led to a field goal.

The Chiefs worked their way into position to break a tie with a late field-goal attempt, but defensive lineman Jay Ratliff hurdled the line and blocked the kick, which set the Cowboys up at their own 36-yard line with 3:09 left on the clock. Three plays later, Romo found Austin, who broke a tackle and sprinted 59 yards for a go-ahead touchdown. The Chiefs would then rally for a late score of their own to tie the game and force overtime.

Austin finished regulation with nine catches for 190 yards and a touchdown, but it wasn't enough. The headshaking in the press box was contagious. No one could believe that a guy with 23 catches in 41 career games could now have nine receptions in just four quarters.

If the bundled-up fans at Arrowhead Stadium were confused as to who this No. 19 was, they weren't getting much help from the Chiefs public address announcer. Even in overtime, an intended pass by Romo went to "Austin Miles."

But the world was about to know exactly who he was. Lining up at his own 40-yard line with 8:33 left in the extra frame, Romo went back to a bread-and-butter play to Austin, who caught a comeback curl on the right sideline, and his tremendous balance and lower-body strength

In his first 41 games, Miles Austin accumulated just 435 receiving yards. Then with a franchise-record 250 yards against the Chiefs, including a game-winning touchdown, Austin instantly became a star.

allowed him to break a tackle by Brandon Flowers and cut up the field. That's when Austin's speed took over. No one was about to catch him. "Miles Austin made the play. Miles Austin saves the day," was the radio call by the Cowboys' longtime play-by-play voice, Brad Sham.

And Austin did save the day. And maybe even the season. The Cowboys were able to get to the bye week at 3–2 and eventually made the playoffs with an 11–5 record, going on to win their first playoff game since the 1996 season. "I'll never forget being on the bottom of that pile after the touchdown," Austin recalled. "I hadn't really produced consistently to that point. For it to come together that day, it was a special moment. I felt like I really contributed to a big win for us. I think it was the turning point in our season but definitely the turning point for me in my life."

The 250-yard receiving day broke Bob Hayes' 43-year-old single-game record set in 1966. Austin's mark still stands as a franchise best, and he backed it up the next game with 171 yards against the Falcons, as he stayed in the starting lineup even after the return of Williams. Austin continued his success all year, making the first of two Pro Bowls after finishing 2009 with 81 catches for 1,320 yards while also tying for fourth in the NFL with 11 receiving touchdowns.

After his record-breaking performance against the Chiefs, superstardom hit Austin quicker than his 60-yard jaunt to the end zone. With his blue eyes, huge smile, and runway model looks, he immediately became a fan favorite. The crowd would go crazy when Austin's face was shown on the video board at home games, and his off-the-field life became a hot topic as well, especially in 2010 when he was reportedly dating celebrity Kim Kardashian, who even attended one training camp practice in San Antonio. But it all started on an overcast day in Kansas City.

Wrong Injury, Wrong Time

No matter the day of the week or month of the year, 7:45 PM is usually a pretty quiet time at Valley Ranch. On this particular late-October Thursday, the regular season was in full swing, but the training room was nearly empty. Tight end James Whalen really has no clue who was still around. His face has been buried in a training-table pillow while his nagging right hamstring received much-needed treatment.

This wasn't a new injury by any means. Whalen had been dragging through practice for the past five weeks. His leg wasn't strong enough to get in the games, but the ultra-competitor who had longed for a shot to prove his NFL worth figured he could fight through this and get back on the field soon enough.

That's when he heard his name being called from a distance.

"Whalen!"

He knew the voice without looking, but he popped his head up anyway. Whalen was certainly not a rookie, but the fourth-year veteran here in 2003 was like everyone else in the building, a Parcells rookie. They were all trying to feel their way around the new coach and his unique ways of motivating, masterminding and sometimes bullying.

"Yes, coach?" Whalen responded, balancing his neck up to make eye contact with Parcells, who had just come out of the whirlpool. And while it wasn't exactly a pretty sight, Whalen's view wasn't as bad as what he next heard: "What the fuck good are you to me now?"

Whalen didn't respond, but it might not have mattered as the disgusted coach had already walked away. "Looking back now, I should've said something right then," Whalen said. "I should've said something about me busting my ass for the last two months, dragging my leg around for him when I should've just rested it for a couple of weeks and I'd be fine. I should've came right back at him. And now that I realize how he was, that's exactly what he wanted me to do. He wanted you to fight back."

Whalen saw that firsthand a year later in the 2004 offseason. He was on the field the day wide receiver Antonio Bryant had run enough routes without getting the ball that he threw his jersey down, had it tossed back into his chest by Parcells and then forcefully threw it back into the head coach's face. That prompted quite a scene and ultimately got Bryant kicked out of practice. "I picked up AB and got him away from Bill," Whalen recalled. "They went at it that day, but he didn't get cut. I think Bill liked the fact that [Bryant] went back at him. If I had done that, I probably wouldn't have been cut."

But it hadn't been that long ago when Whalen was seemingly one of Parcells' favorites. The coach knew he had to get rid of several players from the previous regime, a group that went 5–11 three straight years, but some of the holdovers were useful to Parcells, who liked Whalen's versatility. At 6'2", 240 pounds, Whalen was your classic tweener: not fast enough to be an outside receiver but not quite big enough to consistently block on the line of scrimmage as a tight end. But he could catch the football. There was no doubt about that.

Whalen walked on at the University of Kentucky and became a consensus All-American in 1999 when he caught 90 passes, which still stands as an NCAA single-season record for tight ends. He is also the only tight end in school history to surpass 1,000 yards in a season.

A fifth-round pick of the Buccaneers in 2000, Whalen fought through injuries in Tampa Bay and was then sent to Dallas, where he would later miss all of 2001 with an Achilles injury. But that occurred after a grueling summer in NFL Europe competition, where he teamed up with Cowboys quarterback Clint Stoerner to lead the league in catches for the Scottish Claymores.

When he was healthy, there was no one better at catching the ball—at least on the Cowboys' roster. "I felt like if it was close—high, low, behind me—I was going to catch it," Whalen said. "I never felt I wouldn't catch a ball and I hated any time the ball hit the ground."

Most of the passes intended for Whalen didn't touch the ground. And that's what Parcells liked—along with his ability to play special teams. Whalen could run down on kickoffs and could block on both the return teams. Parcells called Whalen a "satellite" player, meaning he was a hybrid who could play off the line of scrimmage and make plays in space.

But injuries can change a coach's tune real quick, especially with Parcells. When Whalen missed nine games during the 2003 season and rookie Jason Witten emerged with 35 catches, Parcells eventually thought Whalen was expendable.

Sharp enough to understand the business side of the game, Whalen could accept that even if he didn't agree. But what still bothers him to this day is the timing of Parcells' decision. "I'm sitting in the cold tub about five days before the start of training camp," Whalen said of the 2004 season. "I get a call on my cell phone from Bill's assistant, Laura. She asks me if I could stop by, and I told her I was in the building and would come right over. She said to just get dressed and head that way. At that point I didn't think it was anything bad because we were so close to the start of camp."

Whalen quickly got changed and headed to Parcells' office, where the head coach wasted little time in delivering the news. "James, we're going to go in a different direction," Parcells said. "We're doing it now so we can give you a chance to catch on with another team before camp starts."

Whalen was stunned. He couldn't believe this was true. There were so many things he wanted to say. Questions he wanted to ask, including why now? Why right before camp and not a few months earlier when he could've possibly signed with a team and actually opened up a playbook before workouts began.

But his parents didn't raise him to talk back. Instead, he took a big picture approach and thanked Parcells for the opportunity to play for the Cowboys. He got up and tried to regroup. Luckily, his agent got on the phone quickly and before the day was over informed him that some teams were interested. Cincinnati was one of them, and that's where Whalen ended up just two days before the start of the Bengals' training camp. "That first week the tight end coach would tell me in the huddle, 'Run a corner route' or 'Block the linebacker,'" Whalen said. "I didn't know the plays, even though I learned quickly."

What he also learned in a few weeks was how the NFL can be a cruel, cutthroat world that doesn't always play by rational rules.

Whalen suffered a knee injury in the third preseason game, and it was decided he had a cartilage issue. The dilemma was simple. The doctors told him they could repair the cartilage with surgery, and he would be out the entire season. The Bengals would've either placed him on injured reserve or waived him injured with a settlement. Either way, he was likely going to receive a sizable salary for that season.

The other option was to have the cartilage removed. "They told me I could play in six days if I did that," Whalen said. "So I did that. I wanted to play. I wanted to make the team."

Whalen did play with that injury. He suited up for Cincinnati's fourth and final preseason game. By doing so, he was deemed healthy—healthy enough to cut without any financial obligations from the Bengals. Whalen was waived, a move that cost him dearly financially. "If I don't have that surgery, I'm there in Cincinnati all year and I get about $450,000," he said. "Instead, I played, got cut, and got nothing."

Whalen went to training camp the next year with the Eagles but once again was released before the start of the season. And with that he never played again. James Whalen is living proof that succeeding in football isn't always about speed, strength, or skill. Good timing can be rather important as well.

Take My Number

For some players, their jersey number is a huge deal. Deion Sanders wasn't going to sign with a team if he couldn't be No. 21—until the end of his career when he came out of retirement to play for the Ravens at age 37 and wore, naturally, No. 37. Chad Johnson changed his name to Chad Ochocinco (eight, five in Spanish) because of his love for the uniform number. But those two were superstars who were looking for ways to market themselves.

Guys like James Whalen were just happy to have any number. In fact, he got four of them. Two other players in Cowboys history have officially worn as many as three numbers (Cornell Burbage wore 15, 82, and

89, and Alundis Brice wore 21, 23, and 29.) But only Whalen wore four and, amazingly enough, he was with the Cowboys for just four seasons, appearing in a total of 26 games.

Somehow he ended up with numbers that those *other* guys wanted. When he came over from the Buccaneers in 2000, all of the uniforms in the 80s were issued out. So the tight end picked up No. 46 and played with it until the season ended. That's when he jumped at the chance to get into the 80s and picked up No. 82. Whalen didn't wear that jersey for long, though, as an Achilles injury in 2001 wiped out his season.

The next year, the Cowboys signed veteran Tony McGee, a former Bengals standout who had ties with offensive coordinator and former Cincinnati head coach Bruce Coslet. McGee had always worn No. 82 and asked if he could get it. The Cowboys' equipment staff of Mike McCord and Bucky Buchanan have always been as accommodating as possible to players' wishes when it comes to jersey numbers, especially the veterans. With Whalen only having a handful of games under his belt, the team gave McGee 82 and put Whalen in 83.

That didn't really matter to Whalen, who at that point was more focused on returning to the field. And in 2002 he was able to do just that, catching 17 passes for 152 yards while playing in all 16 games, which included six starts when the Cowboys went to a spread subpackage.

Whalen was feeling rather comfortable in No. 83 until the next year when the Cowboys traded for a Bill Parcells guy in Terry Glenn, who played six years in New England wearing No. 88. But he went to Green Bay in 2002 and donned No. 83 and apparently wanted that number again in Dallas. So he approached Whalen and offered him $2,500 to switch numbers.

That was a fairly paltry sum of money for a player entering his fourth year, but again, Whalen didn't worry about jersey numbers, especially since he'd already had three. So the Cowboys moved him to No. 81.

However, in early April, after it was clear McGee would not return,

Whalen actually asked McCord if he could go back to No. 82 and was told that would be fine. Since there were no official practices between then and the draft, all of the on-field throwing sessions in which Whalen participated involved T-shirts and shorts.

He figured he would wear No. 82 when the practices picked up again. However, the Cowboys never switched it officially. And later that month, Jason Witten was drafted in the third round. No. 82 was available, and that's the number the Cowboys gave him. "If I had really pushed for it, I would've gotten 82 back," Whalen said. "I was a veteran, and it was open. But I just didn't really ask about it, and then they gave it to Witten. But had I had 82, I bet they would've given Witten No. 81."

Imagine how that would've gone down a few years later when the Cowboys signed Terrell Owens in 2006, another player who valued his No. 81 jersey. That would've been an interesting dilemma, considering Witten would've had three seasons under his belt and two Pro Bowl nods.

But we'll never know, thanks to Whalen, who only played four years in the league after injuries eventually took their toll on his undersized body. "I would've worn 10 jerseys if it meant I would've played 10 years," Whalen said. "I could care less about a number."

Just Like That...It's Gone

To make an NFL roster, it often takes years of commitment, dedication, perseverance, and any other long-worded adjective to describe the grueling journey. It's all worth the trouble if those dreams turn into reality. It might take years to get to that point. But it can be gone in a matter of minutes.

If you open up the Cowboys' media guide to the all-time players section, you'll see over 1,000 names listed, but Darran Hall's won't be there. And it's likely because of a 10-minute time frame one Saturday night in Denver.

In 2000 the Cowboys knew they were playing the season with one hand tied behind their back. Nearly a third of the salary cap was lost due to "dead money," meaning the club still had prorated signing bonus cash on the books for players such as Deion Sanders, Michael Irvin, and Daryl Johnston, even though they were no longer on the team.

So to make up for the lack of talent and cash flow, the Cowboys were looking for diamonds in the rough. As it turned out, they found someone more rough than diamonds. For about three weeks in training camp, however, Hall, a rookie return specialist, was turning a few heads. He was only 5'9", 170 pounds, but he had blazing speed and tremendous quickness, which helped him excel when bringing back kickoffs. He was officially listed as a receiver, but with guys like Rocket Ismail, Joey Galloway, and James McKnight on the squad, Hall's best—and only— chance to make the team would be as a kick returner.

And through the first three preseason games, he was doing just that. Hall had a 62-yard runback against the Steelers and then had 110 yards on four more returns in a loss to the Raiders, including a 39-yarder that nearly went the distance before he was tripped up just before breaking into the clear.

The Cowboys had something here with Hall, who returned to camp in Wichita Falls, Texas, as a newfound media darling. Everyone wanted to learn more about this receiver from Colorado State, where he caught passes, ran reverses and, of course, returned kicks for the Rams. Hall averaged 16.3 yards every time he touched the ball in college.

Two days before the team departed for the Mile High City, head coach Dave Campo told reporters Hall had a legitimate chance to make the team. "He's almost there," Campo said. "If he goes up there in Denver and lights it up again, it's going to be hard to keep him off, but we're going to give him a chance. He'll get most of the returns."

This wasn't just any preseason game but the fourth one also known as the dress rehearsal in which the starters typically played the entire first half. The game officially kicked off at 7:07 Mountain time in Denver. By 7:08 any chance of Hall making the team was probably lost.

By 7:15 it was all over.

What's worse than fumbling the opening kickoff, having it recovered by the opposing team, and the turnover leading to a quick touchdown? Well, that would be having all of those things happen…and then fumbling the next kickoff as well. Hall's second fumble, again recovered by Denver, led to a field goal.

And with that Hall would never gain another yard with the Cowboys. Other than a second-quarter punt return in which he called for a fair catch, Hall never even touched the ball again. He was removed from kick returns completely and two days after the game was among 13 players released.

The speedy receiver bounced around the Canadian Football League, but his days in the NFL were over. It's just another example of how most players have the smallest margin for error. With two fumbles in a span of eight real time minutes, Hall's chances of becoming a Dallas Cowboy vanished.

Chasing Granddad's Star

Ask your average Cowboys fan about quarterback Zack Eskridge and you'll likely get a blank stare. Rightfully so, considering he never played in a regular-season game and won't be listed in any media guide or any website for reference.

But in 2011 Eskridge was one of about 20 undrafted rookies in training camp, trying to make the Cowboys' roster. Although that's normally hard enough, it would be even more of a long shot considering the NFL owners had locked out the players all summer, which meant rookies like Eskridge couldn't sign until the stoppage was over, and that occurred just two days before the start of camp.

So Eskridge, a small-school quarterback from Midwestern State University, a Division II school in Wichita Falls, Texas, had an uphill battle. But since he was a chasing his dream, the challenge was worth fighting for. Unlike the rest of his fellow first-year players, though, Eskridge wasn't only looking to gain a roster spot or even one of the practice squad positions. No, the quarterback also had his sights set on simply wearing the Cowboys' trademark blue star.

It wasn't just an iconic symbol to him. The mark was something created by his grandfather, Jack Eskridge, the Cowboys' first ever equipment manager back in the 1960s. It was Jack who designed the logo we see today, outlining the blue star in white, giving it a 3D effect. "He took it to Tex Schramm and he liked it. And now that's what we use today," Zack Eskridge said at the time. "It has always been an important thing for our family."

And in 2011 Eskridge was about to wear it. However, while the star is important to his family, it's a big deal to the Cowboys, too. Head coach Jason Garrett adopted the approach that Bill Parcells used in his training camps, pulling the emblem off the helmet of every rookie. The idea was the guys had to earn their star.

So it made for a goose bumpy story. Here was a kid who grew up in the Dallas-Fort Worth suburb of Rockwall, idolizing the Cowboys, who have been a part of his family for decades. A long shot to make the team, he was trying to earn the very star that his grandfather created.

The Cowboys would kick off their exhibition play at home against Denver on August 11. And per NFL rules, the uniforms have to be complete so the rookies would get to wear the star—at least for one game.

But before Eskridge's moment in the sun could arrive, he got the dreaded tap on the shoulder with the even more dreaded, "Coach wants to see you. Bring your playbook." Eskridge was released less than a week before the first game. His No. 4 jersey was given to quarterback Tom Brandstater, who was signed the next day and actually played in the preseason tilt. Sometimes even the heart-warming stories never come to fruition.

CHAPTER 8
WHEN LIFE GETS
IN THE WAY

The *metaphorical phrase* If These Walls Could Talk *is a catchy title for this book, suggesting we go inside the walls of Valley Ranch to provide stories and insights that haven't been heard. However, a scenario I never thought I'd have to face, in any setting, was* If These Walls Collapse. *That was the horrific scene we experienced on May 2, 2009, at Valley Ranch.*

In the middle of a rookie minicamp practice at the Cowboys' indoor facility, which was a tension fabric structure, a massive rainstorm swept in with violently strong winds. Inside the building, concern was evident on the faces of just about all of the media members huddled in the end zone area. You could see coaches, players, and scouts all looking up occasionally at the light fixtures that were swaying at a rapid pace.

On the one hand, you worried about being inside a building that seemed a tad fragile. But on the other hand, as we saw a Porta-Potty fly by in the air, being outside didn't look that safe either.

About two minutes later, it didn't matter where we went because we were all outside. Whether it was a tornado, a microburst, or just a strong enough wind current, the entire building came crashing down. I recall looking up, seeing the ceiling shift to the left, and with an awful screeching sound, it just came crashing down on our heads. All I remember was going to the ground, but thankfully I wasn't hurt. I got up and managed to do my normal 1-2-3 check, looking for keys, wallet, and phone, and they were all still in my shorts pockets.

Still trying to make sure this wasn't a crazy dream, I remember getting to my feet and looking for my friends—the ones who were just by my side, but now were all scattered. It was extremely chaotic, and let's not forget it was still pouring down rain.

I remember looking in the distance and seeing my friend, Jancy Briles, running into the main building of the complex. I saw fellow writer Josh Ellis next to me. And then as I'm turning around to survey the scene, I hear a muffled, "Help! Help!" down by the ground.

Earlier in the day, I went to lunch with a colleague, Todd Archer, whom I've been good friends with for about six years. During that lunch is when I first realized he had a small green shamrock tattoo on his ankle. Less than two hours later, I hear a cry for help and look down— only to see two feet. One of them has that green shamrock.

Not that it would've mattered because I'm going to help whoever was there, but knowing it was Todd under a large 16-feet-by-16-feet garage door made it even more surreal. Josh and I tried to lift if off Todd but couldn't. Then two rookie players with full uniforms on—we believe they were DeAngelo Smith and Brandon Williams—jumped in, and the four of us lifted it just enough for Todd to crawl out.

I then remember getting inside and trying to assess the situation. It was complete bedlam, but I'll never forget the leadership of Wade Phillips, the head coach at the time. Say what you want about Wade, and most people have, but watching him that day gave me complete respect for him.

He wasn't just the head football coach. He was the leader. He came into the locker room, trying to get a head count. And minutes later he storms out, yelling, "Where is [Stephen] Hodge and DeAngelo Smith? Have we seen Hodge and DeAngelo Smith?"

Wade rushes back outside. About three minutes later, I go back outside to try and help, and what do I see some 125 yards away, but Wade walking back in…and he's got Hodge and Smith two steps behind him. Without being too cheesy, it was like a war movie where the general has some soldiers missing, and he goes back into the battle to retrieve his men. When I think about Wade Phillips, I'll never forget that moment.

Overall, I had a big scratch on my back that was gone within a couple of days—that's it. I know how fortunate I was. There were much more serious injuries. One person is paralyzed for the rest of his life, and others have chronic injuries that will never be healed. Although those seriously hurt received settlements, I'm sure all of them would give back every dime not to be standing where they were when the walls came down.

It's by far the scariest moment I've ever experienced.

—Nick Eatman

The Next Deion?

In the spring of 2000, the Cowboys parted ways with one of the greatest football players in NFL history. The release of Deion Sanders signaled a changing of the guard on the team's defense. They needed to get younger and better in the secondary, and despite not having a first-round pick because of a trade that sent two first rounders in 2000 and 2001 to Seattle for Joey Galloway, it was clear that cornerback was going to be addressed.

The Cowboys would take three corners out of five draft picks in 2000, starting with Goodrich, a stocky cornerback who was remembered most for his stellar junior season in 1998. He not only starred on Tennessee's national championship team, but he was the MVP of the BCS National Championship Game when he shut down Florida State standout Peter Warrick and had the game-clinching interception return for a touchdown.

Jason Witten was being heavily recruited by Tennessee at that time and remembers the "legend" status Goodrich had in Knoxville. "Everyone always talked about him and having the right approach and working hard every day," Witten said. "He was a guy that everyone viewed as a leader on and off the field."

Although his senior season in 1999 was injury plagued, Goodrich was still drafted No. 49 overall. "I thought I would play for 10 or 12 years, get to a few Pro Bowls, obviously hopefully win a couple of Super Bowls with the Cowboys and stuff like that," said Goodrich, who signed a four-year, $2.4 million contract. "Definitely that's what I thought initially."

But his teammates weren't so convinced. "When I first saw Dwayne Goodrich, I thought he looked like a safety," said Pro Bowl safety Darren Woodson. "He just didn't look like a cornerback. And he didn't really play like one. He wasn't all that fast. But he was a really smart player. I think he would've been a great safety if he had played there the entire time."

Instead he was trying to find his way at cornerback. Needless to say,

Goodrich never found it. Goodrich was nothing but a role player as a rookie in 2000. Instead he sat by and watched the team's other draft picks perform. Kareem Larrimore, a fourth rounder, started four games as a rookie, and then Mario Edwards started later in the season before eventually becoming a regular on the first team.

But Goodrich had little impact as a rookie and then suffered a season-ending Achilles injury in training camp of 2001. Although he battled back to make the 53-man roster in 2002, he was still a reserve player who didn't contribute much on the field. In three seasons Goodrich started only one game and had no interceptions for his career.

So were the Cowboys so wrong in their evaluations of Goodrich? Or did the player fail to meet the expectations or perhaps a combination of both? Goodrich puts the onus on himself. "I didn't set goals when I got here," Goodrich said. "When I was playing in high school and college, I actually set goals. When I got to Dallas, I felt like I already accomplished my goal of getting to the NFL. When I didn't set goals, it allowed a lot of outside influences to get me off track."

Woodson said Goodrich was too worried about other things in his life to be a great player. "He was just young and dumb with money in his pocket," Woodson said. "He went out all the time and he wasn't as focused as he needed to be—just never consistent. One day he'd be pretty good in practice where you think he might be getting it. The next day he'd fall asleep in a meeting."

"I was a bust," Goodrich said. "I really didn't accomplish anything I set out to do." But another tragic reason is why his NFL career ended so soon.

A Tragic Night

Dwayne Goodrich knew he had to get up early the next day. He knew he needed to be with his teammates for an offseason workout. Yet it didn't stop him from sticking to his nighttime routine, which included dinner with friends, several drinks at the club, and closing down the bar with a hefty tab.

This January 13, 2003, evening started out like many others for the Cowboys cornerback. That was his life back then. He partied at night but still managed to get up and be at the Cowboys practice facility the next day. But after Goodrich closed his tab around 2 AM that morning, he made a tragic mistake, which he now describes in detail:

It was January 13, 2003. It was about two weeks after the season. I was at the house with two cousins. We were sitting around the house, playing PlayStation. We decided to head to a few restaurants and a few clubs after that.

So I went out, it was a typical night—about 9 or 10 of us going out. I had about two drinks that night. At about midnight I decided to stop drinking because I knew I had to go home. So about 2:30, I'm heading up I-35, and another accident took place in front of me. And I was following behind an SUV, and when she swerved to the right, I slammed on my brakes, and that's when I finally first saw the car that was stalled in the road. And I couldn't go to the right because there was an 18-wheeler still coming by so I went to the left.

It was lane four and five, and the car was tilted sideways in lane four and five. And then when I went there and that's where the three gentlemen were: Demont Matthews, Joseph Wood, and Shuki Josef. And Shuki Josef actually had his leg leaning out the car. And I struck all three of them. Demont Matthews died instantly. Joseph Wood [died] on the way to the hospital, and Shuki Josef broke a leg. [All three were Good Samaritans trying to rescue an unconscious driver in a stalled car that was in flames on the highway that night.] And I just left the scene.

Leaving the scene, I just panicked. Obviously, I made a selfish decision. I saw everything that I had worked for just flash in my face. I had all these thoughts in my head about *just get to a safe place* and just not knowing how to handle the situation.

When Goodrich got home, he was in a daze and couldn't grasp what had happened. His next call was to his closest friend. "I called my mom. At this point it was about three in the morning, and I told my mom and she said, 'Son, have you been drinking?' I said, 'Yes, ma'am, I had a few drinks.' And that's when she said we have to start the process of getting you a lawyer and turning yourself in."

Initially, Goodrich told the police he thought he had only struck debris with his BMW sedan. But deep down, he knew it was much worse. "At the time I didn't want to realize what had happened," Goodrich recalled. "I don't want to say 'downplay what happened,' but in my mind, I couldn't just bring my mind to say I knew that I actually hit somebody, so that's what I tried to tell myself, *Nah, it wasn't that.* So when I initially talked to the police I told them it was debris or something like that—just not knowing how to deal with that."

With Goodrich not turning himself in until the next day, it could never be proven if he was legally drunk. He was eventually sentenced to seven years in prison for criminally negligent homicide with a weapon—his car. During the sentence five more years were added for failure to render aid.

He said the time before his prison sentence was the hardest moments. He was released by the Cowboys soon after the accident, and his football career was over. In addition to dealing with the uncertainty of his fate and the constant guilt for the accident, Goodrich also suffered his own family loss when his brother, Walter, was killed in a motorcycle accident in 2004.

To make it worse, two weeks after he was sentenced to prison, his second child, Dylan, was born. Once a football star who had his entire future in front of him, Goodrich's world was crashing down like a ton of bricks. "From the time I was 13 years old, you hear how good you are," Goodrich said. "Nobody tells you anything negative. You feel like you can get out of every situation. You think you're physically strong enough to get out of everything."

Well-Known Inmate

Goodrich found out quickly that America's Team is rather popular behind bars, too. "You've got people who will never have the opportunity to make it. So in a sense, they felt like I had made it, and I blew that opportunity," Goodrich said.

While some inmates take to different jobs in prison, Goodrich served as a janitor at the chapel, something that allowed him stay indoors and get some time to himself. Goodrich said he earned respect from the other inmates and possibly the guards and officers with his daily mentality. "When I was in prison and I looked at a lot of guys, they obviously looked up to me because I played football, but then they watched how I carried myself around there," Goodrich said. "At this time I'm 27, 28 years old, and when I see an officer I'm like, 'Yes, sir. No, sir.' And you've got guys from South Dallas, Oak Cliff, they're looking at me like, 'Whoa, here goes this guy who's made a few million dollars, and here he is respecting people.' So they watched how I carried myself, and I think I earned a lot of respect by that. I mean I got up and went to work every day and didn't feel like…I didn't go in there like I'm some athlete so you've got to treat me different. I put on my shoes and my clothes the same way everybody else did and I did my time the way everybody else does."

The parents of the victims sought a harsher sentence and successfully got their wish when Goodrich was sentenced to five more years for failure to render aid at the scene. But it was during that trial where one of the more powerful moments of Goodrich's life occurred.

Still hurting from the broken leg injury and walking slowly with a cane, Josef approached Goodrich at the bench. An emotional scene included Josef saying, "I forgive you...I'm sorry for you," followed by a forceful hug that led to a tearful breakdown by Goodrich. "I mean, that was powerful," said Goodrich, who admitted that moment helped him get over his own bitterness toward his friends and family who had stopped writing and visiting while he was incarcerated. "I'm sitting there getting mad at people. When he said that it opened my eyes to a lot of things and I said, 'How can I hold grudges and not forgive people for not being as supportive as I'd like, but here I am asking these victims' families to forgive me and this victim to forgive me for taking two lives and critically injuring another?' So it kind of put things in perspective for me when he did that. That helped me out a lot."

With no incidents during his prison time, Goodrich was able to get out of prison on parole in October of 2011. Greeted by his mother as he walked out to freedom, Goodrich called it one of the happiest days of his life. But while Goodrich tries to move on, he will never say he wants to forget his past. "I carry it with me. I know a lot of people tell me: 'You should forget that night.' I carry it with me because it keeps me focused," Goodrich said. "It keeps me focused on going out there and making a difference and going out there to be the best positive role model and turning a negative situation into a positive."

When Goodrich returned in 2012 after an eight-year prison term, the former cornerback spoke to the Cowboys' rookies with one short, but powerful message: seize the moment. Goodrich wanted them all to realize how quickly it can end. His moment on the field was fading fast on January 13 as he had yet to come close to reaching the high expectations placed upon him during his three years in the NFL. But by January 14, his career, his good name, and his freedom suddenly vanished—all because of how Goodrich handled…*his moment.*

To this day it's not an easy story for Goodrich to tell, but he tries. "It's definitely hard when you know you took the lives of two people. I don't think it will ever get easy to talk about," said Goodrich, who spent eight years at the Wallace Unit in Colorado City, Texas. "I can't explain it. It's something I don't enjoy talking about, but I know people need to hear it. The first time I told the story, I literally balled for 20 minutes. I'm talking about snot coming out of my nose. But I want people to hear my story and I want people to be able to go out there and not make those silly mistakes."

Although Goodrich isn't selective in who hears his story, he's especially interested in telling his experience to young athletes, particularly the ones who share his background. That's why returning to Valley Ranch in May of 2012 was a special moment for Goodrich and not just because it was his first trip back to his former workplace. "It's a blessing to be able to walk back in and still feel some of the love from some of the guys that I saw when I was playing," Goodrich said. "It's definitely a humbling experience. It still looked the same. They've got a bunch of different pictures now of the current guys and the current team. It looks a little bit different but still pretty much the same."

Obviously nothing is really "the same" in Goodrich's life these days. And it all changed in one moment. That's the point he tried to share with the Cowboys' current rookies. "Every choice you make has consequences, whether it's good or bad," Goodrich said in his message. "And just seize the moment. That's really what I'm on. Whether you're the sixth overall pick or an undrafted free agent, seize the moment. There's no reason why you can't be the next Romo or no reason you can't be the next Miles Austin and make a few Pro Bowls as an undrafted rookie."

Goodrich was a second-round pick in 2000 as the 49th overall selection, but it was the Cowboys' first choice that year, which put even more of a target on his back. "It felt like I was still a first-round pick, so to speak, being that I was the first pick of the team that year," Goodrich said. "For me just the excitement of being there was enough to me."

That was part of the problem. Goodrich admits he didn't seize his moment. He was too excited about being in the NFL and everything that came with it that he didn't take the extra steps needed to take his game to another level. That's the message he's trying to relay these days. Goodrich doesn't just speak to Cowboys players or other NFL hopefuls. He speaks to youth teams, church groups, and anyone else willing to listen.

Goodrich knows firsthand that players aren't always welcoming to stories like his, especially when they don't see a direct connection. Goodrich said he remembered former Vikings and Eagles receiver Cris Carter speaking to his team at Tennessee but that the message didn't hit home like it should have. "Cris came and told us his story about getting suspended out of Ohio State and not being able to play going into the draft and getting picked up by the Eagles [and] his cocaine addiction," Goodrich said. "But that literally went in one ear and out the other because at that time I didn't have any addictions. I didn't do cocaine. I'm thinking, *This doesn't apply to me. It's completely over my head.*"

Now, Goodrich is on the other side of the storytelling and realizes what Carter was saying was more of an example. "It doesn't have to be cocaine. It doesn't have to be alcohol. It could be girls. It could be family members. It could be anything that gets you off focus," Goodrich said. "Anything that gets you to not focus on your goals—any type of outside influence whether it's family, friends, girls, drugs, alcohol. Any one of those things can you get off focus, so I want to touch on all of those things."

3 Chances, 4 Shots, and 9 Lives

Keith Davis only had one real dream. Growing up in Italy, Texas, just 45 minutes south of Dallas, he loved football and in particular the Cowboys. Naturally, he wanted nothing more than to wear that blue star on his helmet. In fact his goal was to grow up and wear No. 28, just like his favorite player, Darren Woodson.

But this dream didn't just become a reality. Davis took it to another level. He couldn't wear No. 28 when he made the Cowboys roster as an undrafted rookie in 2002 simply because Woodson still had it. Davis actually wore No. 40 until switching to No. 29 the next year.

During a game against the Panthers on October 13 in Davis' rookie season, fellow rookie safety Roy Williams went down with an injury, and Davis got to take the field for his very first time. "I went to Bill [Bates] and said, 'I'm ready, Coach,'" Davis said, referring to the former Cowboys safety and assistant special teams coach at the time. "He asked me if I knew the plays, and I said, 'Put me in. I'm ready.' When I walked out onto that field and ran toward Darren Woodson, that was the greatest moment of my life."

Davis won't ever forget it, but Woodson said he also can remember it like it was yesterday. "You should've seen his eyes," Woodson said. "He was so pumped up. But I remember he played his ass off that day. You could tell how bad he wanted it. We just didn't have a lot of guys with that kind of passion, but KD loved the game."

In one night, however, Davis nearly lost his dream, not to mention his life. Less than a month before the start of the 2003 training camp, the team's first under new head coach Bill Parcells, Davis became the latest victim of the dreaded wrong-place-wrong-time scenario. Trying to aide a friend, he was shot twice.

Davis not only survived, but he also vowed not to let that incident ruin his dreams. Of course, the road back to football was much harder than he ever expected. When it comes to the night of June 29, 2003, no one can tell it better than Davis himself:

I was in Italy [Texas] playing in a basketball tournament all day. I made it back to my house, and it was about 12:30 in the morning. I was coming from Italy. My buddy, Cheeta, it was his birthday. He called and wanted me to come out, but I told him I couldn't. I was just too tired from hoopin' all day. "We'll do it again later, another time."

He kept asking, and I kept telling him no. But then it got to be about 1:10 or 1:15 AM, and my phone is blowing up. He's a good friend of mine and he would never call me that many times unless something was wrong. So to me I knew something was up.

I finally answered and asked if he was okay, and he said, "Nah, I'm not doing good KD. I need you. Can you come get me?" I knew the club was about to close, and by the time I got over there, everyone would be leaving. But he said, "Please bro, I need you."

At that point I really didn't know if he was in trouble or wanted me to hang, but I'm always going to be there for my boys. So I got up and went over there. That's it. That's how it happened.

I made it there about 1:45 or so. I go in and probably have about three or four, five shots real quick. It was just a normal night, really. But some chicks in our group, they got into it with some other chicks. And I told the girl I was with, "Hey, we don't need this. Let's get out of here."

I grabbed the chick I'm with and am sort of scolding her a little, saying not to get caught up in some bullshit. But these dudes come driving by in an old school Impala, and I guess they were with the girls who were fighting with our group. They drove by real quick, and at the last minute, I see they were trying to hit us. I jumped out of the way, pushed ol' girl out of the way, and then I said, "What the fuck, bro? That's not necessary."

The guy driving gets out, throws his hands up, and I said to myself, *Oh, shit. Here we go. Here we go.* I'm 23 years old and I'm full of it. So we start jawing, and before I knew it, I hit him. We're fighting. I'm on top of him, and he's trying to crawl back to the car. I thought, *Hell no, he's trying to get to the gun.* I kept hitting him again.

Well, his homeboy in the car was in the passenger seat. The door was open, and I looked up and saw him reach under the seat. He grabbed that pistol, and I was looking right into his eyes. I just threw my arm up and...*Boom!*

It just hit me in the arm, and I took off running. And I didn't even know I was hit in the arm. I kept running as fast as I could. But as I kept running, I kept fading. I was getting weak. I looked down at my arm, and blood was coming out of me like a water fountain. I didn't even know I was hit in the hip until I got in the ambulance.

I can still remember it like it was yesterday. If I don't put my arm up, that bullet hits me right in the head. It was by the grace of God. But I really had nothing to do with that shit. I was in the ambulance just so mad because I knew if I had just stayed at home, nothing would've happened. I was just trying to be a good friend. In 30 minutes my whole fucking life changed.

Davis really didn't know how much his life had indeed changed. Yes, he was shot twice, but once the doctors told him he would be fine, he immediately turned his mind back to football. "I told myself that if Bill [Parcells] was going to cut me, it wasn't going to be because I wasn't ready," Davis said. "Here's a true story: I was in the hospital hallway backpedaling, just to see if I could get myself ready. And I thought I could."

He was released from the hospital but had to return soon afterward after he continued to lose blood from his arm. He was getting chills, and the bullet wounds were infected, so he stayed in the hospital for another week. "Now I'm down to 17 or 18 days to get myself ready," he said. "And when I started training, I would go up to Valley Ranch around midnight. I didn't want anyone to see me. The same brother I picked up that night, Cheeta, was with me the whole way. He ran, lifted, spotted me, everything. He knew he was responsible, so he manned up and did everything with me."

Davis reported to camp in San Antonio and knew he had to clear three obstacles: making weight, passing a physical, and then passing the dreaded Parcells' conditioning test, which consisted of continuous, grueling runs. After making his weight and getting checked out by the team physicians with no problems, Davis passed the conditioning test. "I remember thinking, 'I did it. I made it back,'" Davis recalled. "So I got on the phone with my high school coach, and he was so proud of me. I'm telling him how the hard part is over. That's when I got tapped on the shoulder."

Bruce Mays, the team's director of football operations at the time, was also called the "Turk" because he was usually the person in charge of informing players when they got cut. When he told Davis to bring his playbook, the stunned safety could only shake his head. "I just stood there in shock. I was like, 'Fuck! Are you shitting me? I did all of this shit, and you're gonna cut me?'" he said. "I went from the highest feeling to the lowest in about one minute. I never talked to Bill. I didn't even get to talk to him. I go back to my hotel and I get off the elevator, and the first person I see is Darren Woodson. He couldn't believe it when I told him. He was as sad as I was."

Davis got in his car and drove back to Dallas. He was so defeated that he simply removed each braid in his hair, one by one, as he's driving down the highway. As long as he could remember, Davis had always played football. But in 2003 because the new head coach wanted to make an example out of him, Keith Davis didn't play.

Parcells didn't end his example story right there. He was always about second and third chances if he felt the player was worth it. So the Cowboys re-signed Davis after the 2003 season, and he was sent to play in the now defunct NFL Europe during the spring and summer of 2004. Davis shined overseas, starring for the Berlin Thunder, who won the World Bowl that season while Davis took home All-League honors.

And once again Davis was on Parcells' mind as the team began training camp, this time in Oxnard, California. Parcells had actually grown fond of Davis, whom he called "Muggsy" after former NBA basketball player Muggsy Bogues, who stood only 5'3". "He said I reminded him of Muggsy because I was always frowning like he was on the court," Davis said.

But during the first team meeting of the 2004 camp, Parcells once again made an example out of Davis—only this time in a different way. "Muggsy, hey, you tell these rookies and young kids what happens when you go to places you're not supposed to," said Parcells. "Stand up. Show them. Pull your pants down and show them."

Davis stood on a table and revealed the wounds where he was shot in the hip, a powerful message that Parcells had Davis also deliver in each of the next two years he coached the Cowboys.

Unfortunately for Davis, a similar incident occurred in 2006 when he was shot twice while driving on a Dallas freeway. Although one bullet grazed the back of his head and another hit him in the thigh, he was able to drive himself to the hospital for care. This incident also occurred in the offseason, but Davis didn't miss any time. Still, Parcells wasn't going to initially let him have the starting job that year, giving the spot to rookie Pat Watkins before Davis finally became the starter later in the season.

Davis ended up playing a total of six years, including a run of five seasons, from 2004–08 when he was considered one of the NFL's better special teams players. As a free agent in 2008, he signed with Miami, where Parcells had become that team's vice president. But the Dolphins released Davis at the end of camp, and he re-signed with Dallas, suiting up for one final season.

The former safety now owns and operates a liquor store in a Dallas suburb. His son, Jah'Shawn Johnson, was a standout defensive back at Ennis (Texas) High School and recently committed to Texas Tech on a full scholarship.

Davis has not set foot in AT&T Stadium, but it's more of a coincidence than any personal vendetta against the Cowboys, an organization that actually signed him three different times. "It's just too hard to go back because I miss the game so much," Davis said. "But I always said, there's only two ways I'll ever end up at the stadium. One, if my son plays there. And two, if Darren Woodson gets inducted into the Ring of Honor."

While the latter could and should happen someday, Texas Tech regularly plays Baylor during the regular season at AT&T Stadium. "I guess I'll be there then," Davis laughed. "But it won't be easy."

Why would it be? Nothing in his football career ever was.

Roommates No More

The Saturday morning before a road trip is usually a pretty lively time for the Cowboys' locker room. The practice or walk-through is rather light, and there is typically a sense of excitement about either the upcoming game. Sometimes the chatter turns to what suit or tie a player might sport on the upcoming charter or whose alma mater is going to win in a college matchup that day.

On December 8, 2012, there wasn't anything like that.

Players were indeed talking, but it wasn't too vibrant. Hardly anyone seemed focused on the Bengals, the Cowboys' opponent just 27 hours away. There was a lot of chatter, but most of it was of the whisper variety with fewer smiles than normal.

Everyone knew *something* was up. No one knew exactly what was going on. But as the team conducted their usual walk-through, went through the meetings, and sat around in the locker room, one thing was very apparent to everyone: Josh Brent and Jerry Brown were not at the facility.

And because more than a handful of them were out partying with the two the night before, speculation that an accident might have occurred was starting to creep into everyone's mind. Before too long, those fears became a very harsh reality.

College teammates at Illinois and current roommates in Dallas, Brown and Brent were involved in a fatal one-car accident in the early hours of Saturday morning. According to the police report, Brent was driving at speeds around 90 mph when the car skidded on a highway service road and flipped at least once. Brown was not wearing a seatbelt and was killed instantly. When the police and ambulance arrived on the scene, a distraught Brent was eventually handcuffed and taken to jail and charged with vehicular manslaughter.

One of the first people in the building to find out was Bryan Wansley, the Cowboys' director of player engagement, who knew the two players were not at the facility Saturday morning. So he got in his car to drive to Brent's house when he passed a policeman driving into the complex. Always fearful of an incident involving the players, Wansley turned around to see if he could assist the cop, who indeed was trying to ask a few questions but mainly there to notify the team of the bad news.

Devastated by what he was hearing, Wansley knew he didn't have time to act on his natural reaction of shock. He had to inform the higher-ups, starting with Jerry Jones and Jason Garrett and public relations director Rich Dalrymple.

While word was starting to trickle out about the incident and players were coming by Wansley's office, which is just a few feet from the locker room, Wansley couldn't confirm the situation. "We still hadn't gotten in touch with Jerry Brown's family," Wansley said. "The police had been trying to do that. And they were trying to get information from us. Jerry hadn't been with us very long so we didn't have a lot of information about him or his family. That's why we couldn't tell anyone what had happened right away."

With Brown's next of kin yet to be notified, the Cowboys decided to at least inform the players with the most information they could. Jones, Garrett, Dalrymple, and Wansley stood in the middle of the locker room that Saturday morning and informed them of the accident that involved both Brown and Brent. They were told more information would be delivered when it was available.

And by the time the players and coaches had to leave the facility to get ready for the team charter flight to Cincinnati, no formal announcement had been made, though word of mouth was starting to spread the news, or pieces of it, rather quickly.

About 90 minutes later, when the team gathered at the airplane and every player had arrived, Brown's family had finally been notified of the horrific news. Just a few minutes before the scheduled takeoff, Jason Garrett made a rare announcement over the intercom, ordering all non-football staff to get off the plane and gather down by the runway while a crucial team meeting took place. Confused by this occurrence, media members, some team personnel such as internet and TV staff, along with all sponsors and guests, unbuckled their seat belts and walked down the stairs with puzzled looks.

It was then that Garrett ushered all coaches and staff to the middle and back of the plane—where most of the players sat—and that's when he informed the players of the news most of them had started to gather. Some of the players cried uncontrollably; some sat there in shock. And some of them, including Barry Church and Danny McCray, who were with both Brent and Brown the night before at a Dallas nightclub, could only shake their heads in disbelief.

Garrett conducted a team prayer, while the Cowboys' team psychologist Dr. Jackie Stephens accompanied the team on the charter and offered her support and guidance to all players struggling with the shocking news. One of their teammates had passed. Another was sitting in jail. And somehow the team was supposed to get ready to play a game against the Bengals up in Cincinnati.

As to be expected, the plane ride to Cincinnati was about as quiet as any trip. There was no laughter. No card games. No real response to the movie being shown as well. In fact, many of the players turned down the meal that is given about 30 minutes into each flight.

This wasn't a normal flight. This wasn't a normal road trip. Nothing normal was occurring, though the Cowboys still had to prepare for a football game. In fact, because Brent was slated to start in place of the already injured Jay Ratliff, the Cowboys had to sign Robert Callaway to the roster from the practice squad and get him ready to play in Brent's spot.

Reporters filled the lobby of the team hotel in Cincinnati, but the players chose not to address the topic.

Because the news happened so fast, the Cowboys' equipment staff had no time to come up with any black patch or stripe on the jersey or even a "JB" sticker, which the team actually wore on their helmets a week later. But the staff did get a white jersey with No. 53 and Brown stitched on the back. Since Brown was on the practice squad and had never played in a game, there wasn't a jersey constructed until that Saturday. The Cowboys placed that jersey over the bench on the sideline as a memory and reminder to the team throughout the game.

Garrett gave a heartfelt speech to the team in the pregame locker room, telling the players, "We're a family and families stick together."

And while the Cowboys came out rather flat early and trailed 10–3, a key turning point occurred when cornerback Brandon Carr intercepted an Andy Dalton pass in the second quarter. Carr's runback set up a game-tying touchdown run. Strangely enough, Carr was the one player on the team that wasn't on the emotional charter flight to Cincy with his teammates. Carr, playing his first season in Dallas after coming over from Kansas City, attended a funeral in Austin for Kasandra Perkins, who was killed by Chiefs linebacker Jovan Belcher, a former teammate of Carr's. The cornerback arrived in Cincinnati later Saturday night after flying in on Jerry Jones' private jet.

That play turned the game around and kept the Cowboys close, though they still trailed 19–10 later in the fourth quarter. Despite suffering a broken finger just a few plays before, Dez Bryant managed to catch a touchdown pass with 6:35 left to put the Cowboys down by two.

After a defensive stop, Tony Romo had the ball back in his hands with 3:44 to play. He marched the team down the field, thanks to some clutch passing and nifty runs by DeMarco Murray, setting up Dan Bailey's 40-yard field goal. As the final second ticked off the clock, Bailey's kick sailed right through the middle of the uprights, giving the Cowboys one of the more remarkable victories in recent history.

And it wasn't because they rallied to beat a talented Bengals team on the road. But in a span of about 30 hours, the team dealt with a tragic accident that killed one teammate and altered the life of another forever, but they stayed together long enough to overcome a pair of deficits in the game to win in the final second.

Fullback Lawrence Vickers, who showed his emotions throughout the game from weeping during the national anthem to a passionate speech in the middle of a pregame team huddle, couldn't fight back the tears as he walked off the field and looked up at the sky.

The most moving moment likely occurred when DeMarcus Ware grabbed Brown's No. 53 jersey and held it high in the air as he ran off the field toward a locker room full of players that didn't exactly know how to react. Garrett gathered the team together in a tighter, closer knit circle than normal with a prayer and an emotional speech that had several players, coaches, including himself, in tears. "Jason was awesome that day," Wansley recalled. "There's no way any other coach could've done a better job with that entire situation. Nobody knew what to do, and they didn't know how to handle it either. But he just brought everyone together and got that team ready to play a football game. And then to win it like we did, it was a great game under the circumstances of such a tragic situation."

And it was a situation that didn't go away. Brent was released on bail and was able to attend the memorial service, where Brown's mother, Stacy Jackson, delivered a powerful message to the audience—but specifically the Cowboys' organization— to continue its support of Brent in these tough times.

However, Brent was rather distant from the team, a decision both sides made to try and keep him out of the spotlight. The following July, Brent decided to retire from the Cowboys, a decision that might have ultimately helped him get a shorter prison sentence. On January 24, 2014, Brent was sentenced to 180 days in jail and a 10-year probation for intoxication manslaughter. Even during the sentencing, Jackson was there on Brent's behalf, showing no physical resentment for the loss of her son. "He's still responsible, but you can't go on in life holding a grudge," Jackson told the court. "We all make mistakes."

This is one, however, that will undoubtedly haunt Brent forever. Not only did he lose prime years of his football career, but more importantly, his best friend in the process.

CHAPTER 9
CAN'T WE ALL GET ALONG?

The NFL is all about pressure. The ultimate goal for players, coaches, and everyone else involved is to win games, and the pressure that comes along with that can be overwhelming. But the pressure to succeed isn't always applied to the field. Covering a team can have its challenges, too, and I've seen countless media quarrels over the years. I've even been involved in my fair share of them—some of which can be Googled, but there's no need to drag those back out.

Media vs. media battles notwithstanding, this next chapter focuses only on tiffs that involved players—whether it's players and their teammates or coaches or even players and the media. I'm proud to say that I haven't had many issues with players during my career. Working for the team's website, where you're treated like media but also share planes and sometimes buses—we'll get to that in a second—can blur the lines a little bit. But when you try to be honest in your writing and on radio or TV shows, that's when it can become a tough balance.

One player who didn't exactly understand our role at DallasCowboys.com was safety Roy Williams. Maybe he understood it fine; he just didn't like our stance sometimes. By the 2006 season, Williams was still making Pro Bowls, but his play was certainly declining. Teams were figuring out that while he was a punishing hitter in the secondary, his coverage skills could be tested.

High picks warrant high expectations, so it doesn't take much for even the better players to be criticized, and I'm sure I said a few things on our radio show about Williams' play that weren't favorable. But what usually happens is the player never sees what you write or hears what you say. It's relayed to him by a friend or family member, and we all know that the Telephone game has its shortcomings.

I didn't really know Williams had an issue with me until one game in Atlanta during the 2006 season. I was about to get on the media bus like usual and head over to the Georgia Dome. This was a big game for the Cowboys, who had a chance to clinch a playoff spot with a win.

Just as I was getting on, Bruce Mays, the team's longtime director of football operations, was worried about space issues on that last bus, which is for *media and special guests. Since I was part of the team, he thought I would be fine to ride on the players' bus, which I had done before—and have done so since—but don't like to make a habit of it, especially before a game when the focus is on football...or should be.*

So I head over to the first one and try to act invisible as I make my way down the aisle. There are probably six people on a bus that seats about 80. I can remember Kenyon Coleman sitting a couple of rows behind me. He had headphones on and was staring at the back of the seat in front of him, seemingly absorbed with the task ahead.

Then Williams came aboard and seemed a little flustered since we were about two or three minutes from leaving. He sat down one row ahead and across the aisle from me. About 30 seconds later, I can feel that he's looking at me. Through the corner of my eye, I see him shaking his head as he mumbles something, and when I look over, he said, "Are you supposed to be on this bus?"

I informed him that Bruce had asked me to and followed it up with, "Is that okay?"

"No...no, it's not okay. This is for players and you shouldn't be on this bus."

"Well, I'm just following orders. Good thing it's a short ride, huh?"

I could tell he wanted to say something back but thought better of it. He was wondering why I'm on this bus. I was wondering why he was wondering about that and not about trying to stop Alge Crumpler or corralling Michael Vick.

Later that season, Williams refused to answer a question from me in the locker room. And that went on until the Cowboys' training camp in 2008, which proved to be his last with the team. One day after practice I approached him about a story but knew that we would need to clear the air in order for me to get any usable quotes.

Shockingly, we stayed on the field for about 45 minutes that day. He told me he didn't like how the team reporters were so critical. When I explained the difficulties of working for the Cowboys but also having credibility with readers, he understood. He talked about some of the personal things that were

205

happening in his life, and I actually did as well. As it turned out, we were both going through similar situations off the field—mine just wasn't as public.

We shook hands, and for that season, I think we were on good terms.

Again, considering some of the stories in this chapter, I'm proud to say that's about as chippy as it ever got with me and a player or coach.

—Nick Eatman

Clash of the Titans

Training camp practice has its moments of entertainment, but for the most part, it's rather uneventful. Reporters on the sidelines often come up with games, scenarios, or just hypothetical situations to not only pass the time, but also get people talking and thinking. One day during the 2009 training camp in San Antonio, the question posed to a few media types was simple: *If you were in a fight against two people, which Cowboys player would you want on your side?*

Obviously, most guys in the media would need all the help they could get, so no attribute was spared on this one. Surprisingly, out of the maybe nine or 10 people who were polled, only two names were given in response, and it was pretty much split down the middle. Jay Ratliff and Marc Colombo. They were two of the biggest, but also meanest and nastiest, players in the NFL. They seemed afraid of nothing.

And the debate went on for about a week. Every now and then the question would get posed to someone new to let that person ponder the thought. But without fail, the answer was always Ratliff or Colombo. Naturally, when you're comparing two players, you start to size them up against each other. One person debates Colombo, a rough and tough brawler from the Boston area with an imposing 6'7", 320-pound frame. But then another makes a case for Ratliff, who lacks in size at 6'4" and 300 pounds, but has a mean streak matched by very few.

Again, it was all hypothetical...until one day it wasn't.

The bad blood all started on an interception in practice by linebacker Bobby Carpenter, who finished off his nice play by weaving through the offense for a would-be touchdown during the team drills. Just as it appeared Carpenter had gotten past the last player and was en route to score, Ratliff blindsided Colombo with all of his force, ear-holing the massive offensive tackle off his feet and to the ground.

Colombo got up and immediately attacked Ratliff, throwing a series of haymakers that landed all over the place—some on Ratliff's helmet, some inside his face mask, some around the neck area. It was a wild scene that eventually was broken up by several players. Four-letter bombs were dropped left and right as it took a few minutes to restore order.

But the calm was only momentary. On the next play, Ratliff and Colombo managed to lock up again, and this time Ratliff ended the pushing and shoving with a vicious head slap to Colombo's head. The thud of the slap seemed to echo through the empty seats inside the Alamodome. Everyone assumed Round 2 was about to get just as nasty.

Instead, Colombo stopped. He shook his head and smiled at Ratliff, seemingly more interested in squashing this battle and getting back to practice. And for everyone in attendance, including the media on the sidelines and probably most of the coaches, that's how it appeared to end. Little did anyone know that the battle was about to get a whole lot uglier.

Ratliff was fuming for the rest of practice and, as he walked off the field and into the tunnel, he still had bad intentions on his mind. And though he turned down the hallway seemingly into the locker room, Ratliff never went fully into the room with his teammates. He waited behind a wall, with his helmet off and cocked in his right hand, preparing to swing it at Colombo, who was a few steps behind him.

Colombo, meanwhile, thought the fight had been left on the field, but as he turned the corner to go into the locker room, he saw Ratliff just in time to sidestep a swinging helmet. Had it connected with Colombo's head, one bystander suggested "it might have killed him."

Fortunately, it didn't, but obviously that set off a Round 3 of fireworks that proved to be one of the ugliest, nastiest fights the Cowboys have ever seen, on or off the field. There was simply no stopping this Ratliff-Colombo hurricane. Some players tried, but it was no use, at least not in the early going. They traded punches to the face. They used elbows, knees, feet—anything to gain an edge. Players who tried to get in were shoved aside or simply bounced off this epic donnybrook, which lasted at least four minutes. Just about every player in the room, one that housed more than 90 lockers, had a chance to stop it or get out of the way. In this case the latter decision seemed the wiser choice.

Remember, all of this occurred after a physical two-hour practice that had already included a pair of fights. Finally, the two were separated, though it took about 10 players to settle the scene. Both Ratliff and Colombo were bleeding, and blood was spotted from one side of the locker room to the other.

While the on-field fight was the talk of the day and being reported both on TV and in print, the real story took place afterward in the locker room. However, that street-fight-like brawl never was revealed in the media. Therefore, the situation easily diffused, and since the two players never scrapped with each other again on the field, the one-day confrontation was basically swept under the rug.

In the end, it was a three-round battle that most observers unofficially ruled a draw—albeit agreeing it was officially scary. As for that media debate, the right answer was still unclear, but at least they knew they had picked the right two finalists.

Thankful Miss

When it came to blocks, Flozell Adams didn't miss many. As for helmet swings, fortunately the five-time Pro Bowl offensive tackle wasn't as accurate. The quiet, laid-back lineman was a gentle giant but had a mean streak that occasionally came out on the field—and it didn't matter if it was a game at Giants Stadium or a practice in sunny California.

In 2001 the Cowboys had finished a grueling two-week stay in Wichita Falls, Texas, where temperatures averaged more than 100 degrees during late July and early August. So the decision to split camp and practice for two weeks in Oxnard, California, was music to the ears of all the players, coaches, and staff members, as well as anyone else looking to beat the heat. And while usually the warmer weather ignites more fights, Oxnard was instead the setting for one of the scariest incidents of rage the Cowboys ever witnessed.

During long training camps, resentment between opposing position groups will often form. Offensive tackles and defensive ends square off on every play, and after about four weeks of battle, Adams and Ebenezer Ekuban locked horns once again. Some normal pushing and shoving after a drill turned into face-mask tugging, and eventually Adams yanked Ekuban's helmet right off. But he didn't drop it.

Instead Adams did the unthinkable. The 6'7", 330-pounder with an incredibly long reach whaled back with the helmet in hand and swung it right at the head of the now gearless Ekuban. Fortunately, the intended target maneuvered to the side just enough for the helmet to slam into his shoulder pads. Teammates then quickly intervened to break up the melee.

Head coach Dave Campo, a highly emotional character who regularly lost his voice during games and sometimes even in practice, was outraged. He stopped the workout, huddled the players together, and directed a profanity-laced tirade at them, saying, "We've got enough teams trying to kick our ass. We don't try to hurt our fucking teammates."

There were no lingering problems between Ekuban and Adams, though it wasn't the only helmet swing for Adams in his career. During a joint training camp practice with the Broncos at Denver's practice facility

Known as a rather quiet player off the field, Flozell Adams had a mean streak that occasionally surfaced in games and on practice fields. *(AP Images)*

seven years later, Adams got tangled up with Broncos defensive tackle Marcus Thomas. And just like with Ekuban, Adams ripped off Thomas' helmet and then swung it in his direction. Again the helmet fortunately didn't do any damage, and the fracas was broken up quickly. A few million more viewers saw this second fight, however since HBO's *Hard Knocks* was profiling that 2008 Cowboys camp and cameras were filming the practice.

Trading Jabs

The same day Adams was swinging a helmet around at a Denver lineman, a battle of a different kind was also brewing. This one wasn't about toughness or grit from guys in the trenches, though, but more a case of one-upmanship between two of the NFL's better athletes. Not only were the Broncos' Brandon Marshall and Cowboys' Adam "Pacman" Jones competing against each other, they were also sticking up for their own teammates as well.

To this point Jones hadn't caused any problems in his first training camp with the Cowboys. Still, he didn't bite his tongue, which likely led to some of his off-the-field issues and subsequent one-year suspension by the NFL in 2007 after a series of detrimental-conduct incidents.

But back on the field, Jones was knocking off the rust, practice by practice. He certainly didn't shy away from the media and he had his own lingo, referring to himself once as a "competer." That answer probably stemmed from a question about guarding Cowboys wide receiver Terrell Owens in practice every day. Jones and Owens had some nice battles during camp, but T.O. found himself on the winning end most of the time.

When the Cowboys got to Denver, Jones welcomed the chance to face some new competition, particularly eventual Pro Bowler Brandon Marshall, who like Jones had endured his share of off-the-field issues and had been fined by the NFL. When Marshall lined up against Jones, one reporter watching on the sideline called it "The Roger Goodell Bowl," referring to the league commissioner who handed out the disciplinary punishments.

After the first morning practice, which was more of a feeling-out process, Jones was asked to assess the Broncos receivers. He only had one thing to say about Marshall. "He's nowhere near T.O.," Jones said. "He's a good athlete, but he ain't on T.O.'s level. T.O. is 10 times faster and 10 times bigger. I would say he's nowhere near T.O."

In the afternoon, Marshall didn't say his response but rather wore it. The receiver taped up the back of his shoulder pads, which conveniently were visible, and wrote "21's no Champ." The reference suggested Jones was not comparable to the Broncos cornerback Marshall faced daily in Champ Bailey.

The next day, Marshall wrote another taped message, "Adam's No Pacman." Marshall said: "Since he changed his name back to Adam, he's not as good as Pacman used to be."

Once the cornerback joined the Cowboys in the summer of 2008, he decided to drop the moniker and just go by Adam. That didn't last long, though, and as he remains in the NFL, enjoying a four-year stint with the Bengals, he still goes by both names.

Summer Slam

Like a lot of fights and scuffles, the trouble usually starts out rather playful, but then testosterone takes over. That's what happened in this training camp skirmish between two of the biggest and strongest players in the NFL. The fight wasn't that big of a deal, but it nearly ended disastrously for an innocent bystander.

Just as routine as practice, meetings, meals, and treatment, television live shots are also a normal part of many players' schedules. TV crews from Dallas, along with many of the local stations, set up for their nightly broadcasts with a live interview. Players are asked to join as guests, and the time usually ranges from 9–10 PM.

Some of the more profiled players, such as Jason Witten and DeMarcus Ware, were asked to do anywhere from 10 to 15 different live shots during the three- or four-week duration of camp. On this night Igor Olshansky and Leonard Davis were coming back from a live shot during the Cowboys' 2010 training camp in San Antonio. Olshansky, a beefy defensive end, was considered the strongest player on the team. But not far behind was Davis, a guard who had made the Pro Bowl in each of the last three seasons.

The two typically faced each other in practice, and things had gotten somewhat testy earlier in the day—but nothing too major. During the late walk, Davis and Olshansky were playfully discussing wrestling moves and body slams when a staff member walking with them wondered out loud if Olshansky could slam the 330-pound Davis to the ground. The easygoing Davis shrugged it off and said it wouldn't happen, which seemed to ignite Olshansky.

The next thing anyone knew, Olshansky and Davis were wrestling on the fifth floor of the team's San Antonio hotel just outside the elevators. Olshansky managed to get under Davis and, just as was discussed earlier, he body slammed the massive player in a move that would've made Hulk Hogan proud.

The problem—other than having two starters fighting at night in front of too many witnesses—was that Davis didn't land fully on the ground. No, Davis' back rolled up on an ankle. And not just any ankle either but that of Witten. The star tight end, who was wearing only flip-flops, nearly went to the ground as well.

Witten's ankle was taped more than usual the next day and he was somewhat limited in practice, but fans have seen too many times over the years when serious injuries such as a ruptured spleen or broken ribs didn't keep Witten out of games or even practices. And neither did this ankle injury, but it could've been much worse had the body slam occurred a few inches closer to Witten.

As for the post-slam fallout, Davis obviously got upset, and the fight even moved into the elevator, but somehow the two were corralled and separated enough to bring the skirmish to an end before it escalated even more.

Heavyweight Approval

In 2002 the Cowboys' training camp was seen like never before as HBO's *Hard Knocks* cameras went behind the scenes to film meetings, practices, and locker room banter, as well as many other places that made for great documentary footage. One place was in the weight room, where emotions can often get as edgy as on the playing field.

The HBO crew was everywhere, so it was no surprise that a fight between offensive tackle Javier Collins and linebacker Orantes Grant was caught on tape. Normally, that wouldn't be a big deal except there was a visitor on his way to meet with the team in a couple of days.

By the time former heavyweight champion and business entrepreneur George Foreman made his way to San Antonio, he had heard all about Collins' one punch that floored Grant, prompting several teammates to jump in and break up the fight.

Collins was a project, having played defensive tackle in college at Northwestern but now making the switch to offensive tackle. One of the more reserved players on the team, he obviously had a temper when triggered. Grant, a third-year linebacker at the time after being a seventh-round pick in 2000, was fighting for a roster spot on the field but apparently fighting for more than that as well.

At 6'7" Collins certainly had more reach than the 5'11" Grant, who took the punch square on the jaw before dropping to the ground. That was basically the end of the fight, and for a moment, it appeared to be just another routine battle of egos that would be swept under the rug—if the former heavyweight champ wasn't coming to town.

Foreman, who still enjoys success for his famous grills, has made the rounds as a motivational speaker. He was in San Antonio for business when he stopped by the Alamodome for a visit with the team. As he had the players huddled around him, Foreman had obviously been informed of the fight and had even caught it on tape.

"Where's Javier?" Foreman asked the team, which started hollering and had to shove the rather shy Collins up to the former heavyweight champ. Foreman raised Collins' right arm, symbolizing the winner of a boxing match. "You're the champ," he said. His teammates thought it was hilarious and began chanting Collins' name, bringing some much-needed humor to the camp.

Well, not everyone enjoyed the bit. All Grant could do was sit there and shake his head. The linebacker was soon cut and later picked up by the Redskins.

Terence vs. Goliath

Locker room pranks are a part of football, virtually at every level. Executed properly and to the right people, they can be fun for everyone involved. But like all attempts at being funny, sometimes the joke isn't appreciated. And when that happens, all bets are off.

This locker room incident, which occurred late in the 2006 season, started out playfully enough. Defensive end Chris Canty, one of the bigger players in the entire NFL at 6'7" and about 295 pounds, had been jawing back and forth with some of the defensive backs during the morning walk-through practice. He then decided to put a random hit on one of them during their position meeting.

Cornerback Terence Newman got back to his locker and saw that his items had been tossed onto the floor. All of his clothes, including practice jerseys, sweatpants, sweatshirts, undershirts, gloves, socks, and, of course, all of the many shoes he wore, were out in the middle of the locker room. And it wasn't exactly done with care and grace, considering the clothes were far from being in a neat, condensed pile.

Newman didn't find the humor in it and began asking around, trying to find the culprit. It didn't take long for him to hear Canty's name surface multiple times. So conveniently enough, as Canty was in his own position meeting with the other defensive linemen, Newman proceeded to return the favor. He pulled all of Canty's clothes out of his locker and dumped them on the floor in a similar fashion.

Tit for tat, right?

Only this time Canty apparently didn't like the retaliation. When he confronted Newman, the argument quickly turned physical. Now the tale of the tape between these two couldn't have been much more opposite. Newman was just 5'11", 188 pounds, losing a solid 100 pounds to his adversary. They didn't exactly get nose-to-nose because of this, but before too long, the fight was on.

Luckily for Newman, Canty didn't have time to turn it into a wrestling match, or it likely would've ended much differently. But according to witnesses, Newman used his quickness to land a series of quick shots on Canty, who barely saw them coming before teammates stepped in to break it up.

Speed vs. power is always a tricky balance for any boxing match, and this one was no exception. Onlookers gave the edge to Newman, though his punches did minimal damage to Canty. Then again, that was certainly a good thing for the Cowboys, considering the two were both defensive starters on a team battling for a playoff spot. The two remained teammates through the 2008 season, and no other incidents or any kind of rift ever surfaced.

Write or Wrong

While player vs. player fights are usually the norm, especially in training camp when the monotony can cause tempers to flare, media vs. media quarrels are common as well. Where it gets interesting—and often ugly—is when players and media go at it. Fortunately, there haven't been any recently reported cases where media-player clashes have gotten physical. But it's been threatened a time or two.

In fact, one reporter who had a higher number of run-ins with players and coaches was only around for six years, and he was actually a club employee. Josh Ellis started out as an intern writer in 2007 for DallasCowboys.com. He then became one of three full-time writers the following year and was the main reporter for the team's publication, *Dallas Cowboys Star Magazine*. But he had quite the week for an intern back in 2007 in San Antonio.

Never one to lack sarcasm, Ellis was on the field with a fellow intern one day after practice, throwing a football around on a half-lit Alamodome field. That's when he spotted kicker Martin Gramatica and punter Mat McBriar walking by.

Having joined the Cowboys the previous year after Mike Vanderjagt was waived, Gramatica hit some clutch kicks down the stretch in 2006. But he was also involved in the Tony Romo botched snap at Seattle in the wild-card round and even received some criticism for not attempting to block a defender who eventually caught the scrambling Romo from behind to preserve the win for the Seahawks.

Gramatica was brought back for the next season to compete with rookie draft pick Nick Folk. As the veteran kicker walked off the field, he asked Ellis for the ball so he could throw them a pass, seemingly just for kicks. "Oh, you can throw?" Ellis quipped. "Because I know you can't block."

Gramatica didn't really say anything at the time. He might have had a sour look on his face, but again it was rather dark. He threw a pass, mumbled something, and then walked away with McBriar. Ellis thought he had gotten away with one and laughed it off.

Two days later, it was revealed that Gramatica hadn't laughed it off. In fact, he did some research and when he found out Ellis wasn't even a member of the media but just a team intern he lost it.

Since kickers have more free time during the team period of practice, Gramatica made his way to Ellis, who had likely forgotten about the comment by now. But Gramatica approached him abruptly and wasn't happy. "The other day I thought you were some media guy...I didn't know you were just a piece of shit intern!" said Gramatica rather quietly but still with a stern look on his face. "I'm going to go into that bathroom over there, and if you're a man, you'll meet me in there and settle this. I'm going to kick your ass."

Some of Ellis' colleagues stepped in and tried to diffuse the situation, but the kicker wasn't in a negotiating mood. Eventually, cooler heads prevailed, and apologies were offered, at least by Ellis. Gramatica might have eventually made another scene down the road, but he was released at the end of camp.

The very next day, however, linebacker Bradie James sought out Ellis' full-time co-workers and inquired about him, too. Apparently James didn't like a question from Ellis that suggested he was "the self-proclaimed leader of the defense." But Ellis was a good reporter and an even better writer, and his knowledge of the Dallas Cowboys history, having grown up as a die-hard fan, gave him a boost.

During the 2011 season, Ellis had another incident—this time with tight end Martellus Bennett, who was one of the more unique players the Cowboys have ever had. Bennett was usually fun-loving and goofy, but he had his moments when the jokester wasn't playing around.

One day he was apparently upset with something Ellis had written, probably the grades that appeared in *Dallas Cowboys Star Magazine* after each game. Ellis did those in about five minutes as one of a dozen responsibilities he had on gameday, but for some reason, players and coaches were always upset with how he graded.

Bennett was yelling, "Where's Josh Ellis?" until Josh moseyed over to his locker to see about the latest Marty-B rant. "You're a shitty writer," Bennett told Ellis, who fired back, "You're a shitty tight end."

And that's how it started. It went on for a minute with Bennett spouting off something about having more money than the reporter would ever have. "It's a marathon Martellus, not a sprint."

Moments later, Bennett had heard enough and he charged at Ellis— not really with the intent of doing any harm but just wanting the reporter, who was giving up at least seven inches of height and about 90 pounds, to flinch. Martellus was held back by Marcus Spears and Orlando Scandrick and eventually calmed down. Ellis was sent out of the locker room. The two eventually hashed it out before the end of the season, and no damage was done.

No Backing Down

The Dallas-Fort Worth media has a reputation for having a few bull-dog media types, especially when it comes to covering the Cowboys. It's a cutthroat beat where reporters are often going the extra mile just to keep up. Sometimes, the pressure of breaking stories and getting the inside scoop can make for some tense moments.

One reporter who has never shied away from speaking his mind is Calvin Watkins, a former *Dallas Morning News* reporter who, like many of his colleagues, eventually moved over to ESPNDallas.com. Watkins has a knack for getting under the skin of coaches and a few players, too.

His most infamous battle occurred with one of the most feared players on the team, Jay Ratliff. There were those on the Cowboys who wouldn't have allowed themselves to ever be in a situation where Ratliff was staring them down, much less in front of larger-than-normal media contingent, who had made sure they were at the team headquarters in Valley Ranch on this day in 2010.

The Cowboys had just been spanked by the Packers 45–7, and the rumors were spreading rather quickly that head coach Wade Phillips had been fired and offensive coordinator Jason Garrett was taking over. Those turned out to be true, but at the time of the open locker room period, there was a lot of unknown.

Ratliff was stewing over the fact that Watkins had written a story saying the defensive tackle had been benched, though he said it was simply a rotation that occurred regularly on the defensive line. It didn't take much to get Ratliff upset, however, and he made sure Watkins would feel his wrath. The problem was Watkins wasn't backing down either. Before he covered the Cowboys beat, Watkins was a boxing reporter, so he's seen a fight or 12.

Ratliff tried the intimidating approach and scare tactics such as "I'll piss on your family!" But Watkins, who stands just 5'9" and 170 pounds, wouldn't go away and kept yelling right back: "You're not going to intimidate me, Jay! I'm not scared of you!"

Good for him because the rest of the media was scared for Watkins. He had to be held back, and a few players got between Ratliff and everyone else. The defensive tackle had a crazy look in his eyes, and it's fortunate the players were there to step in before an expected wave of rage ripped through the locker room.

Watkins had a few run-ins with the head coaches as well. He got Bill Parcells upset one day in 2006 after the Cowboys had signed veteran safety Tony Parrish, who had been recently cut by a 5–8 49ers team. Watkins merely wanted to know how a player, who wasn't good enough to stick around on a bad team, could help a playoff-bound contender such as the Cowboys.

Parcells answered it respectfully at the time, but two hours later he was walking through the halls a little peeved by the line of questioning. "I should've told the guy about Colombo," Parcells said, referring to tackle Marc Colombo, who was cut by the Bears after three injury-plagued seasons but joined the Cowboys in 2005 and eventually became a five-year starter.

The fact that quick-on-his-feet Parcells didn't have a response for Watkins right then was a surprise. An even bigger shock was the comeback the more laid-back Phillips had in 2009. After a couple of inquiries by Watkins, questioning Phillips' decision-making, the head coach responded with a press conference no-no. "Well, why don't you coach the team then?" Phillips said to Watkins, who quipped, "Well, maybe I'd have them in the playoffs."

The tension was painfully thick in the press conference area after that dagger, which took a shot at the Cowboys' 9–7 season in 2008 when they failed to make the postseason. And at the time of the statement, the Cowboys were on the outside looking in during the 2009 playoff race, though they managed to win their last three games and win the NFC East division.

Phillips could only stare right back, but some swear they saw red eyes and smoke coming from the head coach's ears. Unlike Ratliff, Parcells, and Phillips, Watkins is still around, entering his ninth year on the Cowboys beat.

CHAPTER 10
ODDBALLS &
ODD STORIES

Over the years, I've had to learn the difference between covering the team and covering the beat. Covering the team is attending games, practices, and random press conferences. Covering the beat is doing all of the aforementioned things but also landing in places you'd never expect to be.

With Tony Romo as the Cowboys' starting quarterback, that includes finding yourself at a golf tournament every now and then. Romo was good enough to compete in qualifying tournaments for the PGA Tour's Byron Nelson Championship held in nearby Las Colinas as well as U.S. Open local qualifying rounds. Covering Romo at those events typically meant standing around for 18 holes, chatting a little as he walks to his ball, talking some about his round and occasionally football, and then hoping he'll talk on the record afterward.

On this day Romo was at a local tournament, which could've qualified him for the regional tournament of the U.S. Open, and my goal was to catch him halfway through the round, see if he qualified, and get some football-related quotes as well.

It didn't go down like that.

Romo finished his round and was right in the thick of the race with a shot to advance to the sectionals, something he'd never done in three previous attempts. But since he finished his round in the early afternoon and plenty of golfers were still on the course, he had to wait it out to see if he was among the top 10 qualifiers. Romo left the course and returned in the early evening to find he was tied with four other golfers for the final three spots.

The only problem was Romo's neighbor, Bob Swanson, who regularly caddied for the quarterback, wasn't able to return for the playoff, so someone had to hold the bag. The logical choice was fellow reporter Todd Archer, a well-respected journalist who was working for The Dallas Morning News at the time. But citing a conflict of interest, Archer couldn't caddy for Romo, who promptly asked if I could. He really didn't need any advice; he just wanted someone to lug around his clubs.

The other issue all of the golfers were running into was daylight, or rather lack thereof. It was approaching 8 PM, and the sun was setting. The first hole wasn't a big problem in terms of visibility, but Romo's monster drive went way, way to the right. Far to the right was a driving range that hadn't been shagged yet. So here we were, about five reporters and Romo, all looking for a "Titleist 9" ball in the midst of the other Titleist range balls.

We finally found it at about 150 yards out, and I grabbed his 8-iron and 9-iron, figuring one of them would be his choice.

"Hmm, gimme the 7," he said, "and I'll spin it back."

Okay, well so much for my golfing tips. Romo hit the 7 and rolled it back 20 feet from the pin. He missed his birdie putt, as did the others, and we all remained tied going to the next hole.

Darkness was now a bigger issue, but we played on. Romo survived a complete duff shot where his chip from behind the green went only two feet. He made a shot to save par and continue playing, though another golfer qualified with a birdie, leaving three golfers for two spots.

It was now about 8:35, and the other two college-aged kids with promising golfing careers ahead of them wanted to call it a night and resume play in the morning. But Romo talked them out of it, and because he's the starting quarterback of the Dallas Cowboys, they didn't argue with him.

We go back to the No. 10 hole, the first one of the playoff, and by now we have our first hazard. The sprinklers have turned on, and there's one shooting right to left across the tee box, making it impossible to drive through. The golf marshal, who was pushing 90 years of age, tried to shut off the water but had trouble.

Another tournament official asked Romo to get his caddie to step on the sprinkler to block it so the golfers can tee off.

I thought, "Yeah, Tony, get your caddie to step...wait, that's me!"

So with the marshal still down there trying to turn it off, Romo said, "Nick, step on it and block it. Let's go."

As I did, I completely redirected the water and drenched this poor old man who never saw it coming. Romo stepped to the box, water was gushing into my right sock and shoes, and the marshal was now fighting off pneumonia. Romo *blasted the ball about 375 yards down the middle of the fairway. I kept my foot on the sprinkler for the other two golfers, and then we sprinted to the ball.*

We could barely see anything, but Romo hit a great approach, sunk a birdie, and made it. The other two golfers stayed out and either played another hole or waited until the morning. We never saw it because we jumped on the back of two carts and were driven into the clubhouse.

With Swanson by his side again, Romo went to Houston a few weeks later in the regional round and made it interesting for a while, but after two lightning delays and a pair of holes on which he scored an 8, Romo had to withdraw from the tournament to return for a Cowboys OTA practice the following day. If he had made the cut in Houston, he would've been able to play in the U.S. Open.

Romo has played a lot more golf since then but apparently has fought off the urge to call me back to caddy, regardless of my impeccable record when holding the bag—or stepping on the sprinklers.

—Nick Eatman

Bailed Out

Some titles within the Cowboys organization are rather clear. Coaches coach the players. Trainers deal with injuries and rehab. Equipment managers handle, well, the equipment, meaning both the uniforms and the gear as well. But the people with the player development staff handle all sorts of things—from being a support group, to assisting players further their education, to even some of the ancillary things that help keep the guys out of trouble.

During a 2011 meeting led by Larry Wansley, the Cowboys' director of team security, and his son Bryan Wansley, who is the Cowboys' director of player engagement, the topic of valid driver's licenses was the discussion. Larry Wansley warned the players to make sure they took care of all unpaid tickets and subsequent warrants that might have been issued.

In particular they hoped wide receiver Kevin Ogletree, who had several parking tickets that were unpaid, was listening. "We warned him about this for a few weeks," Bryan Wansley said. "I kept telling him he had to get this done. And then when we had that meeting, it scared him to death. I think it really opened his eyes."

So Ogletree got up from the meeting and informed the younger Wansley that he was on his way to pay his tickets immediately. He got in his car and took off. "He seemed pretty anxious to get it taken care of," Wansley said.

Probably a little too anxious.

Ogletree was pulled over less than a block away from the Cowboys' training facility in Valley Ranch. He wasn't the only player leaving. Most of his teammates were also on their way out. And many of them saw Ogletree's car pulled over, but not all of them saw him getting handcuffed.

After the police officer ran a statewide check on Ogletree's license, he noticed the unpaid tickets and failure to have an updated license. It didn't matter that Ogletree was on his way to get those matters resolved. (It's likely the officer had heard that story a time or two before.)

No, Ogletree was arrested on the spot and taken away in the patrol car. The only call he apparently made was to have his car towed away from the spot. One person who saw the receiver in handcuffs was his quarterback. Tony Romo couldn't believe Ogletree, one of the top four receivers expected to help the team this upcoming season, had his hands behind his back.

Romo called Wansley and said he wanted to help but was initially told to let Ogletree handle it. That didn't work for Romo. Ogletree was in jail for maybe an hour before his quarterback was there, helping him pay the $750 bond. It's not that Ogletree didn't have the money, but without Romo there on his behalf, he could've sat behind bars for much longer, maybe even overnight.

Ogletree was back with the team the next morning and played in the season opener against the Jets nine days later. We often hear about receivers bailing out their quarterbacks with a diving catch. Sometimes the quarterbacks can return the favor—literally.

Slack-ing Off

When the Cowboys signed Terrell Owens in March 2006, one of the biggest questions that every fan, every media member, and probably even every person in the Cowboys organization wanted to know was just how T.O. would mesh, or clash, with head coach Bill Parcells. Remember, T.O. was sent packing by the Eagles the season before. Now Parcells, who was considered as old school and headstrong as it gets, had the receiving diva on his hands? Everyone just knew it wasn't going to be a completely smooth relationship. Then again, the same was thought three years earlier about Parcells and Jerry Jones, and there was never a major dispute to speak of between those two.

But T.O. was a different beast. And sure enough, the first issue between the player and his new coach occurred a few weeks after he signed his contract and told the world, "Get your popcorn ready because it's gonna be a show."

Owens had not moved to Dallas yet in the offseason and spent most of his time working out in Los Angeles. Of course, to his credit, staying in shape was never an issue for T.O, who even today keeps himself chiseled.

Parcells, who would be categorized as the opposite of chiseled, still wanted every team member, especially the ones expected to be the key cogs, to be involved in the offseason program, which included days where the players simply ran wind sprints on the field. After Owens missed the first two weeks of the conditioning program, Parcells got his operations staff on the horn. "You tell T.O. to get in here and start running with the guys," Parcells said to then operations assistant Steve Carichoff, who promptly called Owens' agent, publicist, and the wide receiver himself.

Although Owens didn't rush himself to the complex the next day, he did tell the Cowboys he would return to Dallas. It was mid-morning when Owens finally arrived, and the first group of runners was already on the field. Wearing khaki slacks and a blue buttoned-up dress shirt with short sleeves, he had a California look about him, even appearing as if he had worn the same attire the night before.

But instead of quickly changing into the team-issued shorts and shirt, and most importantly cleats or tennis shoes, Owens wanted to make a point: *If they want me here running with the guys, then I'm not going to miss another lap.*

So Owens went straight to the field, dress shoes and all, to join his new teammates. They were running 110s, the length of the field and one end zone, when in jumped Owens.

Although no surprise to him, T.O. smoked everyone. And we're talking about cornerbacks, receivers, running backs, all of whom had been working out for a few weeks and were already warmed up for the day. Oh, and they were wearing proper workout attire, too. But it didn't matter to Owens, who likely ruined his nice clothes after sprinting for about 25 minutes.

When he was done, Parcells wanted to visit with Owens in his office. It had nothing to do with his attire but simply an introductory meeting between two personalities who were destined to clash. Owens walked two steps behind Parcells with his chin nearly pointing straight to the ceiling. His strut screamed with confidence.

And why not? He had just walked off a plane and out-run NFL athletes while wearing nothing but dress clothes, proving once again what he already knew and what many of his new teammates had just found out for themselves: T.O. was a bad man.

Costly Sprint

Competitive spirits are typically a good thing for NFL players. If you don't have the willingness to compete, you're probably not going to be very successful. But sometimes competing at the wrong time or for the wrong reasons can expose you in front of the wrong crowd. Case in point: rookie DeAngelo Smith, a cornerback selected in the fifth round of the 2009 draft out of Cincinnati.

One day after training camp practice in San Antonio's Alamodome, Smith was challenged to an old-fashioned foot race. There had been some chatter over the previous few days about just how fast he was in the open field. Being challenged to a race by a teammate is one thing. Being challenged by a kicker is another.

Place-kicker David Buehler was also a rookie fifth-round pick in the Cowboys' 2009 draft class, one that had 12 players total, all of whom were taken from the third round to the seventh. As locker room neighbors at camp, Smith and Buehler engaged in good-natured trash talk about racing each other. For a while Smith acknowledged the lose-lose situation and blew off the notion until one day in practice he had heard enough and agreed to a 50-yard dash, hoping to shut this kicker up once and for all.

Everyone knew Buehler was an above-average athlete, posting a 4.56 time in the 40-yard dash at the scouting combine and even running down on special teams coverage occasionally at USC. But Smith was never worried about losing the race...until he did.

Buehler beat him rather convincingly, drawing quite a roar from the players, including receiver Kevin Ogletree, another rookie that year who had formed a friendship with Buehler. Ogletree yelled at the dejected Smith while racing to congratulate Buehler: "The kicker just got you. He got you."

Head coach Wade Phillips caught the action while sitting in his golf cart, and some of the assistants, including offensive coordinator Jason

Garrett, were amused by the race, at least the result. But the next day Phillips wasn't too excited about what had happened and when asked by reporters said Buehler "knows better" and "won't be doing that again."

First of all, racing after practice wasn't the smartest idea for a rookie, indirectly suggesting the workout wasn't grueling enough if he still had fresh enough legs to run. Secondly, if he's trying to earn a spot on the roster, getting outrun by a kicker isn't going to do him any favors. Eventually, Smith was released later in the preseason. The race wasn't the only reason he didn't make the team, but it certainly didn't help.

Teacher, Horse, and Irony

When the NFL schedule makers decided to place the Cowboys and Redskins on *Monday Night Football* early in the 2001 regular season, no one blinked. Why should they? These were two of the league's most storied franchises, a rivalry that is still one of the best in sports.

But that cliché of "throw out the records when these two meet up" was put to the test in a major way. Washington and Dallas were both 0–4 in 2001 and eyeballing the other for a possible chance to get off the schneid. Something had to give, right? Well, that something was nearly the right foot of the Cowboys' kicker—in pregame warm-ups of all places.

Tim Seder was already a success story. After staying in his Ohio hometown and walking on at tiny Ashland College, he taught high school science for two years while coaching three sports. But after getting an unexpected phone call from Cowboys kicking coach Steve Hoffman in the summer of 2000, Seder decided to try his luck at making an NFL roster one more time and he eventually won the job in training camp.

Seder even scored a touchdown on a fake field goal against the Bengals on November 12 during his first season with the team and then scored another on October 7, 2001, at Oakland, which occurred a week before this game with the Redskins.

In fact, because of the Cowboys' injury woes at both running back and receiver earlier that week, reporters joked with Seder about possibly getting to play on offense, considering he did have a touchdown at least, something that wasn't occurring nearly enough for this winless team.

The easygoing Seder laughed it off, but it wasn't a laughing matter before this Monday night clash when he attempted a field goal in practice, stepped back, and felt an odd object brushing against the back of his leg. He quickly turned around and saw it was…a horse, of course.

As if the Cowboys needed another mascot, they had a horse on the field parading around during some of the pregame festivities. Right when Seder turned around, the horse's foot stepped down on his right kicking foot, though he pulled it away quickly while the rider also pulled back the startled horse. Seder instantly hopped off, not sure just how much damage, if any, had been done. Kickers are taught to kick through all kinds of elements, but a horse on the field was a new one.

Hoffman is about as easygoing as any assistant the Cowboys have ever had, but like any coach, his temper can get put to the test, and he was undoubtedly heated about this one. Hoffman got up yelling at the rider, the horse, and anyone else involved with the on-field skit. Fortunately, when the dust settled, Seder was fine. "It turned out pretty well. It was a little excitement for the pregame," Seder said afterward. "I think maybe the horse rubbed a little luck on me."

Consequently, that little luck rubbed off on the Cowboys, too. Seder was not only able to just kick, he was also good on three field goals, including a 26-yard game-winner as time expired to lift the Cowboys to a 9–7 win. He did miss two kicks from 41 and 52, but his three makes, also from 28 and 39 yards, finally got the Cowboys in the win column. Hours after colliding with a horse, Seder's kicking foot accounted for every one of his team's much-needed points.

Mexico City Blues

The Cowboys are not only America's Team, but also one of the most recognized sports brands in the entire world. And it's not by accident. The Cowboys cater to their international fans, especially south of the border where they know Los Vaqueros de Dallas is the team of choice in Mexico.

In 1994 the Cowboys and Houston Oilers played in the first international game in Mexico, a preseason contest in front of 112,376 fans in Mexico City. Just being there proved to be the most exciting aspect of the trip. The weather certainly didn't cooperate, and consequently, neither did the field. The game turned into the sloppiest, ugliest, clumsiest NFL game you'll ever see. "Before the game we had a walk-through on the field, and you knew it was going to be a problem," equipment director Mike McCord said of the playing surface. "You could basically just peel up the grass off the ground. It was like pieces of carpet were laid down. Sure enough, we got the rainstorm during the game, and it was a mess. A guy would get tackled and slide 10 yards, and the whole turf would just come up. It was ridiculous how bad the field got."

Fans in Mexico were used to low-scoring games as soccer was, and still is, the country's premier sport. And they were not treated to anything different in this first football showcase, as the Oilers won 6–0. From the horrible playing conditions to the rainstorm that doused them all night to the tiny, dungeon-like locker rooms that needed to house more than 80 players on each team, it was clear the Cowboys were ready to simply get through the game and get out of there. That's what happened...unless you were a part of the "Neglected Nine."

The archaic, underground locker rooms at Azteca Stadium were divided into two different rooms. To get to the back area required a 100-foot walk through a narrow, dark hallway, making communication extremely difficult. And that's where most of the non-players and coaches were forced to dress.

Players and coaches are always the first to get on the buses after the game and usually have to wait sometimes as long as 30 minutes for the equipment crew and trainers to pack everything up, get dressed, and get on board.

Nine members of the football staff, which included McCord and fellow equipment man Bucky Buchanan, trainer Jim Maurer, operations director Bruce Mays and his assistant Steve Carichoff, and video director Robert Blackwell, hurried out of the locker room with their luggage in hand, heading to the parking lot. "The buses were gone," Buchanan said. "We got up there and didn't see anyone. The [security guards] told us the buses had left without us."

Now this is 1994 when cell phones are non-existent, especially in Mexico City. And the guys that are in charge of making sure no one is left behind are indeed the ones left behind. So as far as the players and coaches on the other buses knew, they were clear to leave.

McCord said witnesses on the bus blame former defensive coordinator Butch Davis for telling the bus driver, "We're good." And it was the first road game of any sorts for new head coach Barry Switzer, so he didn't know—or didn't care, for that matter—how the process worked.

So four buses left the stadium en route to the airport, but now nine staffers were on a mission to find their way there before the plane took off. "We found a cargo van that we used for customs and got a guy to drive us," McCord said. "It wasn't very big, and we all climbed in there with our stuff. We didn't have a seat, but we made it work."

Dealing with gameday traffic and no police escort, not to mention a language barrier between the guys and the driver they convinced to take them, the Neglected Nine managed to arrive a few minutes before the team was scheduled to head home. However, there wasn't enough room on the planes to get everyone back to the states. McCord had to fly on the Oilers' plane with Buchanan and Carichoff coming back on another flight and meeting up with the team in San Antonio, where they finished the trip with a short flight to Austin. In Austin, the plane landed so hard on the runway that all of the oxygen masks dropped down on top of the passengers.

Despite all that, getting left behind in Mexico City wasn't the biggest problem about the trip for the equipment managers. Because of the conditions in which they had just played, many of the jerseys were so covered with dirt and mud that extra cleaning would be required. They sent all of the uniforms to their normal cleaning specialist just up the road from the Valley Ranch headquarters in Coppell, Texas, and told the lady to do her best to make them white.

"Back then, our jerseys were the screened-on numbers from Russell to take the weight out of the jerseys," McCord explained. "So to get them clean, she had to use so much chemicals that it just stripped the ink off the jerseys. We got the jerseys back, and they were just all white with mesh, leaving a spot where the numbers used to be. She got the jerseys clean. They were white, just all white."

The Cowboys had to replace just about all of the team's white uniforms and had only six days before the next preseason game. And that was just the first trip to Mexico City.

The Cowboys went back in 1998, and after the game, many of the players and coaches noticed that they had been robbed, believing it was an inside job by the local security. All cash was taken along with jewelry and portable CD and movie players. "I remember some of the players saying, 'Buck, have you seen my watch? Have you seen my billfold?'" Buchanan said. "It was one thing after another. It got really weird. Then I went to Mike [McCord], and he said he'd been getting asked about missing things, and then we knew what had happened. We had to alert the security and, of course, nobody knew anything."

The NFL reimbursed the Cowboys for most of the stolen property.

In 2001, the Cowboys and Raiders returned to Azteca Stadium for the second of three games the two teams played that season. Fortunately, the field held up despite a constant rainstorm, nothing was reported missing from the locker rooms (as security was beefed up this time around), and everyone made it on the bus back to the airport.

Still, while the fans might have enjoyed the three visits the Cowboys made to Mexico City, needless to say, a few of the veteran staff members won't be excited to return anytime soon.

Casting a Spell on You

There have been better players to wear a Cowboys uniform than Alonzo Spellman. The team has also certainly had bigger players than Spellman, who was virtually all muscle. Has there been a more intimidating player than Spellman? Well, that one will always be up for debate, but needless to say, Spellman will go down as one of the more unique individuals to ever lace them up for the Cowboys—and he only did so for two seasons.

Spellman suffered from a bipolar disorder that was initially diagnosed during his six-year tenure with the Chicago Bears from 1992–97. His erratic behavior led to a series of disturbing off-the-field incidents, including a standoff with police at his publicist's house. But after it appeared Spellman had gained control of his condition and was taking his medicine regularly, he signed with the Cowboys in 1999 and spent two years as a key rotational player on the team's defensive line.

His time in Dallas was rather uneventful compared to the legal troubles he endured both before and after, but during those two seasons, Spellman provided quite a few stories that his fellow teammates and staff members will never forget.

For starters, Spellman had a menacing presence about him that couldn't be overlooked. With a bald head, the meanest scowl a man could muster, and eyes that seemingly popped out of his head, Spellman's facial features were actually no comparison to his physique. Although he was listed at 6'4", he had the arms of a seven-foot basketball player, which were also larger in diameter and stronger than your average person's thigh.

Spellman used to amaze passengers seated behind him on the team's charter flights. He could open the overhead compartment, grab his bag, get whatever he needed, put it back up top, then close the door, all while never leaving his seat. In fact, he could keep his seatbelt fastened. That's how long and massive his arms were.

Spellman wasn't just huge, though. He was huge and scary. And when he took that anger to the field, he could be a great player—great enough for the Bears to use a first-round pick on him in 1992. Seven years later the Cowboys were hoping he could still rekindle some of that ability he had displayed earlier in his career.

Of course, his off-the-field behavior is what people remember the most.

The operations staff, which handled bed checks during training camp, first noticed Spellman's unusual behavior. Employees Bryan Wansley and Steve Carichoff were shocked one night when they opened Spellman's dorm room in Wichita Falls, Texas, and saw the defensive end sitting on the edge of his bed without a stitch of clothing on. The lights in the room were off, but the bright streetlights outside silhouetted Spellman with an eerie look.

Night after night they found Spellman in the exact same position, wearing no clothes while sitting on the edge of the bed. He usually said nothing when the door opened but would sometimes mumble something to the effect of, "I'm here."

While Wansley and Carichoff tried telling some of their co-workers about this odd sight, no one seemed to realize the awkwardness. They finally convinced their boss, Bruce Mays, the Cowboys' longtime director of operations to come with them and see for himself. Mays was as high-strung as any Cowboys employee, meaning it wouldn't take much to get him riled up. If a team bus was a few minutes late, he would often flip out, bringing even more stress to the situation. He was rarely relaxed and therefore was usually the butt of a good prank.

So as Mays opened Spellman's door on this night, sure enough, there he sat in the dark, nude, and on the end of the bed. But as Mays tried to shut the door, Wansley and Carichoff pushed him inside the dorm room, closing the door behind him. They also prevented the door from re-opening, leaving Mays alone with Spellman for what had to be the longest 10 seconds of his life. "Guys…Guys …Guys open the door," Mays said, on the verge of yelling. "Get me out of here. Let me out!"

Finally they did, and Mays hurried into the hallway, Spellman having never moved.

Some of the players took their chances with Spellman, too. Safety George Teague would often get in the huddle and call him out, referencing his mood swings, which are prevalent with bipolar disorder cases. "Do we have Alonzo or 'Zo' today? Which one is it going to be?" Teague said. "I'm just wondering."

In a home game against the Redskins late in the 2000 season, Teague was already out for the year with a foot injury, and safety mate Darren Woodson was also sidelined with a broken right forearm, leaving the Cowboys paper-thin at safety. Both Woodson and Teague watched the first two quarters from the sidelines but after halftime stayed back in the locker room to catch the second half on TV.

The Cowboys had a comfortable lead in the fourth quarter when they saw Spellman mix it up with Redskins guard Jay Leeuwenburg. Spellman seemingly cared little that Leeuwenburg was wearing his helmet as the defensive end delivered a series of right uppercuts into his opponent's facemask. Both players were ejected, but it took several Cowboys teammates to separate and then control Spellman. "I remember sitting there with Teague," Woodson said. "We were up in the locker room when he got kicked out. I said, 'Man, he went off on that guy. He's crazy. He's… coming up here?'"

They realized the raging defensive end was headed up the tunnel to an empty locker room. Teague and Woodson decided that was the perfect time to bail and head for home. The equipment managers, Mike McCord and Bucky Buchanan, also had no interest in provoking Spellman.

One day at Valley Ranch, while on a massive rage just outside the equipment room, Spellman turned toward them and yelled, "And that goes for you motherfuckers, too!" Everyone's eyes lit up, but no one said a word. Thankfully, Spellman kept on walking, continuing to curse down the hall.

One of the strangest moments for Spellman occurred just a week before that Redskins fight on December 3, 2000, at Tampa Bay. Once the players finish stretching during pregame warm-ups, the equipment guys will return to the locker room for their own final preparations. That's when they noticed something odd.

Spellman wasn't on the field but rather sitting in a chair in the middle of the locker room. He had decided not to warm up with the team. And he was wearing his jersey backward. "I came in and saw 'Spellman' right across his chest," Buchanan said. "We didn't know what to think. But you didn't really say anything to Zo, especially when he was like that."

Spellman eventually started that game and for a guy who didn't want to warm up he certainly wanted to play. In the fourth quarter, the Cowboys tried to rotate two different defensive ends in for Spellman, running Ebenezer Ekuban and then Aaron Fields onto the field for Spellman, who simply waved them off.

For about four straight plays, defensive ends ran into the huddle screaming at Spellman, but he never moved. The replacement would then be forced to run back off the field, where the assistant coaches were waiting to scream at him. That lasted for an entire defensive possession before the offense got the ball back, and Spellman and the defense came off the field.

Those were the kinds of incidents the Cowboys had to endure with Spellman, who had much bigger issues when his football days were over, most notably in 2002 when he once became so belligerent on an airplane that he forced an emergency landing and was later arrested and sent to federal prison. Spellman's legal troubles continue to this day, likely due to the very bipolar disorder he was trying to control during his short stay in Dallas.

Dotted-Line Guys

When signing players to contracts, whether it's free agents from other teams, rookie draft picks for the first time, or even your own players, the biggest obstacle is always getting the two sides on the same page and agreeing to a figure that works. That's what typically takes the most time in any negotiation, but getting the actual signature on the dotted line of the contract can sometimes be a challenge in and of itself.

Jerry Jones and his son, Stephen Jones, make the deals. Guys like Todd Williams, the team's senior director of football administration, and player personnel assistant Adam Prasifka have gone the extra mile—and sometimes literally miles—to get players to actually sign their contracts. "Once you agree on the terms of a deal, you want to get them done as soon as possible," Prasifka said. "You never know what can happen."

The Cowboys agreed on a six-year, $54 million contract with Miles Austin in 2010 just before the start of the season. The wide receiver went from undrafted and a relative unknown in 2006 to then a role player until in 2009 when he blew up one day in Kansas City with 250 receiving yards. Austin turned that opportunity into a Pro Bowl season, which led to his big payday.

Naturally, Austin was out celebrating his new deal with friends at Ocean Prime, an upscale restaurant in Dallas. Since the season was about to start and the team would be heading to Washington soon for its opening game, the Cowboys needed to officially turn the paperwork into the league but couldn't do so without Austin's John Hancock. Prasifka eventually got ahold of the wide receiver, who informed him of his whereabouts. Before the dinner party could get to the main course, Prasifka was in the parking lot with the contract in hand. Austin hurried outside, got in the SUV, and inked the detailed papers before going back inside to finish his meal.

The inside of cars has been a popular contract-signing locale. Flozell Adams once drove his Cadillac Escalade up to the semi-circle entrance at Valley Ranch, where Williams was waiting for him. Like a fast food drive-thru, Adams rolled his window down, signed what he needed to, and drove off.

Before the Collective Bargaining Agreement in 2011 changed the rules, lowering the overall deals of incoming rookies and making them more structured, signing draft picks before the first training camp practice was always an adventure. In 2005 first-round picks DeMarcus Ware and Marcus Spears were getting their ankles taped, sitting on the training table in Oxnard, California, while their teammates were working out when they officially signed their contracts. Each of them ran onto the field halfway through practice.

That same year second-round selection Kevin Burnett, a California resident, drove through the middle of the night after he was informed the terms of his contract had been agreed upon. Burnett showed up at 3 AM with weary-eyed Williams and Prasifka waiting for him to sign.

Later in the regular season of 2005, the Cowboys stayed in the Bay Area between road games with the 49ers and Raiders. Needing to make a change at long snapper, the team found local product Louis-Philippe Ladouceur, who played nearby at the University of California-Berkley. Ladouceur's workout was good enough to land him in the makeshift equipment room, which was really just a doublewide trailer. He signed his contract just before practice and has now been with the Cowboys for the last nine years.

Tracking down Emmitt Smith, the NFL's all-time leading rusher, to restructure his contract in 2000 proved to be a bit of a challenge. *(Dallas Cowboys)*

Williams might have two of the more entertaining stories concerning signatures, both on a pair of restructured contracts with well-known veterans. In 2000 Emmitt Smith was asked to redo his deal, a standard procedure to help move money around and give the Cowboys some cap relief. But instead of driving up to Valley Ranch one day to meet the team's deadline, Smith told them that he might be at the well-known Crescent Hotel in downtown Dallas for meetings with his business associates. So Williams ended up getting a room at the Crescent and waited all evening and night for Smith, who eventually stopped by and signed off.

Going to a Dallas hotel was nothing compared to the road trip Williams made in 1996 to restructure a contract for tight end Jay Novacek, who was on a spring hunting trip. The Cowboys were under the gun to clear some cap space and desperately needed Novacek to sign his new deal. Although Novacek was coming back from Wyoming, he unfortunately wasn't headed to Dallas. "Somehow, we arranged to meet up in West Texas, about two hours from Dallas," Williams recalled. "We met up at a truck stop, and he pulls up with this customized dually truck. He's got about three dogs in there. We go inside, eat a barbecue sandwich, he signed the deal, and he got back in the truck and kept driving. And I hurried back."

Sometimes the adventures don't stop even after the signatures are in place. Prasifka recalled driving rookie cornerback Terence Newman to the bank immediately after giving him a signing bonus check, which after taxes resulted in more than $4 million. "We go to the Bank of America right up the street, and Terence got out and went up to the teller," Prasifka said. "He said, 'I'd like to cash this check, 10s and 20s please.' The lady just looked at him and said, 'Uh sir, we can't do that,' and he was just playing with her. But when he got in the car, I asked him if he got a copy of the check to keep. Man, he ran back in there so fast. It's the fastest I ever saw him run."

Prasifka often had to drive newly signed players to the airport. In 2005, the Cowboys had a crazy day of free agency, inking three veterans—Anthony Henry, Marco Rivera, and Jason Ferguson—to significant contracts. All three also had separate press conferences in one day, a feat media members in Dallas still believe is some kind of Valley Ranch record. Accompanied by his wife and two-year-old son, the jolly Ferguson couldn't stop smiling as he was being introduced.

On his way back to the airport, Ferguson sat in the front seat of Prasifka's SUV with his wife and child in the back. "I'm driving down the highway, going 60 to 70 miles an hour, and all of a sudden, his two-year-old just opens the back door," Prasifka said. "Jason just reached back and grabbed the kid and didn't let him go. We pulled over quick and got it closed. But I've never been so scared. I remember Jason saying, 'Whew, that almost went from a good day to a bad day.'"

CHAPTER 11
OH, THAT WAS
THE GAME...

O f all the questions I've been asked over my years covering the Cowboys, one of the more frequent inquiries concerns the charter flights after a road game. Win or lose, people want to know how the mood was on the plane ride home. Obviously, there is a perception that after a win the players are partying like it's New Year's Eve, and they treat the losses like a family funeral. I learned on my first two road trips back in 1999 how the reality is usually somewhere in between.

To this day, when someone asks me my favorite game, I bring up the season opener at the Redskins on September 12, 1999. Not because it was my first as a member of the Cowboys' staff, but because we saw a 21-point, fourth-quarter comeback, the largest in franchise history.

The Cowboys rallied from a 35–14 deficit to tie the game in the fourth with an Emmitt Smith 1-yard plunge and two Michael Irvin touchdowns. They then needed a botched field-goal snap by the holder—yes, it happens to other teams, too—in regulation to reach overtime. In the extra frame, Troy Aikman found Rocket Ismail for a dramatic 76-yard touchdown catch to cap off an unbelievable comeback for the ages.

I got onto the team bus thinking all of them were going to be going crazy, but I was surprised at the rather subdued nature of the players on the way back. Maybe they were exhausted from the fourth-quarter rally, or maybe by the time we took off—about two hours after the game ended—things had already started to drift back to normal again.

And I saw a similar attitude after an exact opposite ending on the very next road trip. The Cowboys had a 3–0 record and held a 10–0 fourth-quarter lead in Philadelphia against an Eagles team that came into the game at 0–4. Not only did Irvin go down with a neck injury, which caused a few cheers from the Philly faithful, but the Cowboys also found a way to let the lead slip away for a 13–10 defeat.

To make matters worse, Irvin was hospitalized with a spinal cord injury and didn't return with the team after the game. He would never play another down of football and retired after the season.

The Cowboys departed for home without their vocal leader, who had been *carted away on a stretcher with his face mask unscrewed and neck stabilized. But once on the plane, the mood was really no different than the game before in Washington.*

That's when I realized that these players don't exactly treat the games like their die-hard fans do. Oh, they certainly care, but it's really like a job to them. Once the game has been over for a couple of hours, it's usually on the backburner. That's why you'll hear abnormally loud laughing after a disappointing loss. Or you might not see a raucous plane after a thrilling win.

Speaking of which, only once can I recall having changed my story based on a return trip. In 2001 the Cowboys lost another miserable game in Philadelphia, 40–18 on a Sunday night in the pouring rain.

The team actually received two early gifts on a pair fumble recoveries within the first five minutes but only netted two field goals. They came back in the second quarter and turned the ball over three straight times themselves, and then had a zero-yard punt. All of the miscues led to points for the Eagles, who cruised to the win.

On the plane ride home, I had about five paragraphs written when the flight attendant made the usual announcement for the in-flight flick before we departed.

"Tonight's movie is What's the Worst That Could Happen? *starring Martin Lawrence."*

And I just couldn't pass that up. I had to rewrite the story and include the ironic title. Turning the ball over three straight times and having five turnovers overall en route to an embarrassing, nationally televised loss to a hated rival, and doing all of it in the pouring rain… seemed like the worst that could happen to the Cowboys on that night.

If that game is ever brought up, I'm sure I'd start the sentence with, "Oh, that was the time I rewrote the lead to my story because of the movie title."

And there are many games that happened during my career with the Cowboys that I remember for ironic and coincidental items. This chapter will include some of my favorites.

—Nick Eatman

Spying by Admission

September 18, 2000 at Washington Redskins

Long before social media put its stamp on the world and long before cell phones came along with video capability, the NFL put a rule in place that no teams could send scouts, coaches or any other personnel to an opponent's facility to scout practices, even the open ones free to the public. However, it's rather difficult to enforce and even some coaches, such as Bill Parcells, can be suspicious about certain bystanders who they deem to be more than your average fan.

In Oxnard, California, Parcells saw an unfamiliar face with a media badge standing in the corner of the end zone taking notes. It took about five minutes for him to get some operations assistants to investigate and find out it was former University of Houston coach John Jenkins, who was returning to coaching in the Canadian Football League and was looking for some tips as well as probably scouting for some players who might get cut.

Parcells also inquired about Art Briles, the then Houston coach and current Baylor coach whose daughter Jancy worked in the public relations department up until February 2014. Parcells approved those visits, but his paranoia concerning spies at practice is a common thing among coaches. That's why it's forbidden in the NFL. However, there are loopholes like the ones the Redskins created for themselves back in 2000.

Daniel Snyder had just bought the team in 1999 and was still learning the proverbial NFL ropes. Owners in the league get to their position because they have money. And they have money mostly because they know how to make it, invest it, keep it, and make more.

So before the 2000 season, Snyder spent quite a bit of cash in the offseason signing big-name free agents to try to get his team over the hump and back into the playoffs. One of those was Deion Sanders, who had been cut by the Cowboys after five seasons, and the Redskins added Bruce Smith that spring as well.

In an attempt to make a few bucks, Snyder decided to charge admission for fans attending training camp. Not only was it $10 per day to sit and watch players, rarely in pads, go through drills, but it was also $10 to park.

It was an idea that wasn't foreign to the Cowboys, who also inquired about doing so once in the early 1990s when fans flocked to training camps in Austin. But as soon as Jerry Jones and his staff heard that other teams would be allowed to send their scouts to sit in the stands as long as they were paying customers, it squashed that notion right then and there.

Well, wouldn't you know, Jones made sure the Cowboys were well-represented up at Redskins Park in Ashburn, Virginia. And during that time, a friendly but competitive rivalry was brewing between Snyder and Jones. Not only were they owners in one of the most intense rivalries in sports, but they were also a pair of businessmen-turned-owners who were often categorized and described in similar fashions.

Snyder was the new kid on the block—just as Jones was a decade earlier.

In March 2000 Snyder thought he had swung a deal with Mike Holmgren of the Seahawks to land wide receiver Joey Galloway. The swap was supposedly all but done before Jones sweetened the pot and threw in another first-round draft pick for Galloway, who was ultra-talented but desperately wanted out of Seattle. The Cowboys acquired the wideout in a trade that many feel was the demise of the team. But Snyder reportedly had a heated exchange with Holmgren about the deal. And what made it worse, of course, was getting beaten by Jones.

Snyder even felt comfortable enough to call Jones soon after the 2000 NFL Draft in April and tease him for his draft pick of Dwayne Goodrich in the second round, telling the Cowboys owner that the Redskins didn't even have Goodrich on their board.

So Jones would take any chance he had to send a jab right back at Snyder. The Cowboys were also in a bit of a transition that summer. Dave Campo had replaced Chan Gailey as the head coach, and the team needed any edge possible. "We sent several scouts up there to watch, and I'm sure that we were not alone," Jones said at the time. "We're looking at everything. They've got a great team, and we need to do everything we can to compete. You never know, [head coach] Norv Turner may have come up with some great blocking schemes."

The Cowboys indeed sent more than one scout to Virginia, but long-time scouting assistant Larry Dixon was there for all 19 days. He turned in an expense report that included $380 for admission to the Redskins practices, which included parking.

With Washington adding a pair of future Hall of Famers on defense and Galloway joining the Cowboys, their Week 3 matchup on *Monday Night Football* was billed early on as a classic. Instead the Cowboys were 0–2 with both Galloway done for the season due to a torn ACL and quarterback Troy Aikman out with a concussion he suffered in a Week 1 loss to Philadelphia. The Redskins, meanwhile, were 1–1 after a bad stumble at the Lions the previous week.

Heading into the game at Washington's FedExField, the Cowboys were still trying to get Campo his first win. To do so, they would have to beat Turner's bunch, who were seemingly restocked in the offseason simply to beat their division rivals. But in his daily observations of Redskins practices, Dixon noticed a few tendencies about the Washington defense, including the way the linebackers nearly always followed the running backs who went in motion or split out wide. Knowing this, he told the offensive assistants for months that the running backs would be able to catch the ball out of the backfield against the Redskins.

Sure enough, as the Cowboys trailed 7–0 in the second quarter, Randall Cunningham, who was behind center in place of Aikman, sent tailback Chris Warren, a veteran backup for Emmitt Smith, in motion to the left side. Even though Cunningham initially dropped the snap, Warren was left open down the sideline where he caught an easy 76-yard touchdown to tie the game.

Dixon's observations also said that the Redskins' back-side defense did a poor job of back-side containment and was vulnerable to throwback passes, something better-suited to Cunningham's style than Aikman's. And in the fourth quarter, Cunningham took advantage of a broken play and fired a ball deep to the opposite sideline for Rocket Ismail, a completion that broke the Redskins' back.

The Cowboys held on for a 27–21 victory to give Campo the first win of his head coaching career. Dixon didn't make all the road trips, but he wasn't missing this one. He and Campo shared a hug on the way off the field, and Dixon received a celebratory game ball in the locker room.

In 2001 Redskins fans could attend training camp practices free of charge once again. And they haven't had to pay a dime to watch or park ever since.

QBs Going in Opposite Directions
November 11, 2001 at Atlanta Falcons

The No. 1 overall pick that season was making his NFL starting debut at quarterback for the Falcons. A former No. 2 overall pick who didn't pan out with his previous team was making his debut with the Cowboys, who just eight games into the season were already using their fourth starting quarterback.

Fox Sports sent their No. 4 television announcing crew to the Georgia Dome for the Michael Vick vs. Ryan Leaf showdown. As it turned out, the network probably made the right choice. But there was plenty of irony and memorable milestones.

Vick didn't set the world on fire, but after sitting behind Chris Chandler for seven games, it was time for the No. 1 pick to be thrown into the fire. He had his moments of brilliance and excitement, but he also looked like what he was—a rookie making his first start. On the flip side, Leaf seemed like a guy who just didn't have the same tools that made him San Diego's first-round pick in 1998, No. 2 overall just behind Peyton Manning. But Leaf had a wrist injury that became more troublesome and eventually led to his release by the Chargers.

Since this was Year One of the post-Troy Aikman era, owner Jerry Jones was trying anything and everything at quarterback, having already used Quincy Carter, Anthony Wright, and Clint Stoerner behind center. But while Leaf occasionally showed flashes of promise, eventually reality set in.

Midway through the third quarter, Leaf had a wide-open Joey Galloway streaking down the right sideline for a would-be score—if he could just get the ball to him. Instead Leaf's pass went into the second row of the stands. After the play Leaf was banging his hand against his hip pads, and initially it appeared the hot-tempered quarterback was simply throwing a tantrum for missing Galloway.

Actually, Leaf's wrist had popped out of joint during the throw and the only way to get it into place was for him to pop it back in himself. After about four good jolts to his hip, the wrist was again in alignment. Leaf then finished the game, but that missed opportunity proved to be costly.

Later on that same drive, the team had to settle for a 36-yard field-goal attempt with the hopes of building on their 13–10 lead. But 2001 was the first time in 12 seasons that the Cowboys were playing without veteran snapper Dale Hellestrae, and rookie Randy Chevrier rolled the snap past holder Micah Knorr and kicker Tim Seder, who managed to pick up the ball only to be smashed by two Falcons defenders. Seder suffered a broken foot on the play, went on injured reserve, and never kicked again for the Cowboys. Chevrier was cut that following week and replaced by Mike Solwold.

The Falcons eventually scored 10 points in the fourth quarter and led 20–13 with just more than a minute left to play. Leaf worked the Cowboys in position to possibly tie the game, though it would've been an adventure for Knorr, the punter, to attempt an extra point with a backup holder. But it never got that far as Leaf's final pass was intercepted by a young Falcons defender, Keith Brooking, who would end up joining the Cowboys in 2009 and helping the team win its first playoff game since 1996.

That day in Atlanta proved even the most meaningless of games, from a big-picture standpoint, can be filled with coincidental anecdotes.

Biased Broadcaster?
September 29, 2002 at St. Louis Rams

The Cowboys were now two years removed from the Troy Aikman era, but he was far from forgotten. The previous season the club used four different starting quarterbacks, and none of them had a winning record in what turned out to be a 5–11 disappointment. Aikman retired before the 2001 season, and by 2002 Quincy Carter had taken over as the full-time starter. But he clearly wasn't Aikman. Then again, nobody was.

The Cowboys missed Aikman, and while his job title as a Fox Sports game analyst wouldn't allow him to publicly say so, he still missed the Cowboys, too. Before this game pitting a struggling Dallas squad against the defending NFC Champion Rams, Aikman was on the field chatting with some of his former coaches and teammates when he spotted third-year tight end James Whalen, who joined the team during the middle of Aikman's final season in 2000. Whalen was a college All-American at the University of Kentucky, a sure-handed pass catcher who fell somewhere between a prototype tight end and a possession receiver.

Through the first three games, Whalen had no catches for an offense that was still finding its own identity. With headphones on during his pregame warm-ups, Whalen felt someone grab his arm from behind. He turned to see Aikman, who wasn't really smiling. "Hey, Whalen, when are you going to step up and be the player you're supposed to be?" Aikman asked in a fierce tone.

With this interception Darren Woodson and the Cowboys' defense helped stop the Rams' "Greatest Show on Turf" and rally for a stunning road win in 2002. *(Dallas Cowboys)*

Caught somewhat off guard, Whalen wasn't offended by the remark. He knew it was one Cowboy talking to another. "Hopefully today, Troy," said Whalen, who proceeded to have the best game of his short career, catching five passes for 38 yards, including a key second-half grab to move the chains on a drive that eventually ended with a game-tying field goal.

Aikman wasn't with the Cowboys anymore and was being paid by Fox to be objective. "It was good to know that he still cared," Whalen said. "I don't know if that changed over time, but right then, I could see on his face that he was still a Dallas Cowboy. And it mattered to him."

Now, Aikman didn't have enough time—or hands—to grab every player on that 2002 team who needed to step up his game, but he could've definitely done so to third-year cornerback Dwayne Goodrich, who hadn't come close to meeting the Cowboys' expectations. There had been games in which Goodrich, a second-round pick in 2000, was either inactive or even failed to just step on the field.

Confidence for the young player was an issue from the start, and never was that more apparent than in the second half of this Rams game when starter Mario Edwards left with an injury. His primary backup was Goodrich. "He didn't put his helmet on," recalled safety Darren Woodson. "We had to yell at Goody on the sideline to get in the game. He kept looking at us and asking the coaches if he should go in. We're like, 'Goody, get your ass in here. You're up.' That right there just told me that he really wasn't in the right frame of mind. You should've seen his eyes. They were so big when he got on the field. He had no clue what to do."

Goodrich didn't play long that day as the Cowboys switched up coverages to keep his snaps to a minimum. In fact he didn't play much the rest of the season, which eventually proved to be his last after a deadly hit-and-run accident when he struck and killed two people and injured a third after a night out on the town in January 2003. Goodrich left the scene but later turned himself in to police. He spent six years in prison for criminally negligent homicide before being released in 2011.

Another player whose career would end on a sour note was Carter, but on this day in St. Louis, he rose to the occasion with a late fourth-quarter drive, managing the clock just enough to get kicker Billy Cundiff on the field for the game-winning field goal.

The undrafted rookie from Drake University nailed a 48-yarder as time expired to give the Cowboys a 13–10 win over the Rams, who played most of the game without starting quarterback Kurt Warner. The reigning NFL MVP was knocked out of the game early with a broken finger, which occurred on a blitz by rookie safety Roy Williams.

Trap Game, Foreign Calls, & Rare Praise
October 19, 2003 at Detroit Lions

As winners of five Super Bowls, the Cowboys are one of the most glorified franchises in the NFL. Conversely, the Lions are one of four teams that have never even played in a Super Bowl. Despite the organizational differences, though, winning in Detroit isn't something Dallas has done often.

The Cowboys had lost seven of their previous nine trips to the Motor City, but in 2003 they had just pulled off a dramatic 23–21 win the week before against the division-rival Eagles and were about to face a 1–4 Lions team coming off a bye.

First-year head coach Bill Parcells was shocked that he was about to pull out a certain trick from his bag so early into his tenure with a club that finished 5–11 the previous three years. This was a maneuver for a veteran team that was having a lot of success. But needless to say, the Cowboys were shocking the league with a 4–1 record, having won four straight.

So as the players entered their practice facility on the Wednesday before the Lions game, they noticed a few things hanging from the ceiling of the locker room as well as inside the team meeting room.

They were standard mousetraps hanging upside down. "Don't eat the cheese," recalled Tony Romo, who was just a rookie third-string quarterback that year. "Bill always used to say that when he wanted us to focus. He didn't want the media to fill our heads with stuff, so he'd always say, 'Don't eat the cheese.'"

For a moment, it appeared the Cowboys came to Detroit for the sole purposes of munching on a big cheese tray. A Troy Hambrick fumble was returned for a touchdown by the Lions' Dre' Bly with the Cowboys then fumbling the ensuing kickoff only to have their rookie linebacker, Bradie James, recover it. Down 7–0 the team finally got it in gear and scored 38 unanswered points to win. Three touchdown passes from Quincy Carter, all to wide receiver Terry Glenn, were the highlight of the game.

On defense the Cowboys actually scored as many touchdowns as Detroit did after cornerback Mario Edwards returned an interception for a touchdown.

But Dat Nguyen, who had played with fellow linebacker Dexter Coakley for five seasons, had been trying to loosen up his sidekick since the day he got there in 1999. "Dexter was a military guy, and everything had to be so perfect," Nguyen said. "He was so focused all week and for the entire game. And late in the game, we're winning big, and I'm surprised we're even still out there. But I thought I'd have some fun with Dexter. So we get in the huddle, I get the call from the sideline and I just call the play in Vietnamese. And I just break the huddle, and everyone goes to their positions. But Dexter is freaking out.

"What's the plaaaaaayy? What's the callllll?" Coakley shouted. "Guys, what are we running?"

Finally, Nguyen just yelled out the real play about one second before the snap, and like it had been doing all day, the defense held up and made the stop. Not until after the game did Coakley find it remotely funny, though Nguyen says his friend "loves to tell that story to this day."

Associate trainer Britt Brown, the director of rehabilitation who oversees injured players returning to the field, recalled a different aspect of the game. His memory involves a rather obscure defensive tackle named Daleroy Stewart, a sixth-round pick in 2001 who hadn't produced much of anything until Parcells arrived two years later. Stewart was big, powerful, and hard to move, but he had an ankle injury that had Parcells worried all week. "Britt, you've got to get Daleroy ready to play this week," Parcells told Brown. "We've got to have him out there. Make sure he's ready."

Although it was nearly a game-time decision, they managed to not only get Stewart ready to play, but he also played well. The Lions rushed for 83 yards total and only managed 157 offensive yards overall. Stewart wasn't the only factor in the middle, but he provided plenty of depth.

On the charter flight home to Dallas, Brown was notified in mid-flight that Parcells wanted to see him. And the way the seats were arranged, the two sat on opposite ends of the plane. Brown was often in the last row of the coaches' section with the rest of the veteran staff personnel while the coaches were in first class with Parcells always sitting in the first seat, assuming he wasn't up in the cockpit talking to the pilots. "I walked up there, not knowing what he wanted, and he leaned over and stuck his arm out for a fist bump," Brown said. "He said, 'Britt, I appreciate everything you're doing. You got Daleroy ready, and he played great.' Yeah, I'll always remember that. You can cuss me all you want if you're going to pull me up there and recognize that I'm doing a good job. That might be a little thing, but it was a big deal to me."

Turnovers, Turnaround, & Double Game-Winner
October 8, 2007 at Buffalo Bills

The Cowboys were no strangers to primetime games regardless of their record. But it didn't hurt that they were 4–0 and looking for their first five-game winning streak to open a season in 24 years. Now the folks in Buffalo were strangers to the spotlight. This *Monday Night Football* game was the first in their city since the 1994 season.

Needless to say, the fans were well prepared for the showdown. In fact, they were much more prepared than the Cowboys' equipment staff, which is always responsible for bringing the offense's game balls on the road. Teams use their own balls—Dallas' are branded with the Cowboys' logo—which are worked up and scuffed to the quarterback's liking.

Longtime equipment assistant Bucky Buchanan had noticed a trend every time the Cowboys went to an AFC stadium. Because of the NFL's scheduling, teams only visit the inter-conference stadiums every eight years, which makes the Cowboys logo balls more of a collector's item. Whether the balls were stolen, misplaced, or whatever the reason might be, he always came back with far fewer footballs than he took to an AFC site. "That was the game I decided to only bring 12 footballs," Buchanan said.

That was also the game quarterback Tony Romo decided to have six turnovers, throwing five interceptions, and losing a fumble. And when defensive players get their hands on the ball, you never know what they might do with it, especially if they find the end zone. The Bills had two defensive touchdowns and a kickoff return for a score in the game, which helped build a 24–13 lead in the third quarter.

While the Cowboys were losing on the scoreboard, they were losing in another department, too. "Our ball boy for the game came up to me and said, 'Buck, we're running out of balls. We only have about four left for the second half,'" Buchanan said. "So I was sweating that out. Tony threw those five turnovers, and we lost all of the footballs."

Fortunately for the Cowboys' team and team managers, Romo didn't lose another one. And the Cowboys also rallied in the fourth quarter. Romo recovered to lead the offense to a touchdown in the final minute with the team then recovering an onside kick to set up rookie Nick Folk for a 53-yard field-goal attempt.

Folk drilled the kick, but Bills head coach Dick Jauron managed to call a timeout just before the snap. The attempt to freeze the rookie kicker didn't work, nor did the Bills' equipment staff failing to retrieve the previous ball that was just used.

Typically teams use only one kicking ball as long as it's available. So while Buchanan and Mike McCord were trying to get the ball boys under the goal post to throw back the original ball, a new one was tossed in from the sideline. And the Cowboys had seen that business the season before in the playoffs at Seattle when Romo dropped a field-goal attempt with a brand new ball that had never been used before or even been broken in.

But none of the drama seemed to bother Folk, as he booted the field goal for a second time to give the Cowboys a 25–24 win as time expired. In the postgame press conference, wide receiver Terrell Owens told reporters they had just witnessed history. "You just saw the longest field goal ever, 106 yards," Owens quipped. "He made the 53-yarder twice."

The players' joyous plane ride back wasn't shared by one of their teammates, however. Running back Marion Barber was informed by team security in the locker room that his home in Dallas had been broken into. He was unsure of the valuables that were taken and because the team arrived at 4 AM Tuesday morning, Barber didn't feel comfortable going into his home for the first time at such a late hour. He instead was sent to the hotel where some of the rookies stayed and spent his Tuesday day off dealing with police detectives to report what was missing.

It was just another example of how even in the game of football, real life never stops.

Doors Open, Record Crowd, & Eli's Signature
September 20, 2009 vs. New York Giants

No NFL regular-season game has ever had more fans in attendance than the Cowboys' 2009 home opener against the Giants at their brand-new stadium in Arlington. Despite local fire marshals nearly preventing the record by halting several thousand people from initially packing the end zone "Party Pass" area, a total of 105,121 fans made their way into the game that night. At the time the team's home was aptly dubbed Cowboys Stadium before the club sold the naming rights in 2013, and it became AT&T Stadium.

Of course, nobody seemed to care about the actual name. Fans loved the state-of-the-art palace, which still managed to keep some of the trademark features of Texas Stadium with its hole in the roof and the arches in between. However, the retractable roof and the 60-yard-wide, high-definition scoreboards, not to mention the countless club and field-level suites and party-like end zones, didn't just separate the new stadium from the old one in Irving, Texas, but every other venue in the NFL and all of sports as well.

The scoreboards were owner Jerry Jones' pride and joy. During the first couple of years the stadium was open, he took pride in having the largest video board in sports. When he introduced the screen to a new onlooker, whose mouth probably touched the floor with amazement, Jones would usually utter the same line: "There's only one other video board in the world like that one...on the other side."

If Jones told that joke once, he told it 500 times. But it was true then, though the video board is now ranked as the ninth largest in the world and second in the NFL (to the Texans). As for the actual game, it was a classic in the Giants-Cowboys rivalry, which had heated up again after the Giants knocked off Dallas in the 2007 divisional round of the play-offs en route to an improbable Super Bowl XLII title.

Kicker Lawrence Tynes said the Giants used the fact that they were even playing in the first ever game at the stadium as motivation. "They treated us like a homecoming game, thinking they would win," he said.

The back-and-forth affair saw the Cowboys grab a late lead on Felix Jones' touchdown run with 3:40 to play, but Giants quarterback Eli Manning had plenty of time for one last drive. The result was a game-winning kick by Tynes as time expired. The visitors became the ultimate party crashers for what was still an epic night in Cowboys history.

After the game, a locker room attendant asked Manning to sign a wall in the visitor's locker room, a move that created far more attention than anyone ever imagined, including Manning, who asked the attendant more than five times if he was sure he should write his signature there. Finally, Manning agreed and signed his name across a blank wall. He also wrote the date, "9-20-09" followed by "33–31, First win at the new stadium."

Once the story got out, Manning was criticized by some as it appeared to be a classless act. Of course, for the thousands who loathe the Cowboys and their America's Team moniker, Manning was likely touted as a hero. But in fact Manning was asked to sign it by the Cowboys' clubhouse attendant, who wanted to create a tradition similar to what the Eagles have in the visitors' locker room at Lincoln Financial Field. Hundreds—from opposing NFL teams to soccer players to even musicians who have performed concerts there—have signed their wall. And that was Manning's true intent. He just happened to be the first.

So much controversy and attention was created that it became a spectacle, and the Cowboys, who received numerous requests to film and photograph the signature, eventually painted over it. Manning actually won his first four starts at the stadium and can still claim a 4–0 record under the building's old name. He lost the 2013 season opener, though—the first Cowboys game played since it became AT&T Stadium.

Interim Changes & Smashing Debut
November 14, 2010 at New York Giants

One of the longest weeks in Cowboys history, amidst one of the longest seasons in franchise history as well, ended on a positive note in a place that hadn't been too kind to the Cowboys. But six days after the

Cowboys fired Wade Phillips after a dismal 1–7 start and replaced him with Jason Garrett, it was only fitting the Cowboys would rally around their new interim coach and escape the Meadowlands with a shocking 33–20 victory that improved the team to 2–7.

Garrett, the first former Cowboys player to become head coach of America's Team, was the offensive coordinator for the previous three seasons and he admitted the team's offensive woes were part of the problem during the first half of the season that only produced one win. And Tony Romo sitting injured with a broken collarbone that ultimately sidelined him the rest of the season didn't help matters as well.

But the previous Monday, it was evident Garrett was ready for the challenge. The Cowboys fired Phillips after an embarrassing 45–7 loss in Green Bay on national television, and it became clear Garrett was getting the job, whether he deserved it or not. The Cowboys didn't have a lot of options at that point, but it was obvious a change was needed.

That afternoon, owner Jerry Jones addressed the team after his decision to fire Phillips, and one offensive player said, "It was the most upset I'd ever seen Jerry. He was never like that." According to hearsay, Jones ripped his players, telling them, "I had to fire a damn good football coach and a damn good friend today." He basically put all of the players on watch as well before storming out of the team meeting room.

As the media huddled around the news conference that afternoon, which turned into early evening by the time Garrett came out, they knew there would be changes before he arrived. The standard table and chair that both Bill Parcells and then Phillips used for daily press conferences had been removed—replaced by an upright podium and microphone.

To this day Garrett continues to use the podium for all press conferences, seemingly putting him in more command and control of the room. It was subtle and poignant at the same time. "The Giants don't care about this coaching change," Garrett said. "The Giants are preparing for Sunday, so we've got to be ready. We're going to be ready to play at 4:15 on Sunday afternoon at the Meadowlands against the New York Football Giants."

If Garrett said 4:15 once that day, he said it probably 10 times the rest of the week, already adjusting to the Eastern time zone in his Princeton-graduate brain. For the coach who had interviewed twice for head coaching jobs the past two years in both St. Louis and Baltimore, his moment had arrived. And it just so happened to be against the Giants, not only the team Garrett left Dallas for in 2000 and for whom he played three seasons, but also the team that led the division with a 6–2 record.

On the Cowboys' first offensive play, running back Felix Jones started over Marion Barber. While Garrett and the coaching staff contended it was just a situational switch, there were rumblings that Barber did not adhere to Garrett's new dress-code policy for the team charter. Garrett wanted a more professional look on the plane, even demanding team officials and media members wear slacks, coat and tie, and dress shoes.

However, Barber was seen wearing a sport coat but with blue jeans and sneakers. The ironic part of Barber's attire was that he was usually one of the more decked-out players on the team with snazzy, colorful suits, and gaudy shoes. So it seemed like Barber was making some kind of statement.

Garrett and the Cowboys matched it by playing Jones. Whether or not that was a spark, it was obvious the Cowboys were playing inspired football. Dez Bryant had two unreal catches in the first quarter, including a touchdown grab in the end zone that was initially ruled incomplete but reversed by replay officials.

The Cowboys led 9–3 midway through the second quarter when it appeared their momentum was about to slip away. Eli Manning had his Giants on the Cowboys' 2 on third and goal when he fired a slant over the middle for Hakeem Nicks at the goal line. But faster than you can say "rookie free agent," Bryan McCann had other ideas, stepping in front of the pass for an interception that he returned 101 yards for a touchdown.

Giants fans were stunned. Cowboys fans were stunned. The press

After replacing Wade Phillips earlier in the week, Jason Garrett made his coaching debut against the Giants in 2010 and led his 1–7 Cowboys to a shocking road upset.

box was completely stunned. In no other game in franchise history has the word "who?" been uttered so often and so quickly.

McCann, a rookie from SMU who had made a few plays back in the preseason, was released before the season began but called up to the roster the week before because of injuries. McCann actually fumbled a kickoff against the Packers that led to a Green Bay touchdown. But forced into defensive duty on this day, McCann read Manning's eyes and jumped the route—and jumped straight into the Cowboys' record books with the longest interception return in franchise history. (McCann's big-play heroics carried over the next week against Detroit when he alertly scooped up a deflected punt and raced 97 yards for a game-turning touchdown.)

Instead of the Giants taking the lead at 10–9, the Cowboys led 16–3. Could this really be happening? Could the change to Jason Garrett as the new interim coach make that much of a difference?

The strange events continued in the second half. Two plays into the third quarter, some of the lights went out in the stadium, causing a small delay. However, play resumed with the less than 100 percent lighting as Jon Kitna dumped off a pass to Jones, who went 71 yards for a touchdown—his only rushing touchdown of the season. The Cowboys were indeed playing "lights out" and led the Giants 26–6 when the entire power went out briefly a few plays later.

Just before the snap, MetLife Stadium went completely dark, creating an eerie feeling for everyone, whether you were on the field, in the stands or in the press box, which is located eight floors above ground level. DallasCowboys.com staff writer Rob Phillips not-so-playfully referenced the Tom Clancy novel *Sum of All Fears*, which includes a scene where terrorists plant a bomb inside a football stadium.

For a few seconds, it was scary, but the lights quickly came back on. When they did, Cowboys defensive players were surprised to see safety Alan Ball, perhaps trying to make himself less of a target in the event of a terrorist attack, face down on the ground. Like everyone else, Ball had no clue what has happening around him. His teammates got a major kick out of his response.

After a seven-minute delay, the game resumed, and the Giants started turning the tide. They trimmed the lead to 33–20 and were driving for touchdown to get back in the game. But Manning was picked off near the goal line by none other than Ball, who after the game, playfully jabbed back at his ribbing teammates with a "Who's laughing now?" response.

The Cowboys won the game 33–20, giving Garrett his first win as head coach. The usually stoic coach acknowledged the accomplishment of winning a game on the road amidst a week full of emotion. But he channeled them enough to point out another obvious: "The Lions are coming to town this week and they don't care what happened this week."

ACKNOWLEDGMENTS

When I was in the fourth grade, I tried to purposely wait until after my youth league basketball game to reveal a less-than-impressive report card to my parents. I had it all planned out to conveniently wait until we got home. But the plan was foiled when my mom spotted my brother's report card on the table, which prompted her to ask me about mine.

While I still got to play, I'll never forget her frustrated rant in the car ride to the gym. She wanted me to focus less on my passion and more on my schoolwork. "You can't just work for the Dallas Cowboys someday. You have to study, get good grades to get a job."

Who knew? To this day, nobody could've guessed I'd be a sportswriter for DallasCowboys.com—a job I didn't know existed when I first got to college in 1994, a time when the Internet was barely getting off the ground.

But as fate would have it, I picked a school—Midwestern State University in Wichita Falls, Texas—where the Cowboys decided for some reason to hold training camp. And it just happened to coincide with my graduation, allowing me to slide right into a brand new position, one that has changed over the years but one I've never relinquished.

A few days after my "dream job" hire, as my friends and family would call it, my father told me to keep a journal. He said, "You're going to write a book someday and you'll want to remember everything."

I didn't keep a journal. I should've, proving once again how you should always listen to your parents.

Writing this book has allowed me to go back down memory lane and revisit some stories I hadn't thought about in years. When I was first approached about this project, I told myself I wanted to dig deep and tell some of the more obscure stories about players most people either never knew or had forgotten long ago. I wanted to share those ironic, coincidental stories more than just relive the greatest games or greatest players. And since I've covered this team in a time period that has seen just one playoff win, obviously I had to do my share of digging to come up with suitable, yet entertaining, stories.

When it comes to thanking people for this book—or any book—I will never overlook the opportunity I received from Baylor head coach Art Briles, who allowed me to write his authorized biography. Not only was it an honor to tell the amazing story of an amazing person, but it obviously opened up doors for me that I'm not sure would've been opened without him.

With that, I want to thank Tom Bast at Triumph Books for having the faith in me to write this second book even before I finished the manuscript on the first book.

This Cowboys book was obviously a lot easier in terms of research, considering I've lived all of these moments. But I got some great insight from people who've been here just as long, if not longer. Guys like Todd Williams, Bucky Buchanan, Mike McCord, Britt Brown, and Bryan Wansley were all helpful in sharing their memories.

Former players such as Keith Davis, James Whalen, Dat Nguyen, and Darren Woodson were more than helpful in telling their stories. Woody has always been one of my favorite players, and I can't wait for the day when he sees his name in the Cowboys' Ring of Honor.

One of the most unique parts of my job, and something that continues to be a struggle, is the constant balancing act between being team employees and the media. Some days we're treated like team officials, and other times we get kicked out of the locker room just like anyone else. And trust me, there's good and bad to that. But I've had some media members that have really been blessings to work with. Newspaper guys like Clarence E. Hill and Jean-Jacques Taylor took me under their wings early on. JJT taught me the difference between "covering the team" and "covering the beat." Chip Brown taught me how to take the job seriously without taking yourself too seriously in the process. And Todd Archer, to me, is the most professional reporter I've ever seen. I have the utmost respect for him because he's probably the most fair and honest journalist I've ever seen. I've learned a lot from him whether he knows it or not.

Also coming to the Cowboys in 1999, my boss Derek Eagleton has been here every step of the way. He's been one of my best supporters, and his excitement over this book, and anything that might enhance my own career, is something that I'll forever cherish.

My current colleagues Rowan Kavner, Ed Cahill, Bryan Broaddus, David Helman, Shannon Gross, Chris Behm, and Lindsay Meares have helped pick up the slack when I've needed to balance my everyday work duties and squeezing in time to do an interview here or there. Former co-workers Rob Phillips and Josh Ellis not only helped provide support but proved to be content subjects as well.

One of the best employees the Cowboys have ever had recently left the organization. Jancy Briles' departure will hurt around the building, especially to our website. Before she left, and even afterward, she was extremely helpful lining up interviews for this project. She'll be missed as a colleague but will always be a great friend. I might owe her the most gratitude of anyone else in becoming a published author.

Kurt Daniels has now had editorial duties for both of my books, and I still consider that to be one of the best decisions I've ever made. I couldn't have asked for a more professional, competent person to review my work. If he's willing, Kurt will have a part in every book I write from here on out.

My friends and family are an amazing group. My mother, Camille Williams, and her husband, Mark, not only are great supporters but pretty good copy editors, too. My dad, Tim, and wife, Sharon, make sure my dreams stay big.

My precious daughter, Olivia, thinks it's "pretty cool" that her daddy can write a book, especially one that features her favorite player, "Tony Womo," on the cover. Her mother, Josie, couldn't have been any better in her flexible schedule to help me get through this project.

My lifelong pals—Tony Domenella, Drew Myers, and Chris Fisher are proud of my career but ultimately still know me as the skinny kid from MSU with the Vanilla Ice haircut. One of the worst phone calls I've ever had was to Chris in the 2006 playoffs in Seattle. NFL Films even captures me in the background on the phone as Tony Romo drops the snap for a potential game-winning field.

"Oh my god, Fish. Romo dropped the snap."

"You're lying."

"I wish I was."

"Stop playing."

"Can you hear this crowd?"

After a silence on the other end, his TV delay caught up to the harsh reality, all I could hear was a sick groan and I believe he hung up the phone.

But to this day, I don't know if anyone has had a friend as loyal and supportive as Chris Fisher. I'm sure I haven't.

Julie Acosta once again provided a backbone of encouragement every step of the way. Her sense of understanding is amazing. She's been there through two book projects in less than a year and she's been an unbelievable rock of support. I know her daughter, Marisa, will be eager to have a new bedtime book.

But none of these acknowledgments would be possible had the Jerry Jones family not given me an opportunity some 15 years ago. I wouldn't be here today had Jerry Jones Jr. not taken a chance on a kid from Wichita Falls.

The kid that could multiply by seven before any other number because he would rack up touchdowns in the backyard, idolizing Danny White and Tony Dorsett, suddenly had a front-row seat to America's Team. And 15 years later, still roaming the halls of Valley Ranch.

Hopefully, we just made the walls talk just a little bit.

SOURCES

Books

Engel, Mac—*Tony Romo: America's Next Great Quarterback*; Triumph, Chicago, 2007

Dallas Cowboys Media Guide; Irving, Texas, 2013

NFL Communications Department; *2013 Official NFL Record and Fact Book*; New York, N.Y., 2013

Periodicals

The Associated Press

Fort-Worth Star-Telegram

The Dallas Morning News

Austin-American Statesman

San Antonio Express-News

Lubbock Avalanche Journal

Wichita Falls Times-Record News

Amarillo Globe News

Sports Illustrated

Dallas Cowboys STAR Magazine

Websites

DallasCowboys.com

Profootballreference.com

NFLGsis.com

ESPN.com

CBSSports.com